AF600362

THE CATHOLIC UNIVERSITY OF AMERICA
CANON LAW STUDIES
No. 177

Synodal Examiners and Parish Priest Consultors

AN HISTORICAL SYNOPSIS AND COMMENTARY

BY

REV. JOHN PATRICK CONNOLLY, S.T.L., J.C.L.
Priest of the Archdiocese of San Francisco

A DISSERTATION

Submitted to the Faculty of the School of Canon Law of the Catholic University of America in Partial Fulfillment of the Requirements for the Degree of Doctor of Canon Law

THE CATHOLIC UNIVERSITY OF AMERICA PRESS
WASHINGTON, D. C.

1943

Nihil Obstat:
EDUARDUS ROELKER, S.T.D., J.C.D.,
Censor Deputatus.

Imprimatur:
✠ JOANNES J. MITTY, D.D.,
Archiepiscopus Sancti Francisci.

Sancti Francisci, 19 aprilis 1943.

Printed by
THE PAULIST PRESS
New York, N. Y.

51

TABLE OF CONTENTS

PART II

CANONICAL COMMENTARY

CHAPTER IV

CHAPTER VI

CHAPTER VII

FOREWORD

The curial offices of synodal examiner and parish priest consultor are certainly less known than many of the other offices of the diocesan curia. This is understandable in view of the relatively greater importance of these other offices, for example, that of the vicar general, or that of the *officialis*. Still, it should be born in mind that the Church always has a special and an important reason for creating an ecclesiastical office, and in the case of the two offices considered in this work there is no exception to this general rule. The duties of the synodal examiner are much more numerous than those of the parish priest consultor. In fact, the ministry of the latter official is used but rarely. His duties are concerned with but two of the administrative procedures given in Book IV, Part III, of the New Code of Canon Law. Though the parish priest consultor is called upon but infrequently to aid the Ordinary, still a little consideration of his duties will suffice to show the importance of his office. The synodal examiner, on the other hand, is given a number of duties. He is to take a part in the election of pastors, in most of the administrative procedures just referred to, and the law recommends him to the Ordinary for the purpose of conducting a number of examinations, such as the one for the Junior Clergy, the one for candidates for Orders, etc. The nature of these duties is proof that the synodal examiner really is an important curial official.

In the present work an attempt has been made to give a study of the offices of synodal examiner and parish priest consultor, and also of the duties incumbent upon those elected to these offices. This treatise is divided into two parts. The first considers the history of these offices and of the duties of the officials. The second part is a canonical commentary, in which an attempt has been made to give the law of the Code on these offices and duties together with an interpretation of this law.

In connection with the duties of these officials it has been imperative that there should not be an attempt to give in full the law of the complete procedures in which the work of the officials in question is but a part. At times it has been useful and possible to refer briefly to matters not immediately connected with the duties of the examiners or consultors, but this was only possible on rather infrequent occasions. To have done so regularly would have been to lose sight of the direct object of the present work. Much, therefore, is of necessity left to further investigation for the one who would know not only the duties of the synodal examiners and of the parish priest consultors, but also the whole of each procedure in which these duties are but a part. Consequently, if this work often projects itself, with but a brief introduction, into the middle of a procedure, it can only plead in excuse the limited scope of this study.

The duties of the synodal examiners in the concursus are exactly the same in the new law as in pre-Code legislation. For this reason it has been considered sufficient in the canonical commentary to refer to what is written on this subject in the historical section, and to give a few additional considerations. In the United States the law of the concursus is no longer in effect, and consequently it is of only historical interest in this country.

The writer takes this opportunity to acknowledge most sincerely his gratitude to the Most Rev. John J. Mitty, D.D., Archbishop of San Francisco, California, for the opportunity of further studies in Canon Law. Appreciation is also acknowledged for the interest shown in this work by the Most Rev. Thomas A. Connolly, D.D., J.C.D., Auxiliary Bishop of San Francisco, California, and Titular Bishop of Sila. Finally, a debt of gratitude is due to the Faculty of the School of Canon Law of The Catholic University of America for assistance in the preparation of this study.

Part One

Historical Synopsis

INTRODUCTION

THE offices of synodal examiner and of parish priest consultor are both of recent origin. The office of synodal examiner traces itself back to the Council of Trent (1545-1563).[1] The Council[2] instituted this office for a very particular and important duty connected with the new procedure for the election of pastors. This new procedure was prescribed because the Fathers of the Council were most anxious to insure the placing of none but worthy and capable clerics in the office of pastor, to care for the salvation of souls. Prior to the Council of Trent there was, indeed, an obligation upon the bishops to confer benefices only upon those who were worthy by reason of their theological learning and other merits,[3] and there did exist an examination of candidates. Innocent III[4] numbered among the duties of the archdeacon that of examining candidates for benefices and of presenting them to the bishop. With the gradual decline of the juridiction and office of the archdeacon and the substitution instead of the vicar general, this examination seems to have been given by the latter, except when the bishop reserved this to himself.[5] Briefly, this was the procedure in use at the

[1] *ASS* (41 vols., Romae, 1865-1908), VII, 378-379; Wernz-Vidal, *Ius Canonicum*, II, *De Personis* (2. ed., Romae: Apud Aedes Universitatis Gregorianae, 1928), n. 650; d'Angelo, *La Curia Diocesana a norma del Codice di diritto canonico* (Giarre, Sicilia: Lisi, 1922), pars I, p. 34. (Hereafter this work is cited *La Curia Diocesana.*)

[2] Conc. Trident., sess. XXIV, *de ref.*, c. 18.

[3] *ASS*, VII, 378-379; d'Angelo, *Parroco e Parrochia nel Codice di Diritto Canonico, Nomina del Parroco, Esame, Concorso* (Giarre, Sicilia: Lisi, 1921), p. 25. (Hereafter this work will be cited *Parroco e Parrochia.*)

[4] C. 7, X, *de officio archideaconi*, I, 23.

[5] *ASS*, VII, 378-379; d'Angelo, *loc. cit.*, p. 25.

time of the Council of Trent. With the Council the unique form of the concursus for the election to parochial benefices was first introduced and prescribed.[6] It was in this legislation on the concursus that the office of synodal examiner was created.

The sole duty of the synodal examiner until the decree *Maxima cura,* in 1910,[7] was in connection with the concursus for vacant parishes. With this decree, however, the duties of the examiner were extended to include a part in the administrative procedure for the removal of pastors.

The office of the parish priest consultor is of very recent origin, finding its beginnings in the above-mentioned decree "*Maxima cura.*"[8] That this office was not in existence previous to this decree is an accepted fact.[9] The parish priest consultor had but the one duty to perform, which was in connection with the administrative removal of pastors.[10]

In the first part of this work an attempt is made to treat the origin and historical development of these two offices and of the functions performed by the incumbents of these offices. A study of the duties of the synodal examiners leads necessarily into the history of the concursus, and also into a minor part of the history of the administrative removal of pastors. The study of the duties of the parish priest consultors leads likewise into a part of the history of the administrative removal of pastors. Only by deviating from our particular subject could a complete history of the con-

[6] Fanfani, *De Iure Parochorum ad Normam Codicis Iuris Canonici* (Taurini: Marietti, 1924), n. 103 (hereafter cited as *De Iure Parochorum*).

[7] S. C. Consist., decr., *Maxima cura,* 20 aug. 1910—*AAS,* II (1910), 636-648; *Codicis Iuris Canonici Fontes cura Emi. Petri Card. Gasparri Editi* (9 vols., Romae: Typis Polyglottis Vaticanis, 1923-1939. Vols. VII, VIII et IX, *ed. cura et studio Emi. Iustiniani Card. Serédi*), n. 2074 (hereafter cited *Fontes*).

[8] S. C. Consist., decr., *Maxima cura,* can. 32 cum can. 4.

[9] Cappello, *De Administrativa Amotione Parochorum seu Commentarium in Decretum "Maxima Cura"* (Romae, 1911), p. 73. (Hereafter this work will be cited *De Admin. Amotione Parochorum.*) Connor, *The Administrative Removal of Pastors,* The Catholic University of America Canon Law Studies, n. 104 (Washington, D. C.: The Catholic University of America, 1937), p. 92. (Hereafter this work will be cited *Adm. Removal of Pastors.*)

[10] Wernz-Vidal, *Ius Canonicum,* II, n. 650.

cursus and of the administrative removal of pastors be attempted. It is unfortunate yet necessary that only an incomplete picture of these two canonical procedures be given. The scope, then, of this historical synopsis is to study only those parts of the concursus and of the administrative procedure in the removal of pastors which touch upon the duties of either the synodal examiners or the parish priest consultors.

CHAPTER I

SYNODAL EXAMINERS FROM THE COUNCIL OF TRENT TO THE CONSTITUTION "CUM ILLUD"

ARTICLE 1. TRIDENTINE LEGISLATION

A. *The Concursus*

BEFORE taking up the study of the synodal examiners it is necessary to give a brief description of the concursus as established by the Council of Trent.[1] The Council legislated that as soon as a vacancy occurred in a parochial church the bishop should appoint, if necessary, a suitable vicar, who would be in charge of the parish until a pastor was appointed. Then the bishop, or anyone possessing the right of patronage, was required within ten days, or such other term as the bishop might prescribe, to designate, in the presence of those to be delegated as examiners, certain clerics as capable of governing the vacant parish. Furthermore, others also, who might know of any clerics who were fit for the office, were permitted to make known their names, so that a careful investigation might be made as to the age, morals and qualifications of each. But if in accordance with the custom of the country it should appear more suitable to the bishop, or to the provincial synod, those who wished to be examined might be summoned by public notice. At the expiration of the period assigned for the presentation of names there was to be held an examination. This examination was to be conducted by the bishop, or, if he was impeded, by his vicar general, and by at least three of the examiners. The candidates were to be

[1] Conc. Trident., sess. XXIV, *de ref.*, c. 18. (Use has been made of the translations of the text of the Council of Trent by Schroeder, *Canons and Decrees of the Council of Trent* [St. Louis, Mo.: Herder, 1941], and by Waterworth, *The Canons and Decrees of the Sacred and Oecumenical Council of Trent* [London, 1848]). Since the concursus is treated only in this session and chapter of the Council further footnotes are omitted in this description of the concursus.

examined in regard to age, morals, theological learning, prudence and other qualifications suitable for ruling the vacant church. When the examination was completed the examiners were required to make known to the bishop how many they had judged fit. From these the bishop was required then to choose the one whom he judged the more competent. To this person and to none other was the conferral of the church to be made.

If the church was under ecclesiastical patronage and the appointment belonged solely to the bishop, the patron was to choose the more worthy from amongst those who had been approved by the examiners, and he was then to present this person to the bishop for appointment. If, however, though the church was under ecclesiastical patronage, the appointment was to be made by some one other than the bishop, the latter was the one who was to choose the worthier. The patron was then to present the candidate chosen to the person to whom appointment belonged. When the church was under lay patronage, the one presented by the patron was to be examined, as above, by those delegated thereto, and was not to be admitted unless found competent. No appeal, even to the Apostolic See, or to the legates, vice-legates, or the nuncios of the Holy See, or to any bishops or metropolitans, primates or patriarchs, was to be allowed to hinder or suspend the execution of the report of the examiners.

The Council of Trent was very clear in regard to the obligation of the respective superiors to hold this concursus. It stated that all provisions or appointments made otherwise than in accordance with the prescribed form were to be regarded as surreptitious. All exemptions, privileges, indults were revoked. The following exceptions were nevertheless permitted: if the revenues of the parochial churches should be so scanty as not to bear the burden of all this examination, or if no one should care to undergo the examination, or if by reason of open factions or dissensions, which were met with in some localities, more grievous quarrels and disturbances might easily be stirred up, the Ordinary was permitted to omit this formality and have recourse to a private examination, if in conformity with his conscience and with the advice of the examiners he should deem this expedient.

A final statement by the Council of Trent on the subject of the concursus is worthy of mention. It decreed that if the provincial synod should judge that in the above regulations concerning the form of examination something ought to be added or omitted, it was given the authority to do so.

B. *The Office and Duties of the Synodal Examiners*

Attention is turned now to the specific legislation of the Council of Trent on the office of the synodal examiners and on their duties in connection with the concursus which has just been described. With regard to the office of the examiners the Council made the following laws:[2]

(a) At least six examiners should be proposed annually by the bishop, or by his vicar general, in the diocesan synod. Those proposed must prove satisfactory to the synod and must be approved by it;

(b) those to be elected synodal examiners should be masters, or doctors, or possessed of the degree of licentiate, in Sacred Theology or Canon Law. Other clerics, however, who did not possess such a degree, but who appeared most competent for the office, might also be elected. Regulars, even though members of mendicant orders, as well as the secular clergy, were eligible;

(c) those who were elected were required to take an oath to fulfill their duty faithfully, without respect to human considerations. This oath had to be taken on the Holy Gospels;

(d) the synodal examiners were not to receive anything whatsoever by reason of an examination, either before or after the examination. Those violating this precept, both the givers and the examiners, were to be considered as guilty of simony. From this guilt they might not be absolved until such time as they resigned the benefices which they in any manner whatever possessed before the act of simony. The guilty also became disqualified to possess other benefices in the future;

[2] Conc. Trident., sess. XXIV, *de ref.*, c. 18. All statements of law in this section are from this same session and chapter of the Council of Trent. Consequently further footnotes are omitted in this section.

(e) the examiners besides being bound to render an account to God for their actions in office, were also held to give account of their actions to the provincial synod, if this were asked for. This synod might punish severely, according to its own discretion, any violation of duty on the part of the examiners.

As to the duties of the synodal examiners, the Council of Trent legislated as follows: when a parish church had become vacant the designation of candidates by the bishop, or by the one who possessed the right of patronage, was to be made in the presence of those who were delegated as examiners. Such a procedure was not necessary if a summons of candidates was made by public notice. The bishop was to delegate three of the examiners to conduct the examination with him. He was left free to choose the same three to conduct a succeeding examination if he so desired.

The Council made no laws to govern the actual examination. It did not state whether it should be oral or written, whether all were to be examined at the same time, how long the examination should last, etc. All that it stated was that the candidates were to be examined in the matter of age, morals, theological learning, prudence and other qualifications suitable for ruling the vacant church. Once the examination was completed the Council directed that the examiners should make known to the bishop as many as had been judged fit by them in the above-mentioned qualifications.

If the vacant church should be under ecclesiastical patronage those presented by the ecclesiastical patron were to be examined in the usual manner by the synodal examiners. When it was a question of a church under lay patronage, the one presented by the patron was to be examined and approved by delegated synodal examiners before he could be appointed by the bishop.

Article 2. Legislation of Pius V and Clement VIII

Pius V (1566-1572) in a Constitution, *"In conferendis,"*[3] decreed that since parish churches are to be conferred not only upon the worthy but upon the more worthy, therefore if a bishop should choose a less worthy candidate for the parochial office, those who

[3] 18 mart. 1567, n. VII—*Fontes,* n. 119.

were rejected might appeal from such an election to the Metropolitan, or if the one whose choice was questioned was the Metropolitan, or if he was exempt from a Metropolitan, then the appeal would go to the nearer Ordinary. Otherwise it would be to the Holy See. Such an appeal carried with it the right to cause the one who had been chosen to undergo a new examination before the judge of appeal and his examiners. Appeal from this judge was to be made to the Holy See.

In another Constitution, "*Apostolatus officium,*"[4] a change was made in the legislation of the Council of Trent. In the Council of Trent it was stated that the *provincial synod* had the power to punish severely, according to its own discretion, any breach of duty by the examiners.[5] Pius V, however, gave this right to punish to the *diocesan synod,* though the severity of the punishment was left to the judgment of the bishop. That this change became law is quite clear from the concluding paragraph of this Constitution.[6]

Clement VIII (1592-1605) in a decree, which may be found in a response of the Sacred Congregation of the Council,[7] made provision for possible deficiencies in the number of synodal examiners in a diocese. According to this decree, if all the synodal examiners should die within the year following their election, the bishop should substitute not less than six others in their place. These substitutes were to be selected from amongst those who had previously held the

[4] 19 aug. 1567—*Bullarum Diplomatum et Privilegiorum Sanctorum Taurinensis Editio* (24 vols. et Appendix, Augustae Taurinorum—Neapoli, 1857-1872), VII, pp. 606-607. (Hereafter this work will be cited simply *Bull. Rom. Taur.*)

[5] Sess. XXIV, *de ref.*, c. 18.

[6] *Bull. Rom. Taur.*, VII, p. 609: "*non obstantibus quibusvis aliis constitutionibus, ordinationibus apostolicis, indultis, privilegiis, etc.*"

[7] *Civitaten.*, 3 iul. 1593—apud Pallottini, *Collectio Omnium Conclusionum et Resolutionum Quae in Causis apud Sacram Congregationem Cardinalium S. Concilii Tridentini Interpretum Prodierunt ab eius institutione anno MDLXIX ad annum MDCCCLX, distinctis titulis alphabetico ordine per materias digesta* (17 vols., Romae, 1868-1893), X, "examinatores synodales," nn. 40-41. (Hereafter this work will be cited *Pallottini.*) Garcia, *Tractatus de Beneficiis Ecclesiasticis* (Coloniae Allobrogum, 1636), pars IX, caput II, n. 72. (This work will be cited henceforth as *de Benef.*)

office of synodal examiner. If six such former examiners did not exist, then the bishop was to take as many as did remain and complete the number of six by choosing new examiners, to be approved by the chapter. If no former examiners remained, the bishop was to substitute new examiners, men fit for the office by reason of probity of life and knowledge. The chapter was given the right to approve these new examiners. They were to be not less than six in number. When the time came for a new synod, that is, one year after the previous synod was held, the office of all these substitute examiners automatically ceased.

ARTICLE 3. CURIAL PRACTICE AND CANONICAL TEACHING FROM THE COUNCIL OF TRENT TO THE CONSTITUTION *"Cum Illud"*

In the years following the decree of Clement VIII until the reign of Benedict XIV (1740-1758) there was no pontifical legislation in regard to the synodal examiners or to their duties in the concursus. During this period, however, many questions were settled by some of the Sacred Congregations, in particular by the Sacred Congregation of the Council, and some also by the Sacred Roman Rota. Further, the great canonists and commentators of the period wrote not a little on the subject. In this fashion some doubts were cleared up and a certain practice was developed with regard to the office and duties of the synodal examiners.

A. *Practice and Teaching Regarding the Office*

In the question of the appointment of synodal examiners, it was understood that they might be appointed not only by those with episcopal dignity but also by abbots and other prelates who, though inferior to bishops, nevertheless possessed quasi-episcopal jurisdiction over a separate territory, were not subject to any bishop, but were immediately subject to the Holy See, and possessed the right to convoke a synod.[8] During a vacancy in the episcopal see it was

[8] S. C. C., *Forosemproniens.*, 18 mart. 1591 et *Castri Durantis*, 30 apr. 1611 —apud Ferraris, *Prompta Biblioteca, Canonica, Iuridica, Moralis, Theologica necnon Ascetica, Polemica, Rubricistica, Historica* (9 vols., Romae, 1885-1899), II, "concursus," n. 8. (Henceforth this work will be cited *Biblioteca.*)

the vicar capitular who proposed the names to the diocesan synod.[9]

If the bishop appointed, with the approval of the synod, less than six, every subsequent concursus would be invalid even though there were three examiners present.[10] It was stated by the Sacred Congregation of the Council, however, that more than six might be appointed to the office, but that there should not be more than twenty.[11]

The proposal by the bishop, or his vicar general, had to be specific. The name of the individual was to be clearly indicated, not merely the title or office that an individual held. Deputation of a synodal examiner under the name of a dignity in general was invalid.[12] The approval or rejection by the diocesan synod of the names proposed for the office could be by secret or open vote.[13]

The question of the appointment of examiners outside the time of the synod created a certain amount of difficulty. This difficulty arose because of the fact that at times the number of synodal examiners was depleted either entirely or in part by death, grave illness, incapacity or departure from the diocese. The Sacred Congregation of the Council was insistent that others than those deputed by the diocesan synod could not be considered as true examiners.[14]

[9] S. C. C., *Caurien.*, anno 1593—*Pallottini,* X, "examinatores synodales," n. 8; Barbosa, *De Officio et Potestate Parochi* (Quinta editio prioribus emendatior, Lugduni, 1665), pars I, cap. II, n. 70 (hereafter cited *De Off. et Potest. Parochi*).

[10] S. R. R., *Sempronien.,* 15 ian. 1593—apud Garcia, *de Benef.,* pars IX, cap. II, n. 66; Leurenius, *Forum Beneficiale* (2 vols., Venetiis, 1742), pars I, sect. I, cap. III, paragr. 3, quaest. 186.

[11] *Caesaraugustana,* 13 mart. 1623—Barbosa, *Collectanea Doctorum in varia Concilii Tridentini, Decreta et Canones* (Lugduni, 1657), ad cap. 18, sess. XXIV, n. 85; Leurenius, *loc. cit.*; Benedictus XIV, *De Synodo Dioecesana* (2 vols., Romae, 1806), lib. IV, cap. VII, n. 3.

[12] S. C. C., *in Pennen.,* 14 aug. 1640—*Pallottini,* X, "examinatores synodales," n. 33; Garcia, *de Benef.,* pars IX, cap. II, n. 335; Barbosa, *De Off. et Potest. Parochi,* pars I, cap. II, n. 55.

[13] S. C. C., *Venetiarum,* 11 iul. 1592—*Fontes,* n. 2247; S. C. C., *Fulginaten.,* 3 dec. 1664—*Pallottini,* X, "examinatores synodales," n. 4.

[14] *Toletana,* mense martii, 1595—*Pallottini,* X, "examinatores synodales," n. 9.

The bishop had no power to depute and approve examiners outside the synod.[15] The decree of Clement VIII, referred to above, was the sole exception to this rule. It made no difference whether two years, or even more, had elapsed since the previous synod. Under the law the bishop was powerless to appoint examiners outside of a synod.[16]

If some of the six examiners should have died within the year of their election then the entire faculty of examining pertained to those who remained, together with the bishop, even if only one remained for the duration of that year.[17] If no synod was held at the proper time then if at least six of the examiners appointed in the previous synod remained, these retained their office.[18] If, however, a year after their appointment there remained less than six original examiners, the office of all expired.[19] At times, when no synod was being held and less than six examiners remained, a bishop might petition the Sacred Congregation of the Council for the faculty of deputing new examiners outside a synod. The office of these examiners would last for a year, at the close of which the Sacred Congregation might be petitioned to confirm these same examiners in office for another year. This petition was required each year unless the bishop decided to hold a regular synod and therein depute new examiners or confirm those already in office.[20] It may be noted here

[15] S. C. C., *Zamoren.*, mense decembris, 1583—*Pallottini,* X, "examinatores synodales," n. 11.

[16] S. C. C., *Zamoren.*, mense febr., 1588, dub. 4—*Fontes,* n. 2197; S. C. C., *Toletan.*, anno 1577—Garcia, *de Benef.*, pars IX, cap. II, n. 8.

[17] S. C. C., *Caurien.*, anno 1593—*Pallottini,* X, "examinatores synodales," n. 39; Garcia, *de Benef.*, pars IX, cap. II, n. 69; Leurenius, *Forum Beneficiale,* pars I, sect. I, cap. III, paragr. 3, quaestio 187, n. 2.

[18] S. C. C., *Capuana,* anno 1600—*Pallottini,* X, "examinatores synodales," n. 36; S. C. C., *Montis Regalis,* 2 aug. 1607, ad I—*Fontes,* n. 2367.

[19] S. C. C., *Savonen.*, 5 febr. 1593—*Pallottini,* X, "examinatores synodales," n. 37; S. C. C., *Caurien.*, anno 1593—*Pallottini,* X, "examinatores synodales," n. 36; S. C. C., *in Dubium,* mense nov. 1617—*Pallottini,* X, "examinatores synodales," n. 37; Garcia, *de Benef.*, pars IX, cap. II, n. 75; Barbosa, *De Off. et Potest. Parochi,* pars I, cap. II, n. 59.

[20] S. C. C., *Cassanen.*, 16 dec. 1719—*Pallottini,* X, "examinatores synodales," n. 43; S. C. C., *Aversana,* 2 maii 1739—*Pallottini,* X, "examinatores synodales," nn. 57-58.

that the office of synodal examiner did not cease with the death of the bishop.[21]

The provision made by Clement VIII and this practice of the Sacred Congregation of the Council of granting power to create examiners outside a synod are the origins of the *pro-synodal examiners.* The name does not seem to have been used at first and it is not clear just when it did come into general usage. One thing is certain, that the name was not used in papal legislation until the decree, "*Maxima cura,*" in 1910.[22]

Another question which was settled by the Sacred Congregation of the Council concerned dioceses which were united with equal rights (*aeque-principaliter unitae*). Each diocese was to have its own synodal examiners, and in the event of a vacancy in a parish church in one of the dioceses, the examiners of that diocese had to be used in the concursus which was held. The bishop might, however, hold the concursus in the city and diocese in which he resided.[23]

In regard to the person of the appointee to the office of synodal examiner the Sacred Congregation of the Council as early as 1596 declared that laymen and married clerics were not to exercise the office of synodal examiner.[24]

The question of the oath of fidelity to duty also received attention. If it should happen that the examiners had never, at any time, taken this oath, any concursus in which they had a part was invalid.[25] This oath was more properly taken in the synod, but it sufficed for validity if it were taken before the examiner's entering upon his duties in a concursus.[26] In a synod the oath was to be

[21] S. C. C., in Dubium ad Cap. 18, Sess. XXIV, *de ref.*, Posit. 100—*Pallottini,* X, "examinatores synodales," n. 35.

[22] S. C. Consist., 20 aug. 1910, can. 4, § 2—*AAS,* II (1910), 636; *Fontes,* n. 2074; cf. d'Angelo, *La Curia Diocesana,* I, pp. 35-36.

[23] *Castellan.*, 24 sept. 1639—*Fontes,* n. 2610; *Valven. et Sulmonen.*, 3 sept. 1650—*Fontes,* n. 2711.

[24] *Serguntina,* mense aprilis 1596—*Pallottini,* X, "examinatores synodales," n. 23.

[25] S. C. C., *Bisinianen.*, 12 dec. 1628 et *Illerden.*, 14 mart. 1629—*Pallottini,* X, "examinatores synodales," n. 60.

[26] S. C. C., *in Nullius,* 11 maii 1630—*Pallottini,* X, "examinatores synodales," n. 61; Leurenius, *Forum Beneficiale,* pars I, sect. I, cap. III, paragr. 3, quaestio 189, n. 2.

taken before the bishop, but when one took it outside the synod it was to be before a notary. The testimony of the latter was sufficient proof of the oath's having been taken.[27] It was always to be taken on the Holy Gospels, otherwise it was invalid.[28]

In the matter of recompense for their labors the Council of Trent, as has been noted, was very strict. Interpretations of this law were also very strict. No stipend might be decreed by the bishop for the synodal examiners, and any decree of a diocesan synod which did determine a stipend for them was invalid and was to be abolished.[29] Nor might the examiners receive anything for their labor, or under title of sustenance, from the fruits of the vacant benefice.[30] This strict law held even though an immemorial custom to the contrary existed.[31] It was admitted, nevertheless, that the bishop might make some recompense to the examiners from his own funds (*"de suo"*). This would be given as a reward or stipend, or under title of sustenance.[32] The reason given for this concession was that the prohibition of the Council of Trent was to be understood in the sense that nothing was to be received from the candidates. Hence the bishop might give a recompense from his own funds.[33]

The Sacred Congregation of the Council on various occasions enumerated causes which would impede a synodal examiner from taking part in a concursus. Those examiners who had been condemned by a judicial sentence for the crime of adultery could not

[27] Leurenius, *loc. cit.*

[28] Garcia, *de Benef.*, pars IX, cap. II, n. 358; Leurenius, *ibidem*, n. 3.

[29] S. C. C., *Salernitana—Pallottini,* X, "examinatores synodales," n. 87. The same decision is found in Garcia, *de Benef.*, pars IX, cap. II, n. 374.

[30] S. C. C., *in una Abulen.*—Garcia, *de Benef.*, pars V, cap. VII, n. 11, et pars IX, cap. II, nn. 368-378; Barbosa, *De Off. et Potest. Parochi,* pars I, cap. II, n. 81.

[31] S. C. C., *Civitaten.*, 24 sept. 1592—*Pallottini,* X, "examinatores synodales," n. 90.

[32] S. C. C., *Urgellen.*, ad Cap. 18, Sess. XXIV, *de ref.*, Posit. 100—*Pallottini,* X, "examinatores synodales," n. 94.

[33] S. C. C., *Urgellen.*, ad Cap. 18, Sess. XXIV, *de ref.*, Posit. 100—*Pallottini,* X, "examinatores synodales," n. 94; Garcia, *de Benef.*, pars IX, cap. II, n. 379; Barbosa, *De Off. et Potest. Parochi,* pars I, cap. II, n. 93.

be used in the concursus.[34] The same prohibition held if they had been condemned for the crime of simony.[35] Further, examiners were to be excluded who were legitimately proven to be suspect, whether this was because of the bond of consanguinity with any of the candidates, or for some other reason.[36] Consequently, priests who were candidates for a vacant benefice, which had the care of souls attached, were not to be forced to take the examination before examiners whom they justly affirmed to be suspect.[37]

The synodal examiners not only had the obligation to accept appointment to conduct the examination in a concursus, but at least three might be forced by the bishop to accept, even under threat of penalties, not excluding censures.[38]

B. *Practice and Teaching Regarding the Duties*

It was determined by the Sacred Congregation of the Council [39] that not only bishops, but also abbots and inferior prelates who had quasi-episcopal jurisdiction over a certain territory, who were immediately subject to the Holy See, and who possessed the right to convoke a synod and to elect therein synodal examiners, might conduct the usual concursus with their synodal examiners. When the episcopal see became vacant it was understood that the vicar capitular possessed this right.[40]

[34] *Vasionen.*, 4 dec. 1627—*Pallottini,* X, "examinatores synodales," n. 62.

[35] Cf. Barbosa, *De Off. et Potest. Parochi,* pars I, cap. II, n. 65.

[36] S. C. C., *Bracharen.*, mense sept. 1603—*Pallottini,* X, "examinatores synodales," n. 63; S. C. C., *Lucerina,* 26 nov. 1661—*Pallottini,* X, "examinatores synodales," n. 65.

[37] S. C. C., *Lucerina,* 26 nov. 1661 et S. C. C., *Capuana,* 21 nov. 1739—apud *Pallottini,* X, "examinatores synodales," nn. 64-65; Pax Iordanus, *Opera Omnia* (3 vols., Coloniae Allobrogum et Lugduni, 1729), II, *De Re Beneficiaria,* lib. X, tit. VIII, n. 190.

[38] S. C. C., *Urbaniae,* 24 iul. 1643—*Pallottini,* X, "examinatores synodales," n. 67.

[39] *Forosemproniens.*, 18 mart. 1591 et *Castri Durantis,* 30 apr. 1611—apud Ferraris, *Biblioteca,* II, "concursus," n. 8.

[40] S. C. C., *Elven.*, 1 dec. 1736, ad VII—*Thesaurus Resolutionum Sacrae Congregationis Concilii* (167 vols., Romae, 1718-1908), VII, p. 320. (Hence-

It made no difference how large or how small the vacant parish was, for which the concursus was being held, it was still necessary to have at least three examiners.[41] More than that minimum number, however, might be used.[42] If a bishop should presume to use others than true synodal examiners, both the concursus and the subsequent conferring of the parish were invalid.[43] Even though there might be present the required number of examiners, if others who were not true examiners were also permitted to take part in the concursus and to vote, the concursus was invalid.[44] If, however, one who was not a synodal examiner, for example some illustrious person, was permitted *honoris causa* to assist at the examination of the candidates the concursus was not thereby invalid, provided the outsider did not vote upon the fitness of the candidates. He might even be permitted to question the candidates and to propose cases to them.[45]

As to the actual examination which the candidates were obliged to take on theological learning there was great diversity of practice, since nothing had been determined in the Council of Trent or by Pius V concerning either the matter of the examination or the form it should take.[46] Cases in moral theology, questions in dogmatic

forth this Collection will be cited *Thes. Resol.*) Fagnanus, *Commentaria in Libros Decretalium, Commentarium in Tertium Librum Decretalium* (Venetiis, 1696), *Ne sede vacante,* cap. II, n. 18 sq. The vicar capitular was not free actually to appoint to the vacant parish the one whom he decided was the more fit. He was to report the name of this particular one to the Apostolic Datary—d'Angelo, *Parroco e Parrochia,* I, p. 49.

[41] S. C. C., *Cremonen.—Pallottini,* X, "examinatores synodales," n. 69.

[42] S. C. C., in Dubium ad dictum Cap. 18, Sess. XXIV, *de ref.*, Posit. 100—*Pallottini,* X, "examinatores synodales," n. 68.

[43] S. C. Episc. et Reg., *Casertana,* 9 febr. 1581—*Fontes,* n. 1381; S. C. Episc. et Reg., *Pistorien.*, 14 sept. 1592—*Fontes,* n. 1463.

[44] S. C. C., *Messanen.*, 9 sept. 1628; 15 dec. 1629, et *Carthaginien.*—apud Ferraris, *Biblioteca,* II, "concursus," n. 42.

[45] S. C. C., 2 sept. 1634—apud Ferraris, *loc. cit.*; de Luca, *Theatrum Veritatis et Iustitiae* (16 vols. in 9, Coloniae Agrippinae, 1706), III, pars V, *Annotationes practicae ad Conc. Tridentinum,* discursus XXXII, n. 13.

[46] P. Lambertini (postea Benedictus XIV), *Discursus Secretarii circa Appellationes, quae interponuntur, vel a mala relatione Examinatorum, vel ab irra-*

theology, explanations of the decrees of the Council of Trent, a short sermon, were among the subjects most frequently mentioned as to be treated in the examination, yet there was no determined list of subjects which had to be treated in every concursus. With regard to the form, in some dioceses the examination was given orally; in others it was written. In some the questions were the same for all, while in others different questions were proposed to each candidate. In a certain number of dioceses the custom prevailed of giving identical and written examinations.[47]

Again, there was no uniformity with respect to the amount of time to be allotted for the examination. No set time limit was determined. If it happened that the examination could not be concluded in one day, it might be carried over to another day. In the event that there was any suspicion of knowledge of the questions to be proposed, new questions were to be formulated.[48]

It was necessary for the Sacred Congregation of the Council to reaffirm, on a number of occasions, the fact that the examiners had the duty of exploring not only concerning the theological learning of the candidates, but also concerning their age, morals, prudence and other qualifications.[49] The authors were equally clear on this

tionabili iudicio Episcopi in provisione Ecclesiarum Parochialium per concursum, 1 oct. 1730, nn: XIX-XX—*Thes. Resol.*, I, pp. 375-376. (Hereafter this document of P. Lambertini will be cited simply *Discursus Secretarii.*) Benedictus XIV, Const., *Cum illud,* 14 dec. 1742, § VII—*Codex Iuris Canonici Pii X Pontificis Maximi iussu digestus, Benedicti Papae XV auctoritate promulgatus* (Romae: Typis Polyglottis Vaticanis, 1934), *Documentum IV,* pp. 809-810. (Hereafter this work is referred to as the *Codex I. C.*) Fagnanus, *Commentaria in Libros, Decretalium, Commentarium in Primum Librum Decretalium, de aetate et qualitate,* cap. IV, n. 48; de Luca, *Theatrum Veritatis et Iustitiae,* III, pars V, *Annotationes practicae ad Conc. Tridentinum,* discursus XXXII, n. 14.

[47] P. Lambertini, *Discursus Secretarii,* n. XIX—*Thes. Resol.*, I, pp. 375-376; Bened. XIV, Const., *Cum illud,* § VII—*Docum. IV in appendice ad Codicem I. C.*

[48] S. C. Episc. et Reg., 20 iul. 1592—Barbosa, *De Off. et Potest. Parochi,* pars I, cap. II, n. 53.

[49] S. C. C., *Urbinaten.*, anno 1601, et *Urbinaten.*, 23 iun. 1605, et *Hydruntina,* 19 iun. 1638—apud *Pallottini,* X, "examinatores synodales," n. 70.

point.[50] If it should happen that the synodal examiners considered only the knowledge of the sacred sciences, and not also the other qualifications required in a candidate for a vacant parish, the whole concursus and the subsequent conferral of the benefice were invalid.[51] A final point to be noted in this matter of the qualifications of the candidate for the parish other than that of the theological learning required is that the synodal examiners were allowed to gather information concerning these qualifications from extra-judicial sources, *e. g.*, by private investigation.[52]

When they had completed the examination the synodal examiners were to make their report to the bishop. According to their

[50] Garcia, *de Benef.*, pars V, cap. VII, n. 11; Barbosa, *De Off. et Potest. Parochi,* pars I, cap. II, n. 84; Fagnanus, *Commentaria in Libros Decretalium, Commentarium in Primum Librum Decretalium, de aetate et qualitate,* cap. IV, n. 15; de Luca, *Theatrum Veritatis et Iustitiae,* III, pars V, *Annotationes practicae ad Conc. Tridentinum,* discursus XXXII, nn. 3-4. A brief word may be added here in regard to the various qualifications required in a pastor. A candidate for the office of pastor was required to have entered at least his twenty-fifth year. It was necessary that he be a cleric, that he have received at least tonsure, and that he be able to receive the priesthood within a year after the time he took possession of his parish. The actual reception of the priesthood within that time was demanded by law. It was also required that he be of legitimate birth. His life had to show those virtues which are commensurate with the gravity of the parochial office. His learning had to be such as would make him competent to preach the Word of God, to administer the sacraments and to fulfill personally those other duties incumbent upon the pastor of souls in the vacant parish. He was obliged to know the language of the people of the vacant parish. He was also to be endowed with any other qualities or requisites which particular law might demand in the pastor. Besides these special qualifications which the parochial office as such required, the candidate, quite logically, was obliged to possess those qualifications which were required for the obtaining of ecclesiastical offices in general: he should not be guilty of a crime which would entail deposition, or be under censure, or be irregular, or infamous in law or in fact, or be incapable, either absolutely or relatively, because of a crime, of obtaining an ecclesiastical office. Cf. Wernz, *Ius Decretalium* (6 vols., Vol. II, Romae: Ex Typographia Polyglotta S. C. P. F., 1899), II, n. 826 et n. 294 sq.

[51] Conc. Trident., sess. XXIV, *de ref.*, c. 18: "*Alias provisiones omnes seu institutiones, praeter supra dictam formam factae, surreptitiae esse censeantur*"; S. C. C., *Urbinaten.*, anno 1601 et *Urbinaten.*, 23 iun. 1605—*Pallottini,* X, "examinatores synodales," n. 74.

[52] Barbosa, *De Off. et Potest. Parochi,* pars I, cap. II, n. 85.

findings from the examination given to ascertain the theological learning of the candidates and from the careful scrutiny of the various qualifications in each candidate, the examiners were to pronounce upon the worthiness and fitness of each of the candidates.[53] All the examiners were held to make a report, not merely some of them.[54] The examiners were to vote on the fitness of a candidate with respect to all the qualifications, moral and intellectual. They were not to report a candidate as fit in one or two qualifications, and unfit in others. They were not to report a candidate as fit in the matter of theological learning, but unfit in the matter of his mode of life and his morals. They might not judge on certain requisites and not on others, leaving the latter to the prudence and knowledge of the bishop. In brief, a candidate had to be reported as fit in all the requisite qualifications, else he was to be rejected as unfit.[55] It was not necessary, however, that the synodal examiners should make specific reference to the various qualifications. It sufficed to vote merely: "Titius is approved as fit." [56]

In regard to the method or manner of voting on the fitness of the candidates the Council of Trent made no specific laws. Consequently the examiners were permitted to cast their votes openly or in secret. They might reveal their votes to one another, or they might cast them separately.[57] The more approved method of voting was for the examiners to give their vote openly and then, when they had ascertained which of the candidates had been approved, to in-

[53] S. C. C., *Urbinaten.*, anno 1601—*Pallottini,* X, "examinatores synodales," n. 70; S. C. C., *Urbinaten.*, 23 iun. 1605—*Pallottini,* X, "examinatores synodales," n. 70; S. C. C., *Hydruntina,* 19 iun. 1638—*Pallottini,* X, "examinatores synodales." n. 70.

[54] Leurenius, *Forum Beneficiale,* pars I, sectio I, cap. III, paragr. 3, quaestio 192, n. 3.

[55] S. C. C., *Urbinaten.*, anno 1601—*Fontes,* n. 2340; S. C. C., *Urbinaten.*, 23 iun. 1605—*Pallottini,* X, "examinatores synodales," n. 74; S. C. C., *Hydruntina,* 19 iun. 1638—*Pallottini,* X, "examinatores synodales," n. 73; S. C. C., *Caputaquen.*, 10 iun. 1741—*Fontes,* n. 3516.

[56] Ventriglia, *Praxis Rerum Notabilium Praesertim Fori Ecclesiastici* (2 vols., Venetiis, 1694), II, adnotatio V, § 1, n. 47.

[57] Cf. Garcia, *de Benef.*, pars IX, cap. II, n. 107; Barbosa, *De Off. et Potest. Parochi,* pars I, cap. II, n. 86.

form the notary (or chancellor) [58] that he might write in the acts of the concursus: "Titius was approved; Caius was rejected; etc." [59] Since the approval or rejection of the candidates was a collegiate action the majority opinion ruled. Candidates who received approval by an absolute majority of the votes of the examiners were to be reported as approved.[60]

The duties of the synodal examiners ceased once they had made their report of approval or rejection of the various candidates.[61] It was necessary for the Sacred Congregation to state on a number of occasions that the examiners were not to determine who was the more worthy among the candidates. This choosing of the more fit was not their duty. It pertained to the bishop alone to make this choice.[62]

If it happened that the examiners' votes were equally distributed, or that they were distributed singly, the bishop (or his vicar general, if the latter was conducting the examination due to the fact that the bishop was impeded) might add his vote. This was the law of the Council of Trent.[63] Under no other circumstances could the

[58] Cf. Garcia, *de Benef.*, pars IX, cap. II, n. 107; P. Lambertini, *Discursus Secretarii*, n. XX—*Thes. Resol.*, I, p. 376.

[59] S. C. C., *Cremonen.—Pallottini*, X, "examinatores synodales," n. 76; Garcia, *de Benef.*, pars IX, cap. II, n. 107; Barbosa, *De Off. et Potest. Parochi*, pars I, cap. II, n. 86.

[60] Cf. Garcia, *de Benef.*, pars IX, cap. II, n. 109; Barbosa, *De Off. et Potest. Parochi*, pars I, cap. II, n. 87; de Luca, *Theatrum Veritatis et Iustitiae*, III, pars V, *Annotationes practicae ad Conc. Tridentinum*, discursus XXXII, n. 9; Leurenius, *Forum Beneficiale*, I, III, q. 191, n. 4.

[61] S. C. C., *in Lauden.*, 10 sept. 1672—*Pallottini*, X, "examinatores synodales," n. 77.

[62] S. C. C., *Patavina*, anno 1573—*Fontes*, n. 2123; S. C. C., *Vintimilien.*, mense dec. 1587—*Pallottini*, X, "examinatores synodales," n. 80; S. C. C., *Abulen.*, 1 dec. 1593—*Fontes*, n. 3520; S. C. C., *Conchen.*, anno 1598—*Pallottini*, X, "examinatores synodales," n. 80; S. C. C., *Hydruntina*, 19 iun. 1638—*Fontes*, n. 2592; also cf. Bened. XIV, Const., *Cum illud*, 14 dec. 1742, §§ 10-11—*Docum. IV in append. ad Codicem I. C.*

[63] Conc. Trident., sess. XXIV, *de ref.*, c. 18. The votes of the examiners would be equal, *e. g.*, if Caius was approved by two votes and rejected by two votes. They would be distributed singly, *e. g.*, if when there were three examiners, Caius would be approved by one examiner, rejected by another, while the third neither approved nor rejected him.—d'Angelo, *Parroco e Parrochia*, p. 114.

bishop, or his vicar general, cast a vote with the synodal examiners in the determining of the fitness of the candidates.[64]

The examiners were to cast their votes while they were gathered together with the bishop as a collegiate body. If the situation warranted a vote on the part of the bishop, he was to give this vote while the examiners were still gathered together. This was the interpretation of the authors.[65] However, when the bishop made his choice of the more fit from amongst those approved by the examiners, he was not held to make this decision in the presence of the examiners.[66] Though the examiners had not the duty to choose the more fit, still it was not forbidden to them to note in their report that one candidate was approved unanimously, another was approved by a two-thirds majority, another was just barely approved, etc.[67] Always, however, the bishop remained perfectly free in his choice of the more fit. He was in no way bound to follow such a report as if it were an infallible indication of the more worthy candidate.[68]

When a candidate who had been rejected felt that the judgment of the bishop had not been just he was permitted to appeal his case. In making the appeal, the appellant could demand that the one who had been chosen for the parish should undergo a new examination. This new examination was to take place before the judge of appeal and the latter's synodal examiners. As has been already noted, this legislation permitting appeal was given by Pius V.[69] Appeal against an unjust report on the part of the synodal examiners had previously

[64] S. C. C., anno 1573—*Pallottini,* X, "examinatores synodales," n. 81; Barbosa, *De Off. et Potest. Parochi,* pars I, cap. II, nn. 88 et 90.

[65] Garcia, *de Benef.,* pars IX, cap. II, n. 58; Barbosa, *De Off. et Potest. Parochi,* pars I, cap. II, n. 87.

[66] Garcia, *de Benef.,* pars IX, cap. II, n. 59; Barbosa, *De Off. et Potest. Parochi,* pars I, cap. II, n. 93.

[67] Cf. Garcia, *de Benef.,* pars IX, cap. II, n. 109; Barbosa, *op. cit.,* pars I, cap. II, n. 88; de Luca, *Theatrum Veritatis et Iustitiae,* III, pars V, *Annotationes practicae ad Conc. Tridentinum,* discursus XXXII, nn. 25-26.

[68] Cf. the sources mentioned in the footnote immediately preceding.

[69] Const., *In conferendis,* 18 mart. 1567, n. VII—*Fontes,* n. 119.

been admitted by the Council of Trent itself.[70] In the new examination the synodal examiners were to consider not only the question of theological learning but also the other qualifications required of candidates for a vacant parish.[71]

If appeal was taken to the Holy See the new examination was held in Rome and before the examiners of the Cardinal Vicar.[72]

In this matter of appeal it may be noted that one new examination did not suffice, but according to the practice, a second and a third were not denied until by three uniform decisions it could be determined *ad instar rei iudicatae* concerning the matter of learning.[73]

It is necessary at this point to consider briefly the law and interpretations of the law concerning vacant churches under patronage. According to the Council of Trent [74] if the vacant parish was one subject to ecclesiastical patronage the examiners were to signify their approval or rejection of the candidates presented by the patron. If, however, the vacant parish church was subject to lay patronage, the patron presented his choice to the bishop. The only requisite, in this case, previous to appointment was that the one chosen be examined and found to be fit by the bishop and his synodal examiners. In this instance it was not a concursus that was held but a simple examination to determine that the one presented was actually fit for the parochial office. However, if a number were presented to the bishop by a lay patron, then an examination by means of a concursus was to be held to determine the worthy amongst those presented. In this case the synodal examiners were to be employed as usual.[75] When there was question of a vacant parish of "mixed patronage" there was no need for a concursus. The pa-

[70] Conc. Trident., sess. XXIV, *de ref.*, c. 18. Cf. Bened. XIV, Const., *Redditae Nobis,* 9 apr. 1746, n. XV—*Fontes,* n. 367.

[71] Garcia, *de Benef.*, pars IX, cap. II, n. 252; P. Lambertini, *Discursus Secretarii,* 1 oct. 1730, n. X—*Thes. Resol.*, I, pp. 371-372.

[72] P. Lambertini, *ibidem,* n. X.

[73] P. Lambertini, *loc. cit.*; Bened. XIV, Const., *Cum illud,* 14 dec. 1742, § III—*Docum. IV in append. ad Codicem I. C.*

[74] Conc. Trident., sess. XXIV, *de ref.*, c. 18.

[75] S. C. C., *Vercellen.*, 21 mart. 1643—*Fontes,* n. 2642; cf. Barbosa, *De Off. et Potest. Parochi,* pars I, cap. II, n. 130; cf. also, Garcia, *de Benef.*, pars VII, cap. XVI, n. 19.

rochial church was to be conferred as if it were of purely lay patronage.[76]

In concluding this Article it may be remarked that the Ordinary was not bound to use the synodal examiners, or to hold a concursus, when he examined candidates for parishes whose pastor might be removed at the will of the Ordinary.[77] Nor was there to be a concursus in the conferring of parishes connected with a monastery or with a chapter, when the one who had the actual care of souls was merely the vicar, while the habitual care of souls pertained to the monastery or chapter.[78] At times, too, the bestowal of certain parishes was reserved to the Apostolic See, either because they became vacant in months that were reserved, or for some other reason. In such cases a concursus was, nevertheless, held by the bishop and his examiners.[79]

[76] S. C. C., 5 febr. 1628—apud Barbosa, *De Off. et Potest. Parochi,* pars I, cap. II, nn. 125-126; Bened. XIV, *De Synodo Dioecesana,* lib. IV, cap. VIII, n. 10; Soglia, *Institutiones Iuris Privati Ecclesiastici* (3 vols., Paris., 1842), II, lib. I, cap. III, n. 28, p. 45; Septimius Vecchiotti, *Institutiones Canonicae* (19. ed., 3 vols., Augustae Taurinorum, 1886), I, cap. VIII, n. 87. Cf. tamen, d'Angelo, *Parroco e Parrochia,* I, p. 58.

[77] Cf. Soglia, *op. cit.,* II, appendix, n. XVII, p. 26; cf. also, Leurenius, *Forum Beneficiale,* pars I, quaestio 179 sq.; Coady, *The Appointment of Pastors,* The Catholic University of America Canon Law Studies, n. 52 (Washington, D. C.: The Catholic University of America, 1929), p. 37.

[78] Cf. de Luca, *Theatrum Veritatis et Iustitiae,* III, pars V, *Annotationes practicae ad Conc. Tridentinum,* discursus XXXII, n. 33; Leurenius, *Forum Beneficiale,* pars I, quaestio 120, n. 2; Soglia, *op. cit.,* II, lib. I, cap. III, n. 28, p. 45.

[79] Cf. on this subject: Bened. XIV, Const., *Cum illud,* 14 dec. 1742, §§ XIX-XXI—*Docum. IV in append. ad Codicem I. C.* Here the complete legislation, at least as it stood at the time of this Constitution, is given in regard to the procedure to be followed when parishes were reserved to the Apostolic See. Cf. also, Pius V, Const., *In conferendis,* 18 mart. 1567, §§ II-VI—*Fontes,* n. 119.

CHAPTER II

SYNODAL EXAMINERS FROM THE CONSTITUTION "CUM ILLUD" TO THE DECREE "MAXIMA CURA"

ARTICLE 1. INFLUENCE ON THE NEW LEGISLATION

No papal legislation on the concursus, and more particularly, on the synodal examiners had been forthcoming from the time of Clement VIII (1592-1605). Benedict XIV (1740-1758), however, gave special attention to these matters, and made new legislation which gave to the concursus a much more perfect form.[1]

This new papal legislation was no doubt motivated by previous efforts for reform on the part of Clement XI (1700-1721) and of the Sacred Congregation of the Council.[2] P. Lambertini, later Pope Benedict XIV, was commissioned by the Sacred Congregation of the Council, of which he was the Secretary, to study the question of appeal from the concursus.[3] This question was causing a great amount of difficulty since appeals were becoming too numerous, were allowed very often without proof, from the acts of the original concursus, of a grievance to the appellant, and were causing great harm to the parishes in question.[4] Lambertini submitted his report on October 1, 1720. It contained an analysis of the law concerning appeals,[5] a consideration of the inconveniences and difficulties which came from the law and from accepted interpretations of the law,[6] and finally a set of proposals to remedy these inconveniences and difficulties.[7]

[1] Bened. XIV, Const., *Cum illud,* 14 dec. 1742—*Docum. IV in append. ad Codicem I. C.*

[2] Bened. XIV, *ibidem,* § VI.

[3] Lambertini, *Discursus Secretarii,* 1 oct. 1720, Introd. paragr.—*Thes. Resol.,* I, p. 371; Bened. XIV, *ibidem,* § V.

[4] Bened. XIV., *ibidem,* § III.

[5] Lambertini, *Discursus Secretarii,* nn. I-XI—*Thes. Resol.,* I, pp. 371-374.

[6] *Ibidem,* nn. XII-XVI.

[7] *Ibidem,* nn. XVII-XXIV.

The Sacred Congregation, consequent to its consideration of this report of the Secretary, proposed to itself a set of doubts, in accord with the suggested remedies of the Secretary.[8] It postponed giving an answer to these questions on October 1, 1720, but did give its responses on November 16th of the same year.[9]

In the following year, an encyclical letter was drawn up by the Secretary of the Congregation, P. Lambertini. This was approved by the then reigning Pontiff, Clement XI, and was sent, in the name of the Sacred Congregation of the Council, to the local Ordinaries.[10] It would be a useless repetition to repeat what was said in this encyclical letter concerning the synodal examiners and their duties, since what was proposed therein [11] was made law a brief twenty-one years later in 1742, in the Constitution, *"Cum illud,"* of Benedict XIV.[12] It suffices to make a close study of the new papal legislation as contained in this latter document.

Article 2. New Legislation by Benedict XIV on the Duties of the Synodal Examiners

In order that everything might be done aptly and correctly Benedict XIV prescribed a definite order of action to be followed in the concursus.[13] Herein are given only those parts of the new legislation which touched upon, or were closely connected with, the duties of the synodal examiners:

1. notice of the concursus was to be given by public edict; [14]

[8] S. C. C., Oct. 1, 1720—*Thes. Resol.*, I, p. 368.

[9] S. C. C., 16 nov. 1720—*Thes. Resol.*, I, p. 384.

[10] Litterae Encyclicae S. C. C., 10 iun. 1721—apud Bened. XIV, Const., *Cum illud,* 14 dec. 1742, § VII—*Docum. IV in append. ad Codicem I. C.*

[11] The encyclical letter of the Sacred Congregation, even though approved by Clement XI, did not actually create any new law, since what was contained therein was merely a proposal, a suggestion as to what should be done. Cf. *ASS,* VII, p. 367; Wernz, *Ius Decretalium,* II, n. 827, II; d'Angelo, *Parroco e Parrochia,* I, p. 26.

[12] § XVI, n. 4 et § XVI, n. 6.

[13] Bened. XIV, Const., *Cum illud,* 14 dec. 1742, § XVI—*Docum. IV in append. ad Codicem I. C.*

[14] *Ibidem,* § XVI, n. 2. The legislation is not always given in a verbatim translation, yet an effort has been made to preserve the exact meaning of the law.

2. the examiners were to receive from the chancellor of the concursus copies of a summary made by the chancellor from the documents presented by the candidates and dealing with their merits, qualities and other requisites. This was to be done in order that the examiners might be able to pass judgment on the knowledge, life, morals and other qualifications requisite in the appointee for the ruling of the vacant church; [15]
3. the same questions, the same cases, the same text of the Gospels on which a sermon was to be written, were to be proposed to all the candidates; [16]
4. these cases and questions were to be dictated to all at the same time; also at the same time the text of the Gospels was to be given to all; [17]
5. a definite time was to be set, the same for all, for the solving of cases, the responses to questions and the writing of the sermon; [18]
6. all those examined were to be in the same closed room, and they were not to leave it, nor were others to enter it, till the papers had been completed and handed in. Everyone was to be given writing materials; [19]
7. each was to write in his own handwriting the answers and the sermon, and to sign his name to his responses and sermon; [20]
8. answers were to be in Latin; the sermon in the language ordinarily used in preaching to the people; [21]
9. each response and each sermon, when handed in by a candidate, was to be signed not only by the candidate but also by the chancellor of the concursus, by the synodal examiners and by the Ordinary, or his vicar general, who were present at the concursus; [22]
10. the examiners, in order that they might gain certain and indubitable information concerning the candidate, were to study closely the skill with which each developed and explained orally some point

[15] *Ibidem*, § XVI, n. 3.
[16] *Ibidem*, § VII, n. 1 cum § XVI, n. 4.
[17] *Ibidem*, § VII, n. 2 cum § XVI, n. 4.
[18] *Ibidem*, § VII, n. 3 cum § XVI, n. 4.
[19] *Ibidem*, § VII, n. 4 cum § XVI, n. 4.
[20] *Ibidem*, § VII, n. 5 cum § XVI, n. 4.
[21] *Ibidem*, § VII, n. 6 cum § XVI, n. 4.
[22] *Ibidem*, § VII, n. 7, cum § XVI, n. 4.

of Church doctrine, taken from the Fathers, or from the Council of Trent, or from the Roman Catechism. They were to study carefully the worth of the arguments and the style of writing in the sermon that each had written on a text from the Gospels or on some other theme; [23]

11. furthermore, the examiners were to give just as much, if not greater, care to the scrutiny of the other qualifications requisite for the care of souls; they were to inquire into the good morals of each candidate, the gravity of his character, his prudence, services already rendered by him to the Church, commendation merited by him in other offices, and the practice in his life of all other exceptional virtues which are closely linked to doctrine; [24]

12. when all these matters, taken together as a whole, had been studied, the examiners by their votes were to reject the unqualified, and the qualified they were to report as such to the bishop; [25]

13. once the concursus was completed the synodal examiners were to return to the chancellor the summaries of qualifications which had previously been distributed to them by him. These the chancellor was to burn or keep secretly with the acts.[26]

A study of this papal legislation reveals not so much a change from previous legislation as a clarification of and addition to what had previously been decreed.

It was the appeal which had caused the greatest amount of trouble previous to the time of Benedict XIV, and it was in order to avoid numerous, useless and unjust appeals that the new legislation was issued by Benedict XIV.[27] In referring specifically to the appeal, the new legislation stated that the source of the evil of numerous appeals was the practice of giving orally the examination on

[23] *Ibidem,* § XVI, n. 4. [It is to be noted that Pope Benedict XIV made provision here for an oral questioning in regard to church doctrine in addition to the written questions referred to in §§ 3, 5 and 7. It is also to be remarked that the sermon topic could be from the Gospels or on some other theme. § 4 had only referred to a text from the Gospels.]

[24] *Ibidem,* § XVI, n. 4.

[25] *Ibidem,* § XVI, n. 4.

[26] *Ibidem,* § XVI, n. 5.

[27] *Ibidem,* §§ III-IV.

theological learning.[28] In order to do away with this source of the evil the written examination was made obligatory.[29] With the law requiring the examinations on theological learning to be written and kept in the acts of the concursus, and requiring the testimonials concerning the other requisites to be likewise preserved in the acts the necessity of permitting a new examination was no longer necessary.[30] If one of the candidates should make an appeal, he would have to prove the existence of a legitimate grievance. This grievance would come either from the unjust report of the examiners or from an unreasonable judgment by the bishop as to the more worthy. Judgment as to the existence of a grievance was left solely to the judge of appeal, and his judgment was to be based on evidence found in the acts of the first concursus which were to be transmitted to him. The synodal examiners were to have no part in this judgment.[31] As regards these acts of the original concursus which were to be sent to the judge of appeal, if an authentic exemplar was sent and not the original acts, the synodal examiners were to affix their signature to the exemplar.[32]

This legislation of Benedict XIV *on the appeal* was quite definitely a change from previous legislation. The law previously in effect did not require any proof of a grievance before admitting a new examination before the judge of appeal and his synodal examiners.[33]

Appendix: Summary of Previous Law on the Duties of the Synodal Examiners Which Still Remained in Effect After the Constitution, "Cum Illud"

As is evident from the whole of the Constitution, *"Cum illud,"* which has just been studied, Benedict XIV did not have in mind the repealing of previous law on the concursus, except in the matter of appeal. His main purpose, as has been stated, was to issue such

[28] *Ibidem,* § V.

[29] *Ibidem,* § VII.

[30] *Ibidem,* §§ III et XVI, n. 6.

[31] *Ibidem,* § XVI, n. 6. For further details on the appeal, cf. *ibidem,* §§ XVI, n. 7, XVII, XVIII.

[32] *Ibidem,* § VII cum XVI, n. 4.

[33] Pius V, Const., *In conferendis,* § VII—*Fontes,* n. 119.

additional legislation as was necessary to preclude those evils which had resulted because the law was not sufficiently complete. Conquently, it may be of value to re-state at this point the prescriptions of the Council of Trent and of Pius V which touched upon the work of the synodal examiners and which were still in effect. In this way a fairly complete picture will be had of the law on the duties of the synodal examiners as it stood at the time of the Constitution, *"Cum illud."* Such a re-statement is also of definite value because of the fact that it places in contrast the legislation of the Council of Trent and of Pius V, which was required for validity,[34] and the legislation of Benedict XIV, which, since it contained no invalidating clause, was not considered as binding under penalty of invalidity.[35] We shall also add here, or at least refer to, those previous decisions, of the Sacred Congregation of the Council especially, and those doctrinal interpretations of the law which had a bearing on the law at this time. This will complete the picture of the law on the duties of the synodal examiners as it stood after Benedict XIV's Constitution.

(1) The concursus was to be conducted by the bishop, or, if he was impeded, by his vicar general, and by at least three synodal examiners.[36]

(2) The matter of the examination included: the age, the morals, the learning, the prudence and the other qualifications suitable in a candidate for ruling the vacant church.[37]

(3) Once the examination of the candidates was completed the synodal examiners were to make known to the bishop the names of

[34] Conc. Trident., sess. XXIV, *de ref.*, c. 18: *"Alias provisiones omnes seu institutiones, praeter supra dictam formam factae, surreptitiae esse censeantur."* Pius V, Const., *In conferendis*, § 3—*Fontes*, n. 119, where the identical nullifying clause used by the Council of Trent is renewed.

[35] Cf. *ASS*, VII, p. 350; Wernz, *Ius Decretalium*, II, n. 827, VII. Reclusio claimed that the legislation of Benedict XIV also came under the invalidating clause of the Council of Trent (*Tractatus de Concursibus, Collationibus et Vacationibus Parochiarum Aliorumque Beneficiorum* [Romae, 1774], pars II, tit. IV, nn. 84, 89 et 93), but his opinion is quite definitely disproven by those holding the opposite view. (Hereafter this work is cited *De Concursibus*.)

[36] Conc. Trident., sess. XXIV, *de ref.*, c. 18; cf. also, *supra*, pp. 14-15.

[37] Conc. Trident., *loc. cit.*; cf. also, *supra*, pp. 16-17.

those whom they judged to be possessed of the requisite qualifications.[38]

(4) Synodal examiners might not receive anything for their labor, or as a reward, from the fruits of the vacant parish. Offenders against this law were guilty of simony. A bishop, however, might make some recompense to the examiners from his own funds.[39]

(5) Candidates might object to certain synodal examiners, and, if they gave sufficient proof that the objection was well taken, these examiners were to be excluded. The bishop was the judge in the matter.[40]

(6) The synodal examiners were obliged to take an oath upon the Holy Gospels to fulfill their duties faithfully, all human considerations being put aside. If they had never taken the oath, but nevertheless participated in a concursus, the concursus was invalid.[41]

(7) The synodal examiners were held to render an account of their actions to the diocesan synod whenever this might become necessary, and, if it was found that they had acted contrary to the duties of their office, they might be punished severely, subject to the discretion of the bishop, by this synod.[42]

(8) Provincial synods might add to, or withdraw from, the regulations in the Tridentine form of examination.[43]

ARTICLE 3. CURIAL PRACTICE AND CANONICAL TEACHING FROM THE CONSTITUTION, *"Cum illud,"* TO THE DECREE, *"Maxima Cura"*

A. *Practice and Teaching Regarding the Duties*

What follows is a summary of various solutions to problems

[38] Conc. Trident., *loc. cit.*; cf. also, *supra*, pp. 17-20.

[39] Conc. Trident., *loc. cit.*; cf. also, *supra*, p. 13.

[40] Cf. *supra*, pp. 13-14.

[41] Conc. Trident., *loc. cit.*; cf. also, *supra*, pp. 12-13.

[42] Pius V, Const., *Apostolatus officium*, 18 aug. 1567—*Bull. Rom. Taur.*, VII, pp. 606-607.

[43] Conc. Trident., *loc. cit.* For the law on parishes to which was attached the right of patronage, cf. *supra*, pp. 5, 7, 21. The new legislation of Benedict XIV was, of course, to be applied also to a concursus held in connection with parishes of patronal right. For a statement concerning parishes which might be conferred without a concursus, cf. *supra*, pp. 5, 22.

which arose after 1742 regarding the synodal examiners and their duties in the concursus.[44]

Benedict XIV, in his Constitution, *"Cum illud,"* stated simply that notice of a concursus was to be given by public edict.[45] Such a statement, however, was not meant to set an exclusive method of action. It still remained possible for the bishop to designate within ten days, or such other term as he might prescribe (not to exceed an additional ten days), in the presence of those to be delegated as examiners, certain clerics as capable of governing the vacant church. If this latter method were chosen, others might also present the names of fit candidates.[46] When the vacant church was of ecclesiastical patronage there was to be no edict, but, as previous to 1742, the patron was held to present candidates within the above-mentioned time. These candidates he presented to the synodal examiners.[47]

Another regulation set down by the Benedictine Constitution, *"Cum illud,"* [48] required the signatures of the candidates, the Ordinary (or his vicar general, when the latter lawfully substituted for the bishop), the chancellor of the concursus and the synodal examiners upon each response and upon the sermon when these were handed in by a candidate. Although this was not required under penalty of invalidity, nevertheless the Sacred Congregation was accustomed to nullify a concursus in which this formality was not scrupulously observed.[49]

Whatever form was used by the synodal examiners in arriving at a decision concerning the fitness of the candidates one thing is certain, namely, that in making the final report they were to state simply that a candidate had been judged fit, or had been rejected as

[44] N. B. The history of the duties of the synodal examiners in the concursus is completed in this section, that is, the history is studied from the Constitution, *"Cum illud,"* up to the Code of Canon Law.

[45] § XVI, n. 2.

[46] Cf. discussion in: S. C. C., 3 mart. 1877—*AAS,* X, pp. 129 et 134; cf. also, Conc. Trident., sess. XXIV, *de ref.,* c. 18; Pius V, Const., *In conferendis,* 18 mart. 1567, § V—*Fontes,* n. 119.

[47] Reclusio, *De Concursibus,* pars I, tit. III, n. 47.

[48] § VII, n. 5 cum § XVI, n. 4 et § VII, n. 6 cum § XVI, n. 4.

[49] S. C. C., *Lavinen.,* 3 sept. 1758—*Fontes,* n. 3681; S. C. C., *Beneventana,* 25 ian. 1878—*Thes. Resol.,* CXXXVII, pp. 59-74.

unfit. They were not to report a number of separate decisions, *e. g.*, Titius is fit in learning, unfit in morals, etc.[50]

A question of importance concerning the examination of candidates by the synodal examiners was brought forth in an appeal from a concursus held in the diocese of Brescia, Italy. The doubt proposed to the Sacred Congregation of the Council was whether the method of examining the candidates in a concursus as set down by the bishops of the province of Milan could be approved.[51] The reply was in the affirmative. The method adopted by this province of Milan was to require in every concursus for vacant parishes, except those of least importance, an examination by the synodal examiners not only in regard to fitness in general for the parochial office, but also in regard to fitness relative to the particular church that was vacant.[52] It must be kept in mind that the decision of the Sacred Congregation did not affirm that such a procedure was the only one that could be followed by synodal examiners in any concursus no matter where held. It merely stated that the method in question could be used. It made no further comment. However, the presentation of the case by the consultor who approved of the method under consideration is very interesting.[53] He admitted that at least as far as terminology was concerned, the distinction between an absolute judgment and a relative judgment on the part of the examiners as to the fitness of the candidates was hitherto unknown. The law and the doctors spoke simply of a judgment by the examiners on the fitness of the candidates. But the consultor proceeded to offer proofs that actually the synodal examiners had the duty of giving not only a judgment of fitness for the parochial office in gen-

[50] Bened. XIV, Const., *Cum illud,* § XVI, n. 4: *"Hisque omnibus coniunctim expensis, inhabiles per sua vota reiiciant et idoneos Episcopo renuntient."* Cf. Votum consultoris, n. XVI in S. C. C., *Brixien. et aliarum,* 27 ian. et 22 apr. 1911—*AAS,* IV, pp. 317-318.

[51] S. C. C., *Brixien. et aliarum,* 27 ian. et 22 apr. 1911—*AAS,* IV, pp. 296 sq.

[52] *Regolamento per i concorsi alle parrochie nella provincia ecclesiastica Lombarda,* 1896, n. IV—apud d'Angelo, *Parroco e Parrochia,* I, pp. 168-169.

[53] Votum consultoris, nn. I-XVI in S. C. C., *Brixien. et aliarum,* 27 ian. et 22 apr. 1911—*AAS,* IV (1911), 296 sq.

eral, but that they were also to give a judgment as to fitness for the particular parish for which the concursus was being held.[54]

A further consideration concerning this report on fitness which the synodal examiners were to make to the bishop is that it was required that only the names of those found to be fit had to be reported. The rejected did not have to be mentioned.[55]

Benedict XIV, in his *De Synodo Dioecesana,*[56] stated that the voting was to take place before the synodal examiners and the bishop left the place of examination. Reclusio, however,[57] pointed out that there was nothing in the law which stated exactly the time when the scrutiny of the papers and the voting had to take place. Therefore, he continued, in spite of what Benedict XIV might say to the contrary, the custom of each diocese might be followed in this matter, and it was not at all necessary that this scrutiny, voting and consequent report to the bishop had to be completed by the synodal examiners immediately following the examination and before they left the place of examination. Reclusio pointed to the practice in Rome of waiting a few days for the ultimate disposition of these matters. Nor was it required by law that the candidates be called back for this scrutiny, though this was done in Rome, where each candidate in turn heard his sermon and responses read by the secretary of the concursus, after which he left and the examiners cast their vote. Giraldi likewise admitted that this scrutiny and voting

[54] Authors since have very clearly stated that the words of the Council of Trent, "peracto deinde examine, renuncientur quotcumque ab his (examinatoribus) *idonei iudicati fuerint* aetate, moribus, doctrina, prudentia et aliis rebus *ad vacantem ecclesiam gubernandam,*" did require that the synodal examiners should consider the requisite qualifications in the candidates in relation to the actual parish that is vacant. The question to be answered by the examiners was: "Are the candidates fitted as far as these requisites are concerned to rule this particular parish?" Cf. Discussion in S. C. C., *Romana et Aliarum,* 21 iun. 1919—*AAS,* XI (1919), p. 318 ff.; "Quesiti Minori," n. 17—*Monit. Eccl.* (Romae, 1876—), serie IV, Vol. II (Vol. XXXII della intera Collezione) (1920), p. 197; d'Angelo, *Parroco e Parrochia* I, p. 109.

[55] Reclusio, *De Concursibus,* pars I, tit. V, nn. 12-13.

[56] Lib. IV, cap. VIII, n. 4.

[57] *Op. cit.,* pars I, tit. IV, nn. 2-4.

might take place on another day.[58] The opinion of Benedict XIV seems to have been the prevalent opinion previous to 1742.[59] Although the synodal examiners had no right to determine the more fit from amongst those found to be fit, still there was no law which stated that the bishop might not take into account the votes received by each candidate from the examiners, nor was there any prohibition against the bishop seeking the counsel of the examiners when he was about to make his choice of the more fit.[60]

B. *Practice and Teaching Regarding the Office*

In the interval between the Constitution, *"Cum illud,"* of Benedict XIV, until the Decrée, *"Maxima cura,"* in 1910, there was issued no pontifical legislation concerning the synodal examiners either in regard to their person or in regard to their duties in the special concursus.[61] Consideration has just been given to the curial practice and canonical teaching during this period with regard to the duties of the synodal examiners. Attention is turned now to a study of the few decisions and interpretations on the office of these officials which appeared during this period.

As was mentioned above,[62] the Sacred Congregation of the Council had stated that not more than twenty examiners should be chosen in a synod. In the period following the Constitution, *"Cum illud,"* the same restriction was spoken of by Benedict XIV and by Ferraris.[63]

In the question of approval by the diocesan synod of those proposed by the bishop for the office of synodal examiner, Giraldi noted that an absolute majority was the requisite for approval.[64]

[58] Barbosa, *De Officio et Potestate Parochi, Animadversiones et Additamenta,* Giraldi (Romae, 1831), pars I, cap. II, n. 53, animadversio.

[59] Cf. *supra,* p. 20.

[60] Bened. XIV, *De Synodo Dioecesana,* lib. IV, cap. VIII, n. 6; Ferraris, *Biblioteca,* "concursus," n. 64.

[61] Wernz-Vidal, *Ius Canonicum,* II, n. 827, VII.

[62] Cf. *supra,* p. 10.

[63] Bened. XIV, *De Synodo Dioecesana,* lib. IV, cap. VII, n. 3; Ferraris, *Biblioteca,* II, "concursus," n. 32.

[64] Barbosa, *De Officio et Potestate Parochi, Animadversiones et Additamenta,* Giraldi, pars I, cap. II, n. 56, animadversio.

Benedict XIV remarked that the Sacred Congregation of the Council never refused the faculty to bishops to elect examiners outside of a synod when no synod could be held. He added the usual conditions, that the faculty must be obtained each year, and that approval by the chapter was always required.[65] It was also understood that even if the bishop delayed in making use of this faculty to elect outside a synod, nevertheless, the faculty remained and could be validly used.[66]

A question arose as to what was to be done if the chapter unjustly refused to give its consent when a bishop, with the necessary faculty, would present the names of certain priests for the office of examiner. Reclusio held that if the chapter unjustly refused to approve those who were actually fit, then these were to be considered as approved.[67] Benedict XIV, however, and Ferraris felt that this was a dangerous opinion to follow in practice since the bishop could hardly be a safe judge in a matter which concerned his own choice of candidates. It was better, according to these authors, to do as some bishops had already done, namely, to propose the matter to the Sacred Congregation of the Council and to petition for supplementary consent.[68]

In regard to the oath to fulfill the duties of office faithfully, Benedict XIV and Reclusio held that the synodal examiners might take this oath upon sacred relics as well as upon the Holy Gospels.[69] Another point in regard to the oath is that it sufficed to take it once.[70]

It was decided by the Sacred Congregation of the Council that if a bishop, with the requisite faculty, should propose to the Chapter for approval a number of names for the office of synodal examiner,

[65] *De Synodo Dioecesana,* lib. IV, cap. VII, n. 10.

[66] Cf. discussion in S. C. C., *Melevitana,* 2 iun. et 15 sept. 1764—*Thes. Resol.,* XXXIII, pp. 84 et 133-135.

[67] *De Concursibus,* pars I, tit. III, n. 66.

[68] Benedict XIV, *op. cit.,* lib. IV, cap. VII, n. 10; Ferraris, *Biblioteca,* III, "examen," n. 65 sq.

[69] Bened. XIV, *op. cit.,* lib. IV, cap. VII, n. 6; Reclusio, *op. cit.,* pars I, tit. III, n. 77.

[70] Cf. discussion in S. C. C., *Bisinianen.,* 3 apr. 1756—*Thes. Resol.,* XXV, p. 28; Reclusio, *op. cit.,* pars I, tit. III, n. 78.

amongst which was the name of one of the canons of the Chapter, this particular canon would not be able to vote for himself, but he might vote on the other names proposed.[71]

Article 4. Synodal Examiners and the General Concursus

The laws of the Council of Trent, including, of course, the legislation on the concursus, were not published and received everywhere, and even in some places where they were published the legislation on the concursus was not always observed in the same manner.[72] As a consequence there came into existence what has been termed the *general concursus,* which differed more or less according to places from the concursus instituted by the Council of Trent. (The latter received the name *special concursus.*) The practice of having a general concursus came to be accepted as legitimate by reason either of special apostolic indult or of legitimate custom.[73]

It is not to be imagined that this general concursus was the same in all places. On the contrary, it took different forms in different places.[74] The form which seems to have been more commonly used may be briefly described as follows: the examination on learning was separated from the examination of the other requisite qualifications. The former was held once or twice a year for those who were eligible to become pastors and who presented themselves. This examination on learning was similar to its counterpart in the special concursus. It was held before at least three examiners. Those who were approved by the examiners in this examination remained approved for either a certain period, *e. g.,* for three or six years, or *in perpetuum.* The examination into the other requisite qualifica-

[71] S. C. C., *Iandren.,* 19 maii 1877—*Thes. Resol.,* CXXXVI, p. 286.

[72] Fanfani, *De Iure Parochorum,* n. 104; Wernz, *Ius Decretalium,* II, n. 827, II.

[73] S. C. de Prop. Fide, Instr., 10 oct. 1884—*Fontes,* n. 4906; Vecchiotti, *Institutiones Canonicae,* I, cap. VIII, p. 338; Wernz, *op. cit.,* II, n. 827, scholion.

[74] Wernz, *op. cit.,* II, n. 827; Chelodi, *Ius de Personis iuxta Codicem Iuris Canonici* (2. ed., Tridentini: Libr. Edit. Tridentinum, 1927), n. 225, b; Coronata, *Institutiones Iuris Canonici* (5 vols., vols. I-II, 2. ed., 1939; vols. III-V, 1933-1936, Taurini: Marietti), II, n. 477. (Hereafter this work will be cited *Institutiones.*)

tions of these approved candidates was made whenever a parish would become vacant. In some places it was necessary for the candidates to present themselves for this examination of the other requisites, while in other places this was not demanded. The synodal examiners either approved or rejected the candidates on the basis of the possession or the lack of these other qualifications. Consequent to this examination and report by the examiners the bishop chose the most fit to become pastor of the vacant parish. As has been stated, in certain places the approval in regard to learning lasted but a certain definite period. Once the period was concluded a new examination on learning would have to be taken. However, in some of these places it was possible for a candidate to be exempted from the obligation to undergo a new examination. This exemption was determined by the bishop, after hearing the opinion of the synodal examiners. Reasons for exemption were possession of the office of synodal examiner, the special dignity of an office which the candidate held, lengthy and praiseworthy service in the Church, and evident testimony of the candidate's learning.[75] This type of general concursus existed in Germany and Austria.[76]

Another form which the general concursus took was that there would be held a single concursus whenever a number of parishes had become vacant. The examiners would report the candidates whom they considered fit for the parochial office in general, and the bishop would then choose, from amongst the approved, pastors for the various vacant churches.[77]

In France and Belgium a series of examinations was held at regular intervals, and those who passed these examinations successfully were considered as fit candidates for any parochial benefices which might become vacant within a certain period. Once this period had

[75] Cf. S. C. de Prop. Fide, Instr., 10 oct. 1884—*Fontes,* n. 4906; Wernz, *Ius Decret.,* II, n. 827, scholion; Rossi, *De Paroecia* (Romae: Pustet, 1923), n. 169; Sipos, *Enchiridion Iuris Canonici* (3. ed., Pécs: Haladás R. T., 1936), p. 316. (Hereafter this work will be cited *Enchiridion.*)

[76] Wernz, *loc. cit.*; Sipos, *loc. cit.*; Rossi, *loc. cit.*

[77] Chelodi, *Ius de Personis,* n. 225; Rossi, *op. cit.,* n. 169; Blat, *Commentarium Textus Codicis Iuris Canonici* (5 vols. in 6, lib. II, 2. ed., Romae: Ex Typographia Pontificia in Instituto Pii IX), II, n. 507. (Hereafter this work will be cited as *Commentarium.*)

elapsed a new examination had to be undergone.[78] Apparently these examinations were different from the concursus, whether special or general. It does not seem, for instance, that synodal examiners were required at all.

What has been said concerning the general concursus is very brief. Even more brief has been the description of the duties of the synodal examiners in these types of the general concursus. However, it is hardly possible to give a more detailed description since the procedure appeared to vary according to places. One would have to study this general concursus in each of the forms it took in particular countries or dioceses, in order to see exactly what was required of the synodal examiners. Still, it may be safely said, it seems, that the duties of the examiners remained practically the same as in the special concursus, because in spite of the changes one notes in the general concursus, nevertheless the substance of the law of the Council of Trent appears to have been preserved.

Article 5. Examiners of the Diocesan Clergy in the United States

The II Plenary Council of Baltimore (1866), having in mind the prescriptions of the Council of Trent concerning synodal examiners, *advised* the bishops of the United States to appoint such examiners for the purpose of examining both candidates for Sacred Orders, and priests for the concession of faculties to hear confessions and for the purpose of drawing up testimonial letters. The bishops were advised to nominate these examiners in a diocesan synod or in a meeting of the clergy. It was further suggested that because of the lack of priests, a situation prevalent in almost every diocese, these examiners might at the same time hold the office of consultor to the bishop (diocesan consultor). Mention was made of the fact that the one

[78] Acta et Decreta SS. Concilii Vaticani. Appendix. cf. Postulata Archiepiscopi et Episcopi Belgii—*Collectio Lacensis, Acta et Decreta Sacrorum Conciliorum Recentiorum* (7 vols., Friburgi Brisgoviae: Herder & Co., 1870—1890), VII, p. 875; Wernz, *op. cit.*, II, n. 827, scholion; Bouuaert, *Selecta Capita Codicis Iuris Canonici Analytice Proposita et Brevi Commentario Adaucta* (Gandae, 1919), p. 46.

duty which by common law pertained to the synodal examiners could not be considered as relevant in the United States, since the law of the concursus had no place as yet in the country.[79]

The III Plenary Council of Baltimore (1884) treated the subject of examiners at greater length. It was enacted that each bishop should appoint *examiners of the diocesan clergy (examinatores cleri dioecesani),* after the manner of the synodal or pro-synodal examiners *(ad instar examinatorum synodalium vel prosynodalium).*[80] This definite obligation to create the office of *examiner of the clergy* obviously abrogated the suggestion of the previous Council for the appointment of *synodal examiners.*[81]

It was decreed[82] that for the office of *examiner of the clergy* there should be chosen ecclesiastics commended by their good morals, and, in so far as possible, those who were especially versed in the Sacred Sciences, including canon law. If possible there should be at least six examiners. Appointment was to be made at the diocesan synod, but with the necessary faculty from the Holy See a bishop might choose examiners outside a synod. In such a case he would have to first *hear* the consultors on the matter. Their consent was not required. Whenever vacancies occurred by reason of death, or resignation, or for some other reason, a bishop might, *with the advice* of the consultors, substitute others.[83] Furthermore, continued the Council,[84] those elected to the office of *examiner of the clergy* were obliged to take an oath to fulfill faithfully their duty and not to receive gifts on the occasion of an examination. This oath was to be taken in the synod provided the examiners were elected therein and if they were

[79] *Concilii Plenarii Baltimorensis Secundi, Acta et Decreta, A. D. MDCCCLXXXIV* (ed. altera, Baltimorae: John Murphy, 1894), n. 76. (Hereafter this wor'· will be cited *C. Plen. Balt. II, Acta et Decreta.*)

[80] *Acta et Decreta Concilii Plenarii Baltimorensis Tertii, A. D. MDCCCLXXXVI* (Baltimorae, John Murphy, 1886), n. 24. (Hereafter this work will be cited *Acta et Decreta Conc. Plen. Balt. III.*)

[81] Cf. pp. 44-45.

[82] *Acta et Decreta Conc. Balt. III,* n. 24.

[83] *Ibidem,* n. 25.

[84] *Ibidem,* n. 26.

present; otherwise it was to be taken before the bishop, or his delegate.

The principal duty of these new officials would be to have a part in the particular law concursus held for those missions which enjoyed the privilege of irremovability. It was also suggested that they be used in approving priests for confessions, and in the examinations of candidates for orders, of the Junior Clergy and, finally, of those who wished to be admitted to the major seminary.[85]

The Examiners and the Concursus According to the III Plenary Council of Baltimore

The II Plenary Council of Baltimore did not attempt to introduce the concursus, because, as it stated, the legislation of the Council of Trent on the concursus could hardly be observed even if there were juridical pastors in the United States. Instead this Council enacted that no one should be appointed rector of a church without first being examined by the bishop and two priests designated by the bishop.[86]

The III Plenary Council of Baltimore, however, decreed that there should be held a concursus for vacant missions which enjoyed the privilege of irremovability.[87] This examination or concursus was to take place before the bishop, or his vicar general, and at least three diocesan examiners, in place of the synodal or pro-synodal examiners. The bishop was to designate which examiners would participate.

[85] *Ibidem,* n. 24. These *examiners of the diocesan clergy* were also to assist the bishop in conducting semester or annual examinations of students in major seminaries.—*Ibidem,* n. 175. A specific treatment of the legislation of the Baltimore Councils on the various examinations, *i. e.,* for Orders, for the Junior Clergy, etc., will be given in the Canonical Commentary part of this work.

[86] *C. Plen. Balt. II, Acta et Decreta,* n. 126.

[87] *Acta et Decreta Conc. Plen. Balt. III,* nn. 40-41. The III Plenary Council (n. 41) actually used the Latin equivalent of the English word "mission": *"ad missiones inamovibilitatis privilegio gaudentes."* Barrett uses the term "irremovable rectorships" to designate these *"missiones inamovibilitatis privilegio gaudentes"*—Barrett, *A Comparative Study of the Councils of Baltimore and the Code of Canon Law,* The Catholic University of America Canon Law Studies, n. 83 (Washington, D. C.: The Catholic University of America, 1932), p. 173.

Less than three examiners might not be assigned unless because of the scarcity of priests this number could not be had.[88]

The Council then proceeded to legislate at length concerning this concursus. It seems opportune to give here those parts of this legislation which pertained to, or were closely related to, the duties of the examiners.[89] Thus it will be possible to see at a glance wherein the Common Law on the duties of the synodal examiners in a concursus was followed, and also what additions or changes were introduced.

1. When a mission became vacant which was to be conferred by means of a concursus, the bishop was to appoint a fit vicar in the mission. He was then to announce the vacancy to the clergy of the diocese, at the same time convoking a concursus. The bishop was to allow ten days for the priests to present themselves as candidates, though he was permitted to prolong this term to twenty days. It was regarded as opportune that he should petition the Holy See for the faculty of prolonging this term from ten to thirty days.[90]

2. In order that they might be admitted to the examination priests were required to be of untainted faith and morals, to have laudably exercised the sacred ministry in the diocese for at least ten years, and during these ten years to have had the care of souls, as simple rectors, for at least three years, or in some other manner to have proven their aptitude to govern a mission in spiritual and in temporal matters. Those desiring to be admitted were required to direct an appropriate petition to the bishop, who in turn was to judge whether they should be admitted.[91]

3. In the examination on learning both oral and written answers were required. The questions to be proposed by the examiners were to be taken from theological discipline, especially from moral, dogmatic and liturgical theology and from canon law. These questions

[88] *Acta et Decreta Conc. Plen. Balt. III,* n. 41; cf. also, n. 36. Bishops were given the faculty of appointing the first irremovable rector in the respective irremovable missions without holding a concursus.—*Ibidem,* n. 37.

[89] In giving the legislation a literal translation has not always been made, but at the same time an attempt has been made to give as accurately as possible the actual law.

[90] *Ibidem,* n. 42.

[91] *Ibidem,* n. 43.

were to concern only those matters the knowledge of which was necessary for the proper fulfillment of the pastoral office; the questions were to cover especially those things of which a priest should always possess a ready knowledge, since ordinarily he could anticipate no opportune delay in answering them. Further, there was to be assigned to each candidate one or two questions from the catechism. Each candidate was to explain these catechetical questions so that it might be seen with what method and skill he was able to explain and illustrate Christian doctrine lucidly, clearly and in a manner suited to the capacity of children and unlearned people. Finally, a text from the Gospels was to be proposed on which each of the candidates was to write a sermon, thus proving his ability to preach.[92]

4. The questions and cases which were to be answered in writing by the candidate were to be the same for all and were to be dictated to all at the same time; a certain definite amount of time, the same for all, was to be set for the solving of cases, the answering of questions and the writing of the sermon.[93]

5. The examiners were to fulfill their duties so religiously that no candidate who lacked the necessary learning would have any hope of obtaining a testimonial of fitness.[94]

6. All candidates were to be gathered together in the same room for the examination and were to be under the vigilance of a prefect appointed by the bishop.[95]

7. Each candidate was to write his own answers and after affixing his own signature to them was to hand them to the one deputed as prefect; the responses were also to be signed by the chancellor of the concursus, by the examiners and by the Ordinary or his vicar.[96]

8. For the oral examination there were required to be present, besides the bishop or his vicar general, at least three examiners.[97]

9. In order that the examiners might form a just judgment, they were to weigh diligently the skill of each in evolving and explaining

[92] *Ibidem*, n. 44.
[93] *Ibidem*, n. 45.
[94] *Ibidem*, n. 46.
[95] *Ibidem*, n. 47.
[96] *Ibidem*, n. 48.
[97] *Ibidem*, n. 49.

orally a point of doctrine proposed. They were also to consider the capacity of each to "break bread to the young and to give them the milk of heavenly doctrine." Especially they were to study carefully the written responses. Finally, they were to scrutinize attentively the gravity of delivery, the aptitude of speech, the clarity of exposition and the elegance of style shown in the sermon written by each of the candidates.[98]

10. The examiners once they had studied the question of skill in knowledge and doctrine were required to inquire even more diligently concerning the other qualifications requisite for the office of a rector who would be entrusted with the care of souls, namely, his age, the previous circumstances of his life, duties performed by him, the gravity of his character, his integrity as to morals, his prudence, his skill in the administration of temporal property, and services he had already rendered to the Church. It was to be remembered that the candidates were to be such as would be able, by word and example, to feed their sheep. Information on these matters was to be gathered from testimonials, documents and other sources of a similar nature. All of these were to be free from all fraud. They were to be presented to the bishop before the examination began. The examiners were to consider all these matters as a whole (*"coniunctim"*) and then by their votes to reject the unfit and the unworthy, and to report the fit to the bishop.[99]

11. The examiners were given the right and the duty to report as many as they had judged fit to rule the vacant church. To the bishop alone was reserved the right to choose the one whom before God he considered to be the more fit. However, the bishop, if he should feel it might aid him to act more prudently, was permitted to seek the advice of the examiners before choosing the most worthy from those approved.[100]

12. The examiners were to cast their votes before they left the place of examination and while they were still in the meeting with the bishop or his vicar. It made no difference whether they cast

[98] *Ibidem*, n. 50.
[99] *Ibidem*, n. 51.
[100] *Ibidem*, n. 52.

their votes secretly or openly, but it was considered more fitting that they should communicate their votes to one another.[101]

13. In this judgment of the examiners the bishop, or his vicar, in case the latter assisted at the examination in the place of the bishop, was to have no part, except when votes were either single or equally divided. Then the bishop, or his vicar, was given the right to vote for whom he preferred. When either the bishop or the vicar voted, they were to do so in the presence of the examiners. This pertained to the completion of the examination.[102]

14. A candidate could be exempted from the examination if the Ordinary, having heard the opinion of the examiners, felt that the particular candidate should be exempted because there was available abundant testimony as to his learning either from the dignity of the office which he held, or from the length of services laudably rendered by him to the Church.[103]

The III Plenary Council of Baltimore next made provision for a general concursus, in contrast to the special concursus. The general concursus, however, was permitted only under certain conditions. The Council enacted that if on account of the size of a diocese and the great distance between places, or if because of some other peculiar obstacles, it would be only with difficulty that candidates might convene in one place as often as a church became vacant requiring the appointment of a new rector by means of a concursus, it was permissible to separate the examination as to learning from the examination as to the other canonical requisites. This separation of examinations was to be made in this fashion, that once in the year, at a set time, a general examination on learning was to be held for those missions which might become vacant in the future. This general examination was to be held according to the form prescribed in the legislation on the special concursus, and it had this special object, to explore the degree of learning possessed by those who aspired to the office of irremovable rectorship. The other requisites were to be considered by the examiners when a vacant church was actually to be conferred. Those who had been approved in a previous examina-

[101] *Ibidem*, n. 53.
[102] *Ibidem*, n. 54.
[103] *Ibidem*, n. 57.

tion on learning were to be considered capable in the matter of learning of obtaining any irremovable rectorship which might become vacant within a period of six years. If after six years they had not been given charge of an irremovable mission, they were obliged to submit to a new examination.[104]

Appendix

A question which presents itself concerning the legislation of the III Plenary Council (n. 24) is this: are the *"examinatores cleri dioecesani,"* whose appointment the Council required, the same as the *"examinatores synodales"* of the common law? It does not seem that they were true synodal examiners. The reasons for this statement are these: (a) if the Council wished to have the bishops create true synodal examiners it would have proceeded most logically by decreeing simply that *"examinatores synodales"* should be appointed. Instead, however, the Fathers of the Council decreed that *"examinatores cleri dioecesani"* should be appointed. (b) The Council further stated that these *"examinatores cleri dioecesani"* were *"ad instar examinatorum synodalium vel prosynodalium."* This manner of designating their office seems clearly enough to be a contrasting of two different offices. The wording of the decree of the Council is as follows: *"Constituant singuli Episcopi examinatores cleri dioecesani pro concursibus ad missiones, in quibus rectori privilegium tributum est inamovibilitatis, ad instar examinatorum synodalium vel prosynodalium."* (c) In speaking specifically of the concursus for irremovable rectorships in n. 41, the III Plenary Council again seemed to contrast the two offices: *"Examen seu concursus ad missiones inamovibilitatis privilegio gaudentes institui debet coram Episcopo vel eius vicario generali et tribus saltem ex dioecesanis examinatoribus loco synodalium vel prosynodalium constitutis, quos Episcopus designavit.* (d) In other places in which mention is made of the office required by this Council of Baltimore, in all but one place the terminology *"examinatores cleri dioecesani," "examinatores cleri," "examinatores"* is used, not the name *"examinatores synodales vel prosynodales."* It is true that in n. 152 the Council uses the name *"examinatores synodales*

[104] *Ibidem*, n. 59.

vel prosynodales" when referring to the office: "*Insuper mandamus, ut nullo loco horum Statuum in seminarium maius admittantur alumni, nisi ab examinatoribus facto scientiae periculo probentur. Hi examinatores poterunt esse examinatores synodales vel prosynodales illius dioecesis in qua seminarium illud maius situm est.*" Why the Council should use this terminology in this place is not evident, but it does not seem correct to deduce from this single use of the name which is proper to the office of the common law that therefore the III Plenary Council of Baltimore intended that the bishops should appoint true synodal examiners. Surely in the face of the discrepancy in the terminology used by the Council the question of its intention should be settled by the terminology used in that place in the acts where the office as such is treated. And in n. 24, where the nature of the office is specifically treated, there definitely seems to have been in the minds of the legislators a distinction between the two offices, as has been already pointed out. The conclusion is, therefore, that the III Plenary Council of Baltimore did not establish true synodal examiners in the United States.

As will be seen, however, it was necessary later on for the bishops of the United States to create true synodal examiners in order to comply with the regulations of the Decree, "*Maxima cura*." That the United States did come under this Decree was explicitly stated in 1911 by the Sacred Consistorial Congregation.[105]

[105] 20 febr., 13 mart. 1911—*AAS*, III (1911), 133.

CHAPTER III

SYNODAL EXAMINERS AND PARISH PRIEST CONSULTORS FROM THE DECREE, "MAXIMA CURA," TILL THE CODIFICATION OF CANON LAW

ARTICLE 1. THE LEGISLATION ON ADMINISTRATIVE REMOVAL

As will be seen, the Decree, *"Maxima cura,"* of 1910,[1] not only gave to the synodal examiners a new function, but it also made a number of changes in the office itself. Then, too, it was with this Decree that the office of parish priest consultor came into existence. Before treating in detail of those parts of this Decree which concerned the synodal examiners and the parish priest consultors it is necessary to touch briefly on the subject of the administrative removal of pastors, since it is of this that the Decree specifically treated. Cappello defines administrative removal, or as it is also called, economic or disciplinary removal, as "an act of the legitimate ecclesiastical authority by which a beneficed cleric, when there is a grave cause, *i. e.*, the good of souls, is removed from the possession of his benefice without any juridical solemnities and is transferred to another benefice or ecclesiastical office or is given a suitable pension." [2]

This administrative removal of pastors was not something that was introduced only at the time of the *"Maxima cura."* Connor, in his work, *"The Administrative Removal of Pastors,"* remarks that in the Decretals there is a certain amount of legislation which, although it did not deal directly with removal, nevertheless as interpreted by the decretalists and later canonists, became the basis of the modern administrative procedure of removal.[3] He points to three separate texts in the Decretals, one from Urban III (1185-1187),[4] another from Clement III (1187-1191) [5] and a third from Innocent

[1] S. C. Consist., 20 aug. 1910—*AAS,* II (1910), 636-648—*Fontes,* n. 2074.

[2] *De Admin. Amotione Parochorum,* p. 5.

[3] Pp. 16-18.

[4] C. 5, X, *de rerum permutatione,* III, 19.

[5] C. 4, X, *de clerico aegrotante,* III, 6.

III.[6] He also notes that the Council of Trent may be interpreted as leaving room for the administrative removal of pastors.[7] Finally, he points out that the teaching of the canonists and the practice of the Holy See give definite proof that administrative removal was actually permitted, especially from the seventeenth century.[8]

In spite of the fact that bishops actually made use of administrative removal, it was nevertheless a fact that prior to the Decree, "*Maxima cura,*" nothing had been determined as to the manner of proceeding in such a removal.[9] This is sufficient proof in itself that the synodal examiners did not, previous to the Decree of 1910, have any part in a procedure for the administrative removal of pastors.

However, at the Vatican Council (1869-1870) there came from the bishops of Germany a suggestion for a mode of procedure in which the synodal examiners would have been given a part. This suggestion read: "*Pariter petimus, ut permittatur translatio parochi non voluntaria, vel dimissio cum pensione congrua, quoties per sententiam sive per vota examinatorum prosynodalium constiterit eundem ad regendam paroeciam non amplius esse idoneum.*" [10] The Council, though, was interrupted and prorogued before any disciplinary matters were taken up.[11] It has been said that this was the first time that any suggestion was made relative to the use of synodal examiners in an administrative removal procedure.[12]

"Not until 1910, however, did the Church have a clear, definite

[6] C. 10, § 5, X, *de renuntiatione*, I, 9.

[7] Conc. Trident., sess. XXI, *de ref.*, c. 6. Cf. Connor, *op. cit.*, p. 18.

[8] Connor, *op. cit.*, pp. 16-36.

[9] Connor, *op. cit.*, pp. 34-35; Cappello, *De Admin. Amotione Parochorum*, pp. 10-11; Ayrinhac, *Constitution of the Church in the New Code of Canon Law* (New York: Benziger, 1925), n. 255. (Hereafter this work will be cited *Constitution of the Church.*) Meier, *Penal Administrative Procedure Against Negligent Pastors,* The Catholic University of America Canon Law Studies, n. 140 (Washington, D. C.: Catholic University of America Press, 1941), p. 70. (Henceforth this work will be cited *Adm. Proc. Ag. Neglig. Pastors.*)

[10] *Collectio Lacensis, Acta et Decreta Sacrorum Conciliorum Recentiorum,* VII, 875.

[11] Connor, *Adm. Removal of Pastors,* p. 35.

[12] Hilling, "Das Spruchkollegium bei Amtsenthebung der Pfarrer im Verwaltungswege"—*AKKR* (Innsbruck, 1857-1861; Mainz, 1862—), XCIII (1913), 157-161.

and precise legislation which determined . . . the administrative procedure to be followed." [13] Consequently, it was not until the Decree of 1910 that the synodal examiners were given a part by law in this procedure.

There is no doubt of the fact that the parish priest consultors had no existence previous to the Decree, "*Maxima cura.*" [14] It has been remarked, though,[15] that this office of parish priest consultor had its prototype in the "*consilium iudiciale*" or "*Commissio Investigationis*" which an Instruction from the Sacred Congregation of the Propagation of the Faith, in 1878, instituted for the criminal and disciplinary cases of clerics in the United States.[16] The procedure referred to in this Instruction was not an administrative procedure but rather a summary judicial trial.[17] The Instruction set down that each bishop should elect in the diocesan synod five priests of most upright character, men skilled in canon law. If circumstances would not permit the appointment of five, then at least three such men were to be chosen. These appointees would form a "*consilium iudiciale*" or "*Commissio Investigationis.*" If for a grave reason the bishop could not immediately have a diocesan synod, he was himself to choose ecclesiastics for the office until such time as there would be a diocesan synod. The Instruction then proceeded to describe the manner in which this "*Commissio Investigationis*" was to aid the bishop in conducting and passing sentence in the criminal and disciplinary trials of priests and other clerics. With regard to the removal of a rector from a mission, the Instruction stated that he might not be removed from his office until the bishop associated with himself at least three members of the "*Commissio Investigationis*" and sought their counsel. In another Instruction from the same Congregation, directed to the bishops of the United States,[18] the question of a summary judicial procedure for the criminal and disciplinary cases of clerics was

[13] Connor, *op. cit.*, p. 36.

[14] Wernz-Vidal, *Ius Canonicum*, II, n. 650; Cappello, *De Admin. Amotione Parochorum*, p. 73; Connor, *Adm. Removal of Pastors*, p. 92.

[15] Hilling, *ibidem*, p. 159.

[16] 20 iul. 1878—*ASS*, XII, pp. 88-92.

[17] Meier, *Adm. Proc. Ag. Neglig. Pastors*, p. 66.

[18] Instr., "*Cum magnopere,*" 1884, n. XII—*ASS*, XXIV (1891-1892), 383-390; *Fontes*, n. 4900.

again treated. In this Instruction the duties which had been given to the *"Commissio Investigationis"* were now given to the officials of the diocesan Curia. It was stated, however, that the previous Instruction would still remain in force in those dioceses where there was no episcopal curia. What has been remarked is but a sketchy description of the *"consultores"* who made up the *"Commissio Investigationis"* in the United States, but it is sufficient, it seems, to show a real relation not only between the offices of parish priest consultor as instituted by the Decree, *"Maxima cura"* and that of *"consultor"* in this *"Commissio Investigationis,"* but also a certain similarity in the duties of the individual members of these two offices. It might be added that the same similarity existed between the work of the members of the *"Commissio Investigationis,"* when there was question of the removal of a rector, and the new duties given by the *"Maxima cura"* to the synodal or pro-synodal examiners.

It may be remarked at the outset that the prescriptions of the *"Maxima cura"* were binding on the universal Church. In the Introduction of the Decree it is stated: *"decretum per hanc (Consistorialem) Congregationem edi iussit (Pius PP. X) quo novae normae de amotione administrativa . . . promulgarentur, eaedemque canonicam legem pro universa Ecclesia constituerent."* Since, however, the Decree was only a positive disciplinary decree which did not make express mention of the Eastern Church it was concluded that its provisions did not bind the Oriental Church.[19] In 1911 the Sacred Consistorial Congregation replied that the Decree applied also to the United States and to England.[20]

Article 2. The Offices of Synodal Examiner and Parish Priest Consultor

Since the legislation of the Decree regarding the person of the synodal examiner and the parish priest consultor was identical,[21] it will

[19] Cappello, *De Admin. Amotione Parochorum,* p. 27.

[20] 28 febr., 13 mart. 1911—*AAS,* III (1911), 133.

[21] Canon 4 of the Decree, which treats of the election to these offices, makes this identity abundantly clear: *"examinatoribus et parochis consultoribus eligendis lex in posterum ubilibet servanda haec est, etc."*

not be necessary to treat the two offices separately. Furthermore, since there was little occasion for much development in the interpretation of the legislation, it will be unnecessary to devote separate sections to a study of the interpretations and decisions of the Sacred Congregations and of the authors who wrote on this legislation. It seems sufficient to discuss what came from these sources along with the presentation of the law of the Decree. The method of procedure will be to quote separately each point of this legislation which touches upon the office or work of the synodal examiners or parish priest consultors and then to give immediately any relevant interpretations or decisions from a Sacred Congregation, as well as the opinions of authors. Where there were changes from the previous law with respect to the synodal examiners this will also be noted.

Canon 4, § 1: Si synodus habeatur, in ea iuxta receptas normas, eligendi erunt tot numero quot Ordinarius prudenti suo iudicio necessarios iudicaverit.

There is no room to doubt that the synodal examiners spoken of in the Decree were the identical examiners constituted by the Council of Trent and were to be used in the concursus as well as in the administrative removal of pastors. This was clearly stated by the Sacred Consistorial Congregation shortly after the Decree itself was published.[22]

If the examiners were elected in a synod then the old law was to be followed and names were to be proposed by the bishop, or by his vicar general, to the synod, and the synod had the right by a majority vote of those present to accept or reject those presented to it.[23] The approbation by the synod might, as previously, be by open or by secret vote. If the synod should reject names proposed by the bishop, the latter would have to propose other names to the synod.[24] The synodal examiners were still to be priests with a degree in theology or canon law, or others, whether regulars or seculars, who might

[22] 3 oct. 1910, ad I—*AAS,* II (1910), p. 854.

[23] Wernz, *Ius Decretalium,* V (Prati: ex officina Libraria Giachetti, Filii et Soc., 1914), n. 913, nota 52.

[24] Cappello, *De Admin. Amotione Parochorum,* pp. 75-76.

be otherwise fit.[25] Regarding the number of examiners to be elected, the law was changed and it was left to the prudent judgment of the bishop to elect as many as he wished. It was logically reasoned, however, that there should certainly be more than two, since the Decree itself, in canon 5, § 1, presupposed a greater number, and since at least three were necessary in the concursus for a vacant parish.[26] It was determined by the Sacred Consistorial Congregation that extra-diocesan priests and regulars might be chosen for the office of synodal examiner or parish priest consultor, provided the diocese in question was small, or if there was some other just cause for making such a choice.[27] The same Sacred Congregation also decided that it was not advisable for the Ordinary to make his vicar general a synodal examiner,[28] that pastors might be chosen for the office of synodal examiner,[29] that the parish priest consultor (as the name implies) had to be a pastor [30] and that one and the same person might be both synodal examiner and parish priest consultor, but not in the same case. On this last point, however, the Congregation added that usually it was not expedient that this should be the case, since many offices should not be accumulated in the same person.[31] There was no prohibition against the chancellor of a diocese being a synodal examiner.[32]

Canon 4, § 2: Examinatoribus et parochis consultoribus medio tempore inter unam et aliam synodum demortuis, vel alia ratione a munere cessantibus alios prosynodales Ordinarius substituet de consensu Capituli Cathedralis, et hoc deficiente, de consensu consultorum dioecesanorum.

The consent of the Cathedral Chapter which is here spoken of

[25] Wernz, *loc. cit.*; d'Angelo, *La Curia Diocesana,* pars I, pp. 37-38.
[26] Wernz, *loc. cit.*; d'Angelo, *ibidem,* pp. 36-37.
[27] 3 oct. 1910, ad V—*AAS,* II (1910), p. 854.
[28] *Ibidem,* ad VI.
[29] *Ibidem,* ad VII.
[30] *Ibidem,* ad IV; d'Angelo, *op. cit.,* pars I, p. 53, nota 1.
[31] *Ibidem,* ad VIII.
[32] d'Angelo, *op. cit.,* pars I, p. 38, nota n. 3.

was required for validity.[33] Where there existed no Cathedral Chapter, but in its place the body of diocesan consultors, in such dioceses it was the consent of this body that was required for the valid election of the substitutes spoken of in this § 2 of canon 4 of the Decree.[34] If the Cathedral Chapter, or the body of diocesan consultors, refused to approve candidates whom the bishop felt were truly fit, the safest mode of procedure would be for the bishop to petition the Sacred Congregation of the Council for supplementary consent. This opinion prevailed previous to the "*Maxima cura*" as to procedure in a similar situation.[35] The right given to the Ordinary by this canon 4, § 2 of the Decree was not restricted to the case where the number of the examiners or consultors became altogether too small. Rather, when any of those in office withdrew, then automatically the Ordinary had the right to replace him.[36]

Canon 4, § 3: Quae regula servetur quoque in examinatoribus et parochis consultoribus eligendis, quoties synodus non habeatur.

This regulation was a marked change from the previous discipline as regards the examiners, for previously it was necessary to petition the Sacred Congregation of the Council for special permission each time an Ordinary wished to elect examiners (pro-synodal) outside a synod. The new law gave the Ordinary this permission with regard to both offices, that of examiner and that of parish priest consultor.[37]

It may be remarked that the obligation of the Council of Trent requiring the holding of a synod every year was not considered to bind strictly any longer. It was felt that although there was still an obligation to hold the synod, still bishops could see to the right gov-

[33] Cappello, *De Admin. Amotione Parochorum,* p. 76; d'Angelo, *La Curia Diocesana,* pars I, p. 45. For a comparison between this legislation and the different previous legislation in regard to the synodal examiners, cf. *supra,* pp. 6; 14-17.

[34] S. C. Consist., 3 oct. 1910, ad IX—*AAS,* II (1910), 855.

[35] d'Angelo, *op. cit.,* pars I, pp. 48-49.

[36] Wernz, *Ius Decretalium,* V, n. 913, nota 53.

[37] Wernz, *op. cit.,* V, n. 913, nota 53.

ernment of their dioceses in other ways, without being obliged to hold a synod every year.[38]

Canon 4, § 4: Examinatores et consultores sive in synodo sive extra synodum electi, post quinquennium a sua nominatione, vel etiam prius, adveniente nova synodo, officio cadunt. Possunt tamen, servatis servandis, denuo eligi.

In the previous discipline examiners remained in office until a new synod was held, provided at least six remained. Pro-synodal examiners, elected outside a synod in virtue of an apostolic indult, remained in office for a period determined in the indult. This discipline gave way to the new discipline of this canon 4, § 4.[39]

The examiners and parish priest consultors might be re-elected, and this as often as desired by the Ordinary. The phrase *"servatis servandis"* referred to the fact that the re-election had to be either in a synod, with the consent of a majority of the synod, or outside a synod, with the consent of the Chapter, or, as the case might be, of the diocesan consultors. In a word, a new election was required, not a mere confirmation in office.[40]

Canon 4, § 5: Removeri ab Ordinario durante quinquennio nequeunt, nisi ex gravi causa et de consensu Capituli Cathedralis, vel consultorum dioecesanorum.

For a valid removal two things were required: a grave cause and the consent of the Cathedral Chapter, or of the diocesan consultors. The grave cause might be a crime, that is, any grave delict, such as simony. Or it might be something involuntary and blameless as far as the office-holder was concerned, for example lengthy infirmity, or prolonged absence from the diocese.[41]

[38] Cappello, *op. cit.*, p. 79; d'Angelo, *op. cit.*, pars I, p. 51, nota n. 1.

[39] d'Angelo, *op. cit.*, pars I, p. 51.

[40] d'Angelo, *loc. cit.*

[41] Cappello, *De Admin. Amotione Parochorum*, p. 79; d'Angelo, *La Curia Diocesana*, pars I, p. 52.

The consent required from the Chapter, or from the diocesan consultors, was to be given by these in their character of moral persons. It would not be sufficient that the individual members be separately consulted by the Ordinary. Furthermore, the decision of these bodies was reached by a majority vote. The actual voting by the members was to be secret. The bishop explained the reasons for his action to the Chapter, and the members of this body were then bound to secrecy if the reasons given were occult. The reason for the secrecy was to safeguard as much as possible the good name of the examiner or consultor who was being removed. It was also suggested that a bishop should, before proceeding to remove one of these officials from office, first ask him to resign his office.[42] One author remarked that if an examiner (and, consequently, a parish priest consultor) should resign his office, it would be sufficient that such a renunciation be accepted by the bishop. It would not be necessary to have the acceptance approved by the Chapter as well, though the Chapter was to be consulted.[43]

Canon 5, § 1: Examinatores et parochi consultores ab Ordinario in causa amotionis assumendi, non quilibet erunt, sed duo seniores ratione electionis, et in pari electione seniores ratione sacerdotii, vel, hac deficiente, ratione aetatis.

This point of legislation restricted the liberty of the Ordinary, for he was held to take the two senior examiners and the two senior consultors in any administrative removal process. Seniority was gauged first by time of election; if the officials were of equal rating in this regard, the norm for seniority was the length of time spent by the official in the priesthood; finally, if there could be no distinction reached by these two norms, seniority was to be judged according to age.[44] Precedence by reason of election was to be considered, with respect to the synodal examiners, as dating only from the promulga-

[42] d'Angelo, *loc. cit.*

[43] Greco, *La rimozione amministrativa dei Parrochi*, p. 57—apud d'Angelo, *op. cit.*, pars I, pp. 52-53.

[44] Wernz, *Ius Decretalium*, V, n. 914.

tion of the new law, that is, all who became synodal examiners at the time of the Decree had equal seniority of election, no matter how long they had held the office previous to the Decree.[45] This regulation to take the examiners by reason of seniority did not mean that the same two examiners (or consultors) were to be chosen for every case, but, according to the better interpretation, that the Ordinary was held to call the examiners (or consultors) in order (of seniority), so that, for the succeeding case, those should be taken who followed the ones who had a part in the case immediately preceding.[46]

If it happened that the bishop either inadvertently or for his own reasons did not follow the order of precedence, as prescribed, the acts of the administrative removal were not thereby invalidated, for it was held that this regulation was to be followed for licitness only, and not under penalty of invalidity. The pastor who was concerned, however, had, at the inception of the process, the right to refuse examiners or consultors appointed otherwise than according to the law of precedence.[47]

> **Canon 5, § 2: Qui inter eos ob causam in iure recognitam suspecti evidenter appareant, possunt ab Ordinario, antequam rem tractandam suscipiant, excludi; ob eamdem causam parochus potest contra eos excipere, cum primum in causa veniat.**

The right was hereby given to the Ordinary to remove from participation in an administrative removal process any examiner or consultor whom he might know to be quite evidently "suspect." The Ordinary could likewise remove any of the officials whom a pastor, when his case was first brought up, might oppose as being

[45] S. C. Consist., 3 oct. 1910, ad X—*AAS,* II (1910), p. 854.

[46] Suarez, *De Remotione Parochorum Aliisque Processibus Tertiae Partis Lib. IV Cod. Iur. Can.* (Romae: Pontificium Internationale Institutum Angelicum de Urbe, 1931), n. 46. (Hereafter this work will be cited *De Remotione Parochorum.*)

[47] S. C. Consist., 3 oct. 1910, ad XI—*AAS,* II (1910), p. 855; Cappello, *De Admin. Amotione Parochorum,* p. 82.

suspect for a manifest reason. The reasons for judging an examiner or consultor to be suspect had to be such as were recognized in law. The Ordinary gave his judgment *"ex officio,"* not by means of any formal judicial process.[48]

Canon 5, § 3: Alterutro vel utroque ex duobus prioribus examinatoribus vel consultoribus impedito vel excluso, tertius vel quartus eodem ordine assumetur.

Whenever an examiner or a consultor was either impeded from acting, or was excluded from participation in an administrative removal process, a third, and if necessary a fourth, were to be assigned to the case. Again, the order of seniority was to be followed. If an examiner or consultor was legitimately impeded he was to be excused from his duty for as long a time as the impediment might last. The bishop was the exclusive judge of the legitimacy of the impediment.[49]

Canon 7, § 1: Examinatores et consultores debent sub gravi dato iureiurando servare secretum officii circa omnia quae ratione sui muneris noverint, et maxime circa documenta secreta, disceptationes in consilio habitas, suffragiorum numerum et rationes.

According to the Council of Trent,[50] the synodal examiners were bound to take an oath on the Holy Gospels to fulfill their duties faithfully, without thought of human feelings. This oath was absolutely required, so much so that if even one of the examiners at a concursus had failed to take the oath, the concursus was considered invalid. The oath needed only to be taken once, and it was considered to continue in effect as long as the office was held, though it would have to be renewed upon re-election. A bishop might, however, require this oath before each concursus, if he so desired.[51]

[48] Wernz, *Ius Decretalium,* V, n. 914; Cappello, *op. cit.*, pp. 80-83.

[49] Cappello, *op. cit.*, p. 82.

[50] Conc. Trident., sess. XXIV, *de ref.*, c. 18.

[51] d'Angelo, *La Curia Diocesana,* pars I, pp. 40-41.

When the Sacred Consistorial Congregation was questioned as to whether the oath mentioned in canon 7 of the Decree had to be renewed before each case, or whether it would suffice to take it once, after the election, or before the first case, the Sacred Congregation replied that it was sufficient to take the oath once, provided it was taken for all cases. The Ordinary might, however, require the examiners and consultors to renew it in particular cases, if he judged this expedient.[52]

A later Decree made a quite definite distinction between the legislation concerning the two oaths, the one to be taken by the examiners to fulfill their duties faithfully in every concursus and the other to be taken by the examiners and parish priest consultors with regard to the administrative removal proceedings. According to this later Decree, which was issued by Pope Pius X, with the advice of the Sacred Consistorial Congregation,[53] it was determined that for the future the synodal examiners and parish priest consultors who took part with the bishop in a decree of removal, or in the revision of the decree, had on each occasion and at the first session, under penalty of invalidity, to take the following oath:

> *"Ego N. N. examinator (vel parochus consultor) synodalis (vel prosynodalis) spondeo, voveo ac iuro munus et officium mihi demandatum me fideliter, quacumque affectione postposita, et sincere, quantum in me est, executurum: secretum officii circa omnia quae ratione mei muneris noverim, et maxime circa documenta secreta, disceptationes in consilio habitas, suffragiorum numerum et rationes religiose servaturum; nec quidquam prorsus, occasione huius officii, etiam sub specie doni, oblatum nec ante nec post, recepturum.*
>
> *"Sic me Deus adiuvet et haec sancta Dei Evangelia, quae meis manibus tango."*

As is evident, this oath differed from the one which the examiners and consultors were previously bound to take, for the new oath included not only secrecy in regard to their duties in the administrative removal process, but also the faithful fulfillment of these duties, and the refraining from receiving anything on the occasion of the exer-

[52] S. C. Consist., 3 oct. 1910, ad XII—*AAS,* II (1910), p. 855.

[53] S. C. Consist., decr., 15 febr. 1912—*Fontes,* n. 2083.

cise of their office, either before or after, even if something were offered to them as a gift. It will be recalled that the examiners were bound by the Council of Trent[54] to avoid receiving anything whatsoever on the occasion of the examination in a concursus. Though there was no oath required on this point by the Tridentine prohibition, nevertheless the penalties were extremely severe for one guilty of accepting offerings, stipends, etc.[55]

Briefly, then, the oath regarding the concursus had to be taken but once during an examiner's term in office, unless the bishop expressly required it to be taken frequently, or even before each concursus. The oath regarding the administrative removal procedure, however, had by law to be taken before every procedure by those examiners and consultors who took part in the case.

The oath of secrecy taken by the examiners and consultors had regard to whatever pertained to their duties, especially regarding letters, denunciations, and other writings of an occult nature; the arguments given by the pastor in his own defense; the testimony of witnesses; all discussions held during the proceedings; the origin and nature of any disputes occurring during the process; the results of the voting; the reasons given for particular votes, etc. It made no difference whether or not some things were publicly known. If they were treated in the case they were not to be discussed as having been treated.[56]

Canon 7, § 2: Si contra fecerint, non solum a munere examinatoris et consultoris amovendi erunt, sed alia etiam condigna poena ab Ordinario pro culpae gravitate, servatis servandis, mulctari poterunt; ac propterea obligatione tenentur sarciendi damna, si quae forte inde sequuta.

[54] Sess. XXIV, *de ref.*, c. 18.

[55] d'Angelo, *La Curia Diocesana*, pars I, pp. 41-42. Cf. *supra*, p. 8.

[56] Gennari, "Sulla Rimozione dall'Officio e Beneficio Curato. Breve Commento del Decreto *Maxima cura*."—*Monit. Eccl.*, Terza Serie, II (1910), (Vol. XXII della intera Collezione), p. 501. (Henceforth this series of articles will be cited *Rimozione dal Benef. Curato.*) Cf. also, Cappello, *De Admin. Amotione Parochorum*, p. 86.

The penalties mentioned here were all *ferendae sententiae*. Therefore, although one who was guilty of breaking the oath of secrecy was to be removed from office (*"amovendi erunt"*), nevertheless until he actually was removed he could validly exercise his office. The various penalties were inflicted by the Ordinary *ex officio*.[57] In order to remove an examiner or consultor from office for breaking this oath of secrecy there was no need of a judicial process. All that was required was that the bishop know for a certainty, from the testimony of witnesses, or from some other reliable source, that the obligation of secrecy had been violated.[58] d'Angelo states [59] that in his opinion it was not necessary for the bishop to receive the consent of the Cathedral Chapter, or of the diocesan consultors, before making this removal from office.

Concerning the additional penalties which this canon 7, § 2, permitted the Ordinary to inflict, it is to be noted that the Ordinary could inflict them, but did not have to. When he did impose additional penalties, he was to measure them according to the gravity of the guilt.[60]

With respect to repairing damage done by the violation of secrecy, it was the Ordinary who would judge from the testimony of witnesses, documents, etc., just how the guilty examiner or consultor was to make reparation.[61]

> Iis autem cito exsequendis quae in hoc decreto statuuntur, SSmus. Dominus Noster mandat ut omnes et singuli Ordinarii quamprimum parochos aliquot consultores, iuxta praescripta can. 4, constituant. Quod vero ad examinatores attinet, si in dioecesi, sive in synodo sive extra synodum electi, habeantur, statuit ut, de cathedralis capituli vel consultorum dioecesanorum consilio, aut eos in officio confirmare (hac tamen lege ut post quinquennium a munere cessent),

[57] Cappello, *op. cit.*, pp. 86-87; d'Angelo, *op. cit.*, pars I, p. 43.

[58] Cappello, *op. cit.*, p. 87.

[59] *Op. cit.*, pars I, p. 43, nota 5; et p. 52, nota 2.

[60] Cappello, *loc. cit.*; d'Angelo, *op. cit.*, pars I, p. 44.

[61] Cappello, *loc. cit.*; d'Angelo, *loc. cit.*

aut ad novam examinatorum electionem, servata regula can. 4, devenire possint, prout prudentia et adiuncta suaserint. Deficientibus vero in dioecesi examinatoribus, ad eorum electionem, servatis superius statutis, sine mora deveniant.

According to this prescription, which comes at the very end of the Decree, the synodal or pro-synodal examiners who were in office at the time the Decree went into force automatically lost their office. The Ordinary, however, was given the faculty of confirming them in office for a period of five years. To do this he had but to *consult* the Chapter, or the diocesan consultors. If he preferred, he might follow the prescriptions of canon 4. If there were no synodal or pro-synodal examiners in any diocese the Decree prescribed that the Ordinary must immediately see to their election according to the regulations of canon 4. With regard to the parish priest consultors, all Ordinaries were to see to it that these were immediately elected according to the rules of this same canon 4.[62]

Article 3. The Duties of Synodal Examiners and Parish Priest Consultors in the Administrative Removal of Pastors

Before treating of the duties of each office separately a brief study must be made of an important fundamental canon relating to both offices.

Canon 6, § 1: Quoties in canonibus qui sequuntur expresse dicitur Ordinario procedendum esse de examinatorum vel consultorum consensu, ipse debet per secreta suffragia rem dirimere, et ea sententia probata erit quae duo saltem suffragia favorabilia tulerit.

[62] As was mentioned *supra*, p. 45, the Sacred Consistorial Congregation, on February 28 and March 13, 1911, replied that the Decree, *"Maxima cura,"* applied also to the United States and to England. Consequently, the prescription relative to the election of true synodal examiners and to the appointment of parish priest consultors was binding upon the bishops of the various dioceses in these countries.

§ 2: Quoties vero Ordinarius de consilio examinatorum vel consultorum procedere potest, satis est ut eos audiat, nec ulla obligatione tenetur ad eorum votum, quamvis concors, accedendi.

§ 3: In utroque casu de consequentibus ex scrutinio scripta relatio fiat et ab omnibus subsignetur.

Whenever a canon required the consent of the examiners or consultors this consent was to be had else the action was invalid. This consent was had when there was a majority, that is at least two votes, of the votes cast by the bishop and the two examiners or consultors. The voting was to be done in secret. Both Cappello and Wernz argued that if the vote was not secret it would be invalid, though Wernz added that a secret re-taking of the vote would be sufficient sanation.[63]

When a canon required merely that the bishop consult the examiners or consultors, it was necessary that the bishop actually consult them, but he did not have to follow their advice. The act was considered invalid by Cappello [64] if the bishop did not consult these officials. Wernz [65] seems to have held the same opinion: "*necessario quidem debet eos audire.*" Gennari likewise seems to have held this opinion: "*Quando si richiede il consiglio, questo può darsi a voce. L'ordinario è obligato di chiederlo.*" [66] In giving their vote, when it was a question of counsel and not of consent, the examiners might vote either openly or secretly.[67]

In either case a written report was to be made of the voting which had taken place. This report was to be signed by all who had a part in the voting, and it was to be kept in the acts of the process.[68]

[63] Cappello, *De Admin. Amotione Parochorum*, p. 89; Wernz, *Ius Decretalium*, V, n. 916, nota 57.

[64] *Op. cit.*, pp. 83-84.

[65] *Op. cit.*, V, n. 916.

[66] "Rimozione dal Benef. Curato"—*Monit. Eccl.*, Terza Serie, II (1910), (Vol. XXII della intera Collezione), p. 501.

[67] Cappello, *ibidem*; Wernz, *op. cit.*, V, n. 916, nota n. 58; Gennari, *loc. cit.*

[68] Wernz, *op. cit.*, V, n. 916.

One of the examiners or consultors when assisting in a case might act as notary, or the Ordinary might appoint a notary.[69]

A. *The Duties of the Synodal Examiners*

Canon 8: Quoties itaque, pro prudenti Ordinarii iudicio, videatur parochus incidisse in unam ex causis superius in can. 1 recensitis, ipse Ordinarius duos examinatores a iure statutos convocabit, omnia eis patefaciet, de veritate et gravitate causae cum eis disceptabit, ut statuatur sitne locus formali invitationi parochi ad renunciandum.

When the bishop felt that with regard to a pastor there was present one of the causes spoken of in canon 1,[70] he was to call together the two senior examiners and to discuss with them whether or not causes for removal were present, whether they were sufficiently grave and, in brief, whether all things being considered the pastor in question should be invited to resign.[71] The examiners who were called by the bishop and who were not impeded were obliged to present themselves, and might even be forced to do so by threat of ecclesiastical penalties.[72]

Canon 9, § 1: Formalis haec invitatio semper praemittenda est antequam ad amotionis decretum deveniatur, nisi agatur de insania, vel quoties invitandi modus non suppetat, ut si parochus lateat.

§ 2: Decernenda autem est de examinatorum consensu.

[69] Gennari, *loc. cit.*

[70] For a discussion of these causes, as well as for a discussion of those other parts of the Decree which have no direct bearing on the duties of the examiners or consultors, cf. *e. g.*, Cappello, *De Admin. Amotione Parochorum*; Gennari, "Rimozione dal Benef. Curato"—*Monit. Eccl.*, Terza Serie, II (1910), (Vol. XXII della intera Collezione), pp. 445-454; 492-502; 535-550; Wernz, *Ius Decretalium,* V, nn. 903-930.

[71] Wernz, *op. cit.*, V, nn. 917-918.

[72] Cappello, *op. cit.*, p. 88.

The important point in this canon in connection with the examiners is that the consent of the examiners was necessary before the bishop might send the invitation to the pastor to resign. This consent was had if the bishop and one of the examiners voted for sending the invitation to resign. Further, the vote had to be taken secretly.[73]

> **Canon 10, § 3: Si agatur de occulto delicto, et invitatio ad renunciandum scripto fiat, causa aliqua dumtaxat generalis nuncianda est; ratio autem in specie cum argumentis quibus delicti veritas comprobatur, ab Ordinario dumtaxat est explicanda, adsistente uno examinatorum qui actuarii munere fungatur, et cum cautelis ut supra.**

If it happened that the cause for removal was an occult crime, a written invitation would mention only a general cause. The real cause, together with the proofs concerning its existence, was to be explained to the pastor afterwards orally and in the presence of a synodal examiner. The latter would draw up a document stating therein that the invitation was also made orally and noting that the true cause was revealed to the pastor at the oral invitation. The bishop, the examiner and the pastor were to sign this document. It was then to be kept in the acts of the Episcopal Curia.[74] In other instances where the bishop would give an oral invitation to resign there would be need of a notary, but the law (can. 10, § 1) made no mention of an examiner for the duty.

> **Canon 12: Fas autem parocho est, invitatione cum assignato temporis limite accepta, dilationem ad deliberandum vel ad defensionem parandam postulare. Quam Ordinarius potest iusta de causa, cum examinatorum consensu, et modo id non cedat in detrimentum animarum, ad alios decem vel viginti dies concedere.**

[73] Cappello, *op. cit.*, p. 89.

[74] Cappello, *De Admin. Amotione Parochorum*, p. 89; Wernz, *op. cit.*, n. 918.

According to canon 10, § 4, the Ordinary was to note in the invitation to the pastor that within ten days of the receipt of this invitation he was either to resign his parish or to demonstrate by conclusive arguments that the alleged causes for his removal were false. Otherwise a decree of removal would be given. In virtue of canon 12, however, the pastor might petition a longer period in which to deliberate or to prepare his defense. This petition the Ordinary might accede to and grant the pastor ten, or at most twenty additional days, provided that there was present a just cause, that there would not thereby be caused any harm to souls, and that he obtained the consent of the examiners.[75]

Canon 15, § 1: Si parochus oppugnare velit causas ad amotionem decernendam invocatas, debet intra utile tempus scripto deducere iura sua, allegationibus ad hoc unum directis, ut causam ob quam renunciatio petitur impugnet et evertat.

§ 2: Potest etiam ad aliquod factum vel assertum quod sua intersit comprobandum, duos vel tres testes proponere, et ut examinentur postulare.

§ 3: Ordinarii tamen est cum examinatorum consensu eos vel aliquot ipsorum, si idonei sint et eorum examen necessarium videatur, admittere et excutere; vel etiam, si causa amotionis liqueat et testium examen inutile et ad moras nectendas petitum appareat, excludere.

§ 4: Quod si, allegationibus exhibitis, dubium exoriatur quod diluere oporteat ut tuto procedi liceat, Ordinarii erit cum examinatorum consilio, etiam parocho non postulante, testes qui necessarii videantur inducere, et parochum ipsum, si opus sit, interrogare.

If the pastor, after receiving the invitation to resign, wished to oppose the alleged causes, he had to present his defense in writing within the prescribed ten days (canon 10, § 4). As was noted under

[75] Wernz, *op. cit.*, V, n. 823, nota n. 65.

canon 12, he might ask for an extension of time, to the extent of an additional twenty days. In order to prove a fact or an assertion in his own favor the pastor was allowed to present two or three witnesses and to ask that these be examined. The Ordinary, with the *consent* of the examiners, was to determine whether or not such witnesses were to be admitted and examined. They had to be fit witnesses. The number *"duos vel tres"* was not understood as a strict limitation.[76] These witnesses were to be rejected by the Ordinary and the examiners if the cause for removal was clearly evident and if it was apparent that the examination of the witnesses would be of no value and was requested merely to cause delays. All or some of the proposed witnesses were to be admitted according as their examination seemed necessary or useful.[77]

If, once the pastor had presented his defense, there arose a doubt which had to be satisfied before the Ordinary could proceed with the case, the Ordinary was permitted, after *consulting* the examiners, to bring in any witnesses who might seem necessary, and he was also permitted to question the pastor. Since the law stated that the Ordinary needed only to consult the examiners in this last mentioned circumstance, it followed from canon 6, § 2, that he was not bound to follow their advice.[78]

Canon 16, § 1: In examine testium sive ex officio sive rogante parocho inductorum, ea dumtaxat serventur quae necessaria sint ad veritatem in tuto ponendam, quolibet iudiciali apparatu et reprobationibus testium exclusis.

§ 2: Eadem regula in interrogatione parochi, si locum habeat, servetur.

[76] Cappello, *De Admin. Amotione Parochorum,* p. 100; Wernz, *Ius Decretalium,* V, n. 923, nota, n. 66; Villien, *Le deplacement administratif des curés,* pp. 156 sq.—apud Wernz, *loc. cit.* Gennari interpreted the law strictly; according to him no more than two or three should be admitted: "Rimozione dal Benef. Curato"—*Monit. Eccl.,* Terza Serie, II (1910), (Vol. XXII della intera Collezione), p. 501.

[77] Cappello, *op. cit.,* p. 100; Gennari, *art. cit.,* p. 540.

[78] Cappello, *op. cit.,* p. 100.

Canon 17, § 1: Si parochus intersit et documenta ac nomina testium ipsi patefiant, ipsiusmet erit, si possit ac velit, contra ea quae afferuntur excipere.

§ 2: Quando vero parochus iuxta can. 9 invitari nequeat ad iura sua deducenda, aut quando iuxta can. 11 testium nomina et aliqua documenta ei manifestari nequeant, ipse Ordinarius curas et industrias omnes adhibeat (seu "diligentias," ut vulgo dicitur, peragat), ut de documentorum valore et de testium fide iustum iudicium fieri possit.

Canon 16 prescribed that the witnesses and the pastor were to be examined by the judge and the examiners, without the formalities of a judicial trial. The only form which had to be followed in making these examinations was that which equity demanded and which would best conduce to the finding of the truth. There was to be no objecting to witnesses. Still this exclusion of objecting to witnesses and of the other solemnities of a judicial trial, for the sake of a more expeditious rendering of judgment, imposed upon the Ordinary and the examiners a greater obligation of examining accurately the probity and honesty of the witnesses, the content, veracity and the value of documents.[79]

Canon 17 determined that when the documents and names of the witnesses were made known to the pastor, the latter might object to what had been brought forth. He might not object to the person of a witness, nor against the fact that the witness was to be examined, but he might make objection to the evidence brought forth by a witness.[80] The Ordinary and the examiners would study any objections made by the pastor, and they were then to admit such objections if they found them to be reasonable, otherwise they were to reject them.[81]

When the pastor, according to canon 9, could not be invited to resign, either because of insanity or because he was absent, and again,

[79] Wernz, *op. cit.*, V, n. 924.

[80] Cappello, *De Admin. Amotione Parochorum*, p. 102.

[81] Gennari, "Rimozione dal Benef. Curato"—*Monit. Eccl.*, Terza Serie, II (1910), (Vol. XXII della intera Collezione), p. 541.

when, according to canon 11, the documents and names of witnesses could not be made known to the pastor, the Ordinary was obliged to take all possible measures to determine the value of the documents and the truthfulness of the witnesses.[82]

> Canon 19, § 1: Omnibus expletis quae ad iustam parochi tuitionem pertinent, de amotionis decreto ab Ordinario cum examinatoribus discutiendum est, et per secreta suffragia iuxta praescripta in can. 6 res est definienda.
>
> § 2: Suffragium autem pro amotione nemo dare debet, nisi sibi certo constet causam parocho denuntiatam vere adesse eamque legitimam.

When everything had been done that pertained to a just defense of the pastor, the Ordinary and the examiners were obliged to study the arguments pro and con to see if the cause alleged in the invitation really existed and was a just cause for removal. After this discussion a secret vote was to be taken. The consent of the examiners was required. Mere consultation was not sufficient.[83] According to Wernz [84] it was the common opinion of commentators that neither the Ordinary nor the examiners were allowed to abstain from giving a vote, either for or against removal.

> Canon 22, § 2: Recursus interponendus est intra decem dies ab indicto decreto; nec remedium datur contra lapsum fatalium, nisi parochus probet se vi maiori impeditum a recursu fuisse; de qua re videre debet Ordinarius cum examinatoribus, quorum consensus requiritur.

Recourse against the decree of removal had to be made by the pastor within ten days. There was no remedy if the fixed legal period of time for making the recourse had elapsed, unless the pastor proved that he was impeded from having recourse. Judgment as to the

[82] Gennari, *loc. cit.*

[83] Cappello, *op. cit.*, p. 105; Gennari, *loc. cit.*

[84] *Ius Decretalium,* V, n. 925, nota n. 71.

existence of such an alleged impediment was made by the Ordinary and the examiners by a secret vote. In this instance it was the consent of the examiners which was required.[85]

> **Canon 26, § 1: Sacerdoti ex facta sibi invitatione renuncianti, aut administrativo modo a paroecia amoto, Ordinarius pro viribus consulat, aut per translationem ad aliam paroeciam, aut per assignationem alicuius ecclesiastici officii, aut per pensionem aliquam, prout casus ferat et adiuncta permittant.**
> **§ 2: In provisionis assignatione Ordinarius examinatores, vel parochos consultores si usque ad eos causa pervenerit, audire ne omittat.**

This particular canon had regard to the provision that was to be made for the pastor who would either accept the invitation to resign or who would be removed from his parish by the administrative procedure. The provision was to be determined by the Ordinary, after consultation with the synodal examiners who had taken part in the case. If, however, the procedure had reached the stage of the revision of the acts then it was the parish priest consultors who were to be consulted. Consultation, not consent, was what the canon required.

Since they were to be consulted on the matter, the examiners, or consultors, were required to keep in mind the prescriptions of canon 27, which stated that the Ordinary should not give a parish to the priest unless he were worthy and fit to rule a parish. According as equity and prudence demanded the Ordinary might give a priest a parish of equal value to the one from which he had been removed, or one of inferior, or even of superior value. An ecclesiastical office or pension might be granted instead of a parish, if the case and the circumstances seemed to call for such a provision. Other things being equal, the Ordinary was to act more favorably in the case of a pastor who renounced his parish than with one who had been removed (canon 27).

The question of provision for the pastor was independent of the

[85] Cappello, *op. cit.*, p. 109; Wernz, *op. cit.*, V, n. 926.

question of removal and was not to retard the actual administrative procedure of removal.[86]

B. *The Duties of the Parish Priest Consultors*

Canon 22, § 1: Contra decretum amotionis datur dumtaxat recursus ad eumdem Ordinarium pro revisione actorum coram novo Consilio, quod Ordinario et duobus parochis consultoribus constat iuxta § 2, can. 3.

Canon 23: Interposito recursu, datur parocho adhuc decem dies ad novas allegationes producendas, iisdem servatis regulis quae superius in discussione coram examinatoribus statutá sunt, salva dispositione § 4, can. seq.

Canon 24, § 1: Consultores, convenientes cum Ordinario, de duobus tantum videre debent, utrum in actibus praecedentibus vitia formae in ea irrepserint quae rei substantiam attingant, et utrum adducta amotionis ratio sit fundamento destituta.

§ 2: Ad hunc finem omnia superius acta et adducta examinare debent atque perpendere.

§ 3: Possunt etiam ex officio ad illa duo memorata discussionis capita in tuto ponenda exquirere et percontari de rebus quas necessario cognoscendas putent, auditis etiam, si opus sit, novis testibus.

§ 4: Parochus tamen ius non habet exigendi ut novi testes inducantur et examinentur; nec ut sibi dilationes ulteriores ad deducenda sua iura concedantur.

After the decree of removal was given the pastor had the right to have recourse to the same Ordinary for a review of the acts. This review would be made by a new council composed of the Ordinary and two parish priest consultors. The Ordinary had to choose the

[86] Wernz, *op. cit.*, V, n. 928.

consultors according to the regulations of canon 5, § 1, that is he had to take the two senior consultors.[87]

The consultors, who were chosen, and the Ordinary had to consider only two things: whether in the preceding acts there were any defects of form which affected the substance of the proceedings,[88] and whether the reason given for the removal actually existed and was a cause admitted in law for administrative removal of a pastor. In order that they might be able to give their judgment, the acts of the case were to be produced and examined. The new assertions of the pastor were to be heard. The Ordinary and consultors might also make further inquiries of the pastor and might hear previous witnesses or new witnesses if they felt that this was necessary. As regards the form to be followed in carrying out this procedure in revision the same rules prevailed as for the previous procedure (canon 23) (cf. esp. canons 16 and 17). The pastor, however, did not have the right to introduce new witnesses, or to petition for an extension of time to prepare his defense. The canon stated that the pastor did not have the right to these, but the interpretation of the canon was that one or two concessions might be made in these matters *ex gratia*, especially when such concessions seemed to the judges to be in the cause of truth.[89]

Canon 25, § 1: Admissio vel reiectio recursus maiore suffragiorum numero est decernenda.

The acceptance or rejection of the recourse depended upon the secret vote of the Ordinary and the consultors. The majority decision decided whether or not the previous decree of removal would be confirmed. The rejection of the recourse meant the confirmation of the decree, the acceptance of the recourse meant the repeal of the decree.[90]

[87] Cf. *supra*, pp. 54-55.

[88] *"Maxima cura,"* canon 2, § 2: *"in quo procedendi gradu regulae infra statutae ita servandae sunt, ut, si violentur in iis quae substantiam attingunt, amotio ipsa nulla et irrita evadat."*

[89] Cappello, *De Admin. Amotione Parochorum*, p. 110; Gennari, "Rimozione dal Beneficio Curato"—*Monit. Eccl.*, Terza Serie, II (1910), (Vol. XXII della intera Collezione), p. 545; Wernz, *Ius Decretalium*, V, n. 927, nota n. 81.

[90] Gennari, *art. cit.*, p. 545; Wernz, *op. cit.*, V, n. 926.

As is evident, therefore, the Ordinary was bound to have the consent of the consultors, and this for the validity of the act.

The vote was given to determine whether the causes alleged for the removal lacked foundation, and whether there existed a substantial defect in form in the first procedure. If the pastor could prove that either was the case the votes had to be cast for acceptance of the recourse, which implied repeal of the decree.[91] According to Wernz,[92] if there had been a defect in form it seemed plausible to hold that the Ordinary and the synodal examiners might retract the defective act and by using the form prescribed convalidate the act. Cappello [93] held this same opinion and even stated that if the decree was repealed because a wrong cause had been given as the reason for the decree of removal, the Ordinary, with the same synodal examiners as had been used might remedy the sentence by adducing a cause admitted in law. In this case the whole procedure, of course, would have to be renewed. If the examiners had been the culpable cause then the Ordinary would have to choose the next two examiners in the order of seniority to try the case with him.

91 Wernz, *op. cit.*, V, n. 926.

92 *Op. cit.*, V, n. 926, nota n. 30.

93 *Op. cit.*, p. 112.

Part Two

Canonical Commentary

CHAPTER IV

THE OFFICE OF SYNODAL EXAMINER AND PARISH PRIEST CONSULTOR

Article 1. The Synodal Examiners and Parish Priest Consultors as Members of the Diocesan Curia

A. *The Diocesan Curia*

Canon 363, § 1: Curia dioecesana constat illis personis quae Episcopo aliive qui, loco Episcopi, dioecesim regit, opem praestant in regimine totius dioecesis.

§ 2: Quare ad eam pertinent Vicarius Generalis, officialis, cancellarius, promotor iustitiae, defensor vinculi, synodales iudices et examinatores, parochi consultores, auditores, notarii, cursores et apparitores.

A diocesan curia is made up of those persons whose duty it is to aid the bishop, or other person ruling the diocese in the bishop's stead, in the administration of the whole diocese. In every epoch bishops have had need of helpers for the dispatch of numerous affairs concerning their dioceses, and history demonstrates that bishops have in fact always made use of the services of others for this purpose. In the first centuries priests and deacons were the bishops' assistants, the former helping in the sacred ministry, the latter giving aid in the administration of temporal affairs.[1] With the growth of the Church there was need for specific officials to whom could be intrusted many

[1] Chelodi, *Ius de Personis,* n. 199; Cappello, *Summa Iuris Canonici,* I (3. ed., Romae: Apud Aedes Universitatis Gregorianae, 1938), n. 405, I, nota 1. (Hereafter this work will be cited *Summa.*)

of the duties that crowded in upon the bishop. The episcopal curia was thus the result of a natural growth and evolution. Among the members of the curia the bishop shared his jurisdiction, measuring this sharing to the extent to which he needed assistance.[2] The most prominent curial office in the Church from the middle of the fourth century to the thirteenth century was that of the archdeacon. His duties were various, and his dignity and authority came first after those of the bishop himself.[3] Pope Innocent III called the archdeacon "*maiorem post Episcopum et ipsius Episcopi vicarium.*"[4] Later there came a division of his office into that of the *archidiaconus principalis* in the cathedral city and that of the *archidiaconi minores* in other districts of the diocese.[5] From the thirteenth century other offices came into existence, including that of the vicar general and of the vicars forane. In the course of time the office of the vicar general supplanted that of the archdeacon.[6] In France, Germany, Spain and England jurisdiction in judiciary matters was given, not to the vicar general, but to another, the *officialis*.[7] The Council of Trent suppressed practically all of the power of the archdeacon,[8] and as a natural consequence the office itself presently ceased to exist.[9] The vicars forane were reduced by the Council to their present status as inspectors and delegates of the bishop in administrative affairs.[10]

The Council of Trent also instituted the office of synodal examiner, to help the bishop in the matter of choosing pastors whenever

[2] Dugan, *The Judiciary Department of the Diocesan Curia,* The Catholic University of America Canon Law Studies, n. 26 (Washington, D. C.: The Catholic University of America, 1925), pp. 9-10.

[3] Wernz, *Ius Decretalium,* II, n. 774, I et n. 800, I-II; Chelodi, *op. cit.,* n. 199; Toso, *Ad Codicem Iuris Canonici Commentaria Minora,* III, pars I (Romae: Ius Pontificium, 1925), p. 5. (Hereafter this work will be cited *Commentaria Minora.*) Cappello, *loc. cit.*

[4] C. 7, X, *de officio archidiaconi,* I, 23.

[5] Wernz, *op. cit.,* II, n. 800, II; Chelodi, *loc. cit.*

[6] Wernz, *op. cit.,* II, n. 800, III-IV; Chelodi, *loc. cit.*; Toso, *loc. cit.*

[7] Wernz, *loc. cit.*; Chelodi, *loc. cit.*

[8] Sess. XXIV, *de ref.,* c. 20; sess. XXV, *de ref.,* c. 3.

[9] Chelodi, *loc. cit.*

[10] Sess. XXIV, *de ref.,* cc. 3 et 20.

vacancies might occur in the parishes of his diocese.[11] In 1910 the office of parish priest consultor was established, to afford the bishop assistance in the new administrative procedure concerning the removal of pastors. At the same time the duties of the synodal examiners were augmented, to include a part in this new administrative procedure.[12]

This is a brief statement of the history of the diocesan curia, with a word added concerning some of its officials.

In the Code of Canon Law canon 363, § 2 enumerates the officials who constitute the diocesan curia of today. These officials may be divided into two groups. In the first are they who aid the bishop in the administration of spiritual and temporal matters in the diocese. Some of these possess jurisdiction. This jurisdiction is voluntary, in contradistinction to jurisdiction enjoyed by others in judicial matters. The officials in this first group are the vicar general, the chancellor, the synodal examiners and the parish priest consultors. The second group is composed of those officials whose duties center about the judicial affairs of the diocese. Whatever jurisdiction is possessed by members of this group is judicial, not voluntary. To this group belong the *officialis,* the promoter of justice, the defender of the bond, the synodal judges, the auditors, the court messengers *("cursores")* and the apparitors *("apparitores")*.[13] The synodal examiners and the parish priest consultors, then, are members of the diocesan curia, and their duties are concerned with the non-judicial matters of the diocese.

Canon 363, § 1, speaks of the diocesan curia helping the bishop, or other person who rules the diocese in the place of the bishop. The "others" referred to may be apostolic administrators,[14] abbots and prelates *nullius,*[15] cathedral chapters,[16] boards of diocesan consultors,[17] and vicars capitular.[18]

[11] Sess. XXIV, *de ref.*, c. 18.

[12] S. C. Consist., decr., *Maxima cura,* 20 aug. 1910—*Fontes,* n. 2074.

[13] Dugan, *op. cit.*, p. 16.

[14] Cf. canons 315, §§ 1-2, n. 1; 431, § 2.

[15] Cf. canons 215, § 2; 323, § 1.

[16] Cf. canons 431, § 1; 435, § 1.

[17] Cf. canon 427.

[18] Cf. canon 435.

B. *The Synodal Examiners and Parish Priest Consultors Possess an "Ecclesiastical Office" in the Wide Sense of the Term*

May it be said that the synodal examiners and parish priest consultors possess a real ecclesiastical office? Yes, but only in the wide sense of the term. Canon 145 states that an ecclesiastical office in the wide sense of the term is any employment which is legitimately exercised for a spiritual purpose. In the strict sense, however, it is a stable position, created as such either by Divine or ecclesiastical law, to be conferred according to the norms of Canon Law, and carrying with it some participation of ecclesiastical power, either of orders or of jurisdiction. Canon 145, § 2, creates a presumption, namely, that in law "ecclesiastical office" is taken in the strict sense, unless the contrary is evident from the context of the law. With respect to the offices of synodal examiner and parish priest consultor the contrary is true as is clear from the context of the law, for an examination of the duties incumbent upon these officials, as expressed in the law, makes it evident that at no time do they exercise ecclesiastical power. Certainly it is not an exercise of ecclesiastical power of orders to aid in the various examinations mentioned in canon 389, or to take part in the administrative procedures spoken of in canons 2147-2185. Nor again may any of these duties of the synodal examiners or parish priest consultors be considered as constituting acts of jurisdiction. In the examinations in which they take part, the synodal examiners merely give to the bishop their prudent judgment on the learning and fitness of candidates. If such a judgment were to imply jurisdiction, whether of the external or of the internal forum, then other teachers who would examine students could also be said to possess jurisdiction. As to the duties of the synodal examiners and parish priest consultors in the administrative procedures of canons 2147-2185, these neither entail the giving of a sentence, nor do they imply a jurisdictional determining or regulating of any particular matter of discipline. In the fulfillment of these duties the synodal examiners and parish priest consultors merely give their counsel. Not even their consent is required. This counsel which is given is not, and may not be said to be, an act of jurisdiction, since only the bishop is competent to give the decision.[19]

[19] d'Angelo, "De Examinatoribus Synodalibus"—*Apollinaris* (Romae, 1928—), III (1930), p. 140.

As a consequence, therefore, if the synodal examiners and the parish priest consultors may in any sense be said to possess an ecclesiastical office (and canon 364, § 1, does refer to them as possessing such an office: *"qui praedicta officia"*), it can only be an ecclesiastical office in the wide sense of the term. It may be added that the offices of synodal examiner and of parish priest consultor, like those of the other officials, are not benefices, since there is lacking the character of stability. Their term of office is not for an indefinite period but is clearly defined in the Code (canon 387). Once the term is completed they automatically go out of office.[20]

Article 2. The Election of Synodal Examiners and Parish Priest Consultors

A. *The Election*

Canon 385, § 1: In quavis dioecesi habeantur examinatores synodales et parochi consultores qui omnes in Synodo constituantur, propositi ab Episcopo, a Synodo approbati.

In every diocese there are to be appointed synodal examiners and parish priest consultors. They are to be appointed in the synod, being proposed by the bishop and receiving the approval of the synod.

"In quavis dioecesi": there is an obligation upon every bishop to see that these officials are appointed in his diocese. If a bishop should rule over two dioceses, even if they be united with equal rights *("aeque principaliter unitae")*, he is to have a distinct body of synodal examiners and of parish priest consultors for each diocese, unless express permission has been obtained from the Sacred Congregation of the Council to employ one body for both dioceses.[21] This is clear from the wording of the canon,[22] and is also the authen-

[20] Cf. d'Angelo, *La Curia Diocęsana,* I, p. 4; Cappello, *Summa,* I, n. 405, III-IV.

[21] d'Angelo, "De Examinatoribus Synodalibus"—*Apollinaris,* III (1930), p. 141.

[22] Cf. canon 18.

tic interpretation given to pre-Code legislation, which in this particular point was the same as the present legislation.[23]

"*... qui omnes in Synodo constituantur*": this part of the canon corresponds entirely with the original law of the Council of Trent, and must consequently, in accord with canon 6, 3°, be interpreted in the same way. Therefore, it is required for validity that the appointment be made in the synod itself.[24] This restriction, however, is greatly relaxed by canon 386, and must be interpreted accordingly. This latter canon gives the bishop the right to elect examiners outside a synod when there is a necessity of substituting a new official for one who has, for some reason or other, ceased to be a synodal examiner, and also when no synod is to be held.

"*... propositi ab Episcopo*": the one change here from the old law is that the vicar general has no right similar to that of the bishop to propose names for approval, unless he has been given a mandate to do so by the bishop.[25] The presentation of names made by the bishop to those present in the synod must be made as before the Code, that is, the bishop must indicate clearly the name of the individual, not merely the title or office that an individual holds. Designation solely by office or by dignity would be invalid.[26] Not only bishops, but also abbots and prelates *nullius* [27] are required to appoint synodal examiners and parish priest consultors in the synod. The same obligation rests upon apostolic administrators, if they are appointed permanently.[28] Apostolic administrators who are appointed temporarily,

[23] Cf. canon 6, 3°; S. C. C., *Castellan.*, 24 sept. 1639—*Fontes*, n. 2610; S. C. C., *Valven. et Sulmonen.*, 3 sept. 1650—*Fontes*, n. 2711.

[24] Conc. Trident., sess. XXIV, *de ref.*, c. 18.

[25] Cf. canon 152.

[26] Cf. canon 6, 3°. S. C. C., *in Pennen.*, 14 aug. 1640—*Pallottini*, X, "examinatores synodales," n. 33; Garcia, *de Benef.*, pars IX, cap. II, n. 335; Barbosa, *De Offic. et Potest. Parochi*, pars I, cap. II, n. 55; Ferreres, *Institutiones Canonicae*, I (2. ed., Barcinone: Subirana, 1920), n. 680, II; Rossi, *De Paroecia*, n. 174, nota n. 95, ad 4; Cocchi, *Commentarium in Codicem Iuris Canonici*, Vol. III (3. ed., Taurinorum Augustae: Marietti, 1931), n. 292, a. (Hereafter this work will be cited *Commentarium.*) Beste, *Introductio in Codicem* (Collegeville, Minnesota: St. John's Abbey Press, 1938), p. 278. (Henceforth this work will be cited *Introductio.*)

[27] Cf. canon 215, § 2; Ferreres, *loc. cit.*

[28] Cf. canon 315, § 1.

cathedral chapters, boards of diocesan consultors and vicars capitular may not at any time appoint synodal examiners or parish priest consultors in a synod for the very reason that they are not permitted to convoke a synod.[29]

"... *a Synodo approbati*": this part of canon 385, § 1, is also taken from pre-Code law.[30] The voting by members of the synod for the approval or rejection of each specific name proposed by the bishop may be either secret or open.[31] Canon 358, § 2, determines who has the right to vote in a diocesan synod. A convenient method of procedure for this voting is to have a list, with the names of those proposed by the bishop, and to distribute this list to the members of the synod. Each of the members could then check off the names of those whom he did not wish to approve.[32]

In order to receive the approval of the synod a proposed name must have at least an absolute majority of the votes cast.[33] After the second balloting, however, a relative majority would suffice.[34] Approval by the Synod is necessary for a valid appointment.[35]

B. *Qualifications*

1. In the Synodal Examiners

With regard to the qualifications which should be found in the

[29] Cf. canons 357, § 1; 315, § 2, n. 1; 435.

[30] Conc. Trident., sess. XXIV, *de ref.*, c. 18.

[31] Cf. canon 6, 3°. S. C. C., *Venetiarum*, 11 iul. 1592—*Fontes*, n. 2247; S. C. C., *Fulginaten.*, 3 dec. 1664—*Pallottini*, X, "examinatores synodales," n. 4; Augustine, *A Commentary on the New Code of Canon Law* (8 vols., St. Louis, London: Herder, 1925-1938), II (5. ed., 1925), p. 420; (hereafter this work will be cited *Commentary*). Rossi, *De Paroecia*, n. 174, nota n. 95; Coronata, *Institutiones*, I, n. 432; Beste, *Introductio*, p. 278.

[32] Mothon, *Institutions Canoniques* (3 vols., Paris: Desclée, de Brouwer & Cie., 1922-1924), I, n. 664.

[33] Barbosa, *De Officio et Potestate Parochi, Animadversiones et Additamenta*, Giraldi, pars I, cap. II, n. 56, animadversio; Augustine, *op. cit.*, II, p. 420; Wernz-Vidal, *Ius Canonicum*, II, n. 652, II; Coronata, *op. cit.*, n. 432.

[34] Canon 101, § 1, 1°. Cf. Wernz-Vidal, *loc. cit.*; Rossi, *De Paroecia*, n. 174, nota n. 95; Coronata, *Institutiones*, I, n. 432, nota 6; Beste, *Introductio*, p. 278.

[35] Cf. canon 6, 3°. Conc. Trident., sess. XXIV, *de ref.*, c. 18.

candidates for the office of synodal examiner, some authors [36] claim that the law of the Council of Trent still holds, namely, that the candidates should be masters, or doctors, or possessed of at least the degree of licentiate, in sacred theology or canon law, though clerics without a degree might also be elected if they appeared more competent for the office. Other authors,[37] and they are more correct, it seems, state simply that the Code is silent concerning requisite qualifications. Since in fact there is no mention of required qualifications anywhere in the Code, it seems to follow quite logically that the opinion of these authors is correct, for canon 6, 6° provides that disciplinary laws, which were in existence previous to the Code, but which are neither explicitly nor implicitly contained in the New Code, are to be considered as having lost all force of law. However, it may be stated that the qualifications formerly required by law would seem still to be required by the very nature of the office of synodal examiner, and by the duties attendant upon this office.

2. In the Parish Priest Consultors

The Code contains no law requiring specific qualifications in the candidates for the office of parish priest consultor. The one thing necessary is that they be pastors, though even this is not stated expressly in the Code. It is implied, however, in the very name given to these officials, *"parochi consultores,"* which is translated "parish priest consultors" or "pastor consultors." The Sacred Consistorial Congregation (October 3, 1910) implied as much when it stated that a religious priest would have to be a pastor in order that he might be elected parish priest consultor.[38] The authors are positive on this

[36] Ferreres, *Institutiones Canonicae,* I, n. 679; Bevilaqua, *De Episcopi seu Ordinarii ex Novo Codice Canonico Iuribus ac Obligationibus* (Romae, Ratisbonae, Coloniae Agrippinae, Neo Eboracei, Cincinnati: Pustet, 1921), n. 235; Ayrinhac, *Constitution of the Church,* n. 181; Wernz-Vidal, *Ius Canonicum,* II, n. 651; Munerati, *Iuris Ecclesiastici Publici et Privati Elementa* (4. ed., Romae: ex schola typographica Salesiana, 1926), n. 301.

[37] Chelodi, *Ius de Personis,* n. 203 et nota 1; Coronata, *Institutiones,* I, n. 432; Sipos, *Enchiridion,* n. 53, IV, 1, nota 37; Cappello, *Summa,* I, n. 408, ad 6.

[38] Ad IV—*Fontes,* n. 2076.

point.[39] Though there is no other qualification required by law, still it seems that the very nature of the office and the duties of a parish priest consultor require that he be a highly respected pastor and a man who knows very well those things which are necessary for the capable administration of a parish.[40]

C. *Exclusion from the Offices of Synodal Examiner and Parish Priest Consultor*

Whenever the question arises as to whether or not certain persons are excluded from the office of synodal examiner, or from that of parish priest consultor, the solution may be found by an application of the following two norms: (1) is there any prohibition in the canons? (2) does the one in question already possess an office which by its very nature would not admit of the simultaneous reception and exercise of the office of synodal examiner, or of parish priest consultor: in other words, does incompatibility exist? [41]

In order to determine the question of incompatibility one must keep in mind the duties of the synodal examiners, or of the parish priest consultors, as the case may be. Briefly, the duties of the former are to examine candidates for vacant parishes, to aid in certain administrative processes, and, if called upon by the bishop, to take part in the examinations for ordination, for the approval of candidates for jurisdiction to hear confessions, or for faculty to preach, and for the annual testing of the Junior Clergy.[42] The duties of the parish priest consultors are very few, namely, to assist in certain administrative procedures.[43] As has been previously pointed out, none of these duties of either official constitutes an act of jurisdiction.

[39] *E.g.*, Wernz-Vidal, *Ius Canonicum,* II, n. 651; Prümmer, *Manuale Iuris Canonici* (4. et 5. ed., Friburgi Brisgoviae: Herder, 1927), quaestio 136; Oesterle, *Praelectiones Iuris Canonici,* I (Romae: Collegio S. Anselmi, 1931), p. 189; Beste, *Introductio,* p. 278.

[40] Wernz-Vidal, *loc. cit.*; Prümmer, *loc. cit.*

[41] Cf. canons 156 and 188, 3°.

[42] Canon 389.

[43] Cf. canons 2153, § 1; 2154, § 1; 2165.

With the above norms in mind it is possible to settle some particular cases:

1. May a priest not of a diocese, or a priest of a religious order or congregation exercise the office of either examiner or consultor? Yes, because first of all there is no prohibition in the Code. Secondly, diversity of diocese, or type of clergy (*i. e.*, diocesan priest, religious priest) are not facts which would imply incompatibility.[44] The Sacred Consistorial Congregation (October 3, 1910) [45] replying to a doubt concerning the decree, *"Maxima cura,"* of August 20, 1910,[46] stated that an Ordinary might choose a priest not of his diocese for the office of synodal examiner, or of parish priest consultor, provided that his diocese was small, or that there was some other just cause for making such a choice. In practice this reply of the Sacred Consistorial Congregation may be applied even today, provided there really exists a sufficient cause.[47] Concerning religious priests the same Sacred Congregation, in reply to another doubt, affirmed without reservation that they might be chosen for either office.[48] Of course,

[44] d'Angelo, "De Examinatoribus Synodalibus"—*Apollinaris,* III (1930), pp. 140-141; "Quistioni minori: Chi puó essere esaminatore sinodale"—*Perfice Munus* (Augustae Taurinorum, 1926—), VII (1932), pp. 598-599.

[45] Ad V—*Fontes,* n. 2076.

[46] S. C. Consist.—*Fontes,* n. 2074.

[47] d'Angelo, *loc. cit.* Gennari gives it as his opinion that a diocese would be considered sufficiently small if it did not have 100,000 people. (It seems that he was referring to Catholic people): "Rimozione dal Benef. Curato"—*Monit. Eccl.,* Terza Serie, II (1910), (Vol. XXII della intera Collezione), p. 433.

[48] S. C. Consist., 3 oct. 1910, ad IV—*Fontes,* n. 2076. The question asked of the Sacred Congregation was whether the Ordinary could appoint any "regular" priest (*"aliquem sacerdotem regularem"*) as examiner or consultor, and the answer similarly referred to a "regular" priest. Browne has, very rightly it seems, argued that the word *"regularis"* may be here taken in the wide sense to include all religious that are otherwise eligible for either office. He gives as his reason the fact that the term *"regularis"* was often used before the Code in a wide sense to signify all male religious, that is, members of Congregations as well as Orders—"Can Religious Be Appointed Diocesan Consultor or Parochus-Consultor?"—*The Irish Ecclesiastical Record* (Dublin, 1864—), XLII (July-Dec., 1933), 5th series, pp. 415-416. An additional reason, not mentioned by Browne, may also be adduced: there does not appear to be any reason why only members of Orders, and not of religious in Congregations as well, should be allowed to be synodal examiners or parish priest consultors.

the religious would have to be a pastor to be taken for the office of parish priest consultor.[49] With regard to the choosing of religious for these offices d'Angelo remarks that in his personal opinion the bishop, at least out of prudence, should rather choose his own secular priests, if they are fit, and if there is a sufficient number in his diocese.[50]

2. May a pastor be a synodal examiner? Yes, for there is neither any prohibition in the law, nor any incompatibility between the two offices. Before the promulgation of the Code the Sacred Consistorial Congregation replied in the affirmative to a question whether some pastors might be numbered amongst the synodal examiners.[51] If it should happen that in a particular case a pastor could not undertake the additional duties involved in his being synodal examiner, this would be a question of fact, not of law, and in such an instance the bishop should refrain from choosing the particular pastor for the office of examiner.[52]

3. May a cathedral canon, or a diocesan consultor be chosen for the office of synodal examiner? Yes, and for the same reasons as given above, namely, that the Code does not place any prohibition, nor is there any incompatibility between the offices. Again, though, it must be remarked that if there would be a specific instance wherein a particular canon, or diocesan consultor, would be unable to perform the duties of both offices, the bishop should under the circumstances refrain from choosing such an one for the second office.[53]

4. May the vicar general, the *officialis,* the chancellor be chosen for the office of synodal examiner? Strictly speaking, yes, for neither canonical prohibition, nor incompatibility stand in the way as obstacles. In practice, however, it is not expedient that they should be chosen. With regard to the vicar general this was the answer given by the Sacred Consistorial Congregation (October 3, 1910).[54] Furthermore, it may be noted that under certain circumstances the

[49] S. C. Consist., 3 oct. 1910, ad IV—*Fontes,* n. 2076; Ferreres, *Institutiones Canonicae,* I, n. 679; Rossi, *De Paroecia,* n. 239, nota 8, ad 3.

[50] d'Angelo, *ibidem.,* p. 141.

[51] 3 oct. 1910, ad VII—*Fontes,* n. 2076.

[52] d'Angelo, *loc. cit.*; *Perfice Munus,* VII (1932), p. 597.

[53] d'Angelo, *ibidem,* p. 142; *Perfice Munus,* VII (1932), pp. 597-598.

[54] Ad VI—*Fontes,* n. 2076.

office of vicar general would be incompatible with that of synodal examiner. For example, the vicar general may preside at a concursus, in place of the bishop, and when this would be the case it would naturally follow that he could not at the same time act as a synodal examiner.[55] As to the *officialis*, he is the ordinary judge in the diocesan court, and the possibility of a conflict between the assignments of a judge and the duties of a synodal examiner suggests that the expedient course would be not to appoint the *officialis* to the latter office.[56] In the case of the chancellor it should be noted that since he may be chosen to act as notary in a concursus and in the administrative processes (a thing which would be apt to happen frequently in small dioceses), it would follow that he could not at the same time fulfill the duties of synodal examiner. For this reason it is recommended that the Ordinary should not appoint the chancellor to the office of synodal examiner.[57]

5. When it is a question of the vicar general, the *officialis*, the chancellor, or a diocesan consultor being chosen for the office of parish priest consultor, an added difficulty presents itself. In order that a priest be a candidate for the office of parish priest consultor he must, of course, be a pastor. When, therefore, one of the above-mentioned officials would become a parish priest consultor he would, at one and the same time, be holding three offices. The answer to the question proposed seems to be that the bishop should, if at all possible, refrain from appointing these officials to the further office of parish priest consultor. This response is dictated by the following reasons: first, the Code itself declares that the office of vicar general should not, except in case of necessity, be given to a pastor.[58] As a natural consequence, therefore, there is all the more reason why an added office should not be given to a vicar general who is also a pastor. Though there is no explicit statement in the Code forbidding the accumulation in one person of the offices of pastor and *officialis*, or of pastor and chancellor, or finally of pastor and diocesan consultor, still the same reasons for a prohibition, which seem to have urged the legisla-

[55] d'Angelo, *La Curia Diocesana*, I, p. 38; d'Angelo, *loc. cit.*

[56] d'Angelo, *loc. cit.*; *Perfice Munus*, VII (1932), p. 598.

[57] d'Angelo, *art. cit.*, p. 143; *Perfice Munus*, VII (1932), p. 598.

[58] Canon 367, § 3.

tion of canon 367, § 3, appear to be also present, if in a lesser degree, with regard to the accumulation of these other offices. Similarly, therefore, the adding of a third office to the person who already possesses the offices of pastor and *officialis,* or the offices of pastor and chancellor, or finally of pastor and diocesan consultor, would seem to be quite clearly a thing to be avoided. Secondly, the principle: *"generatim expedit ne plura officia in una eademque persona cumulentur"* [59] militates strongly against the accumulation in one person of three different offices. Finally the reasons alleged for the conclusion that a vicar general, an *officialis,* and a chancellor should not be given the office of synodal examiner seem to be conclusive also in the question at hand, namely, these officials ought not to be given the office of parish priest consultor.

6. May an ex-religious be a synodal examiner or parish priest consultor? Canon 642, § 1, 3° and § 2 gives the answer: any professed religious who returns to the world is prohibited from any office in episcopal curias, unless he receives a new and special indult from the Holy See. This prohibition applies also to those who pronounced only temporary vows, or took an oath of perseverance, or made other promises according to their constitutions, when they have been dispensed from them, provided, however, that they have lived under these obligations for a period of at least six years. This canon refers to all secularized religious, including dismissed religious, once they have been dispensed from their vows.[60] The prohibition does not affect those professed religious who were not in sacred orders at the time of separation from their religious Order or Congregation. Nor does it affect those who, at the time of separation, were in sacred orders, but had not as yet made their profession, because, for example, they were still in the novitiate.[61] This prohibition does not affect, either, those religious who were able to leave their particular religion, without the necessity of a dispensation, for the reason that

[59] Cf. S. C. Consist., 3 oct. 1910, ad VIII—*Fontes,* n. 2076.

[60] Schäfer, *De Religiosis ad Normam Codicis Iuris Canonici* (3. ed., Romae: Herder, 1940), n. 556.

[61] *The Ecclesiastical Review* (Philadelphia, 1889—), LXXXIX (1933), p. 526; Woywod, *The Homiletic and Pastoral Review* (New York, 1900—), XXXV (1935), p. 1063; Schäfer, *loc. cit.*

the period covered by their vows had elapsed.[62] If the religious profession was invalid, then the prohibition has no effect whatsoever.[63] The Pontifical Commission for the Interpretation of the Code has stated, in answer to a proposed doubt, that those religious who had left their particular religious Order or Congregation, by permission from the Holy See, before the promulgation of the New Code were also bound by the prohibition of canon 642.[64] In spite of this response, however, those ex-religious who had obtained a curial office, such as that of synodal examiner or parish priest consultor, before the promulgation of the Code are not bound now to give up the office. Theirs is an acquired right.[65] The religious who are bound by canon 642, but who would nevertheless obtain a curial office, would do so illicitly, but not invalidly.[66]

D. *The Appointment of Synodal Examiners and Parish Priest Consultors Must Be Put in Writing*

Canon 364, § 1, legislates that the appointment of curial officials is to be put in writing. Contrary to the opinion of d'Angelo,[67] it does not appear to be necessary for validity that the appointment of synodal examiners and parish priest consultors be in writing. It seems rather to be a question of licitness.[68] The reason for differing from the opinion of d'Angelo is that there is no express word, or its equivalent, in canon 364, § 1, which would indicate the notion of invalidity.[69]

[62] Vermeersch, A.-Creusen, J., *Epitome Iuris Canonici* (3 vols., Mechliniae: H. Dessain, 1934-1936. Vol. I, 6. ed., 1937; Vol. II, 5. ed., 1934; Vol. III, 5. ed., 1936), I, n. 799. (Hereafter this work will be cited *Epitome.*)

[63] Woywod, *loc. cit.*; Schäfer, *loc. cit.*

[64] 24 nov. 1920, ad V—*AAS,* XII (1920), p. 573.

[65] Canon 4; Schäfer, *op. cit.*, n. 556.

[66] Cf. canon 111; Schäfer, *loc. cit.*

[67] *La Curia Diocesana,* I, p. 4.

[68] Woywod, *HPR,* XX (1920), p. 644; Ferreres, *Institutiones Canonicae,* I, n. 320; Toso, *Commentaria Minora,* III, pars I, p. 6; Cocchi, *Commentarium,* Vol. II (3. ed., Taurinorum Augustae: Marietti, 1930), n. 65, 4.

[69] Cf. canon 11; Woywod, *loc. cit.*; Toso, *loc. cit.*

E. *Oaths*

According to canon 364, § 2, 1° those appointed to the offices of synodal examiner or parish priest consultor are obliged to take an oath before the bishop to exercise their office faithfully, without respect to persons. In the law of the Council of Trent [70] there was required a similar oath of fidelity to duty, with respect to the duties of the synodal examiners in the concursus. Consequently, since the new law corresponds in part to the old law, it follows that in accord with canon 6, 3° this particular part of the new law is to be interpreted as it was previous to the Code. The important consequence of this is that whenever a synodal examiner, who has not taken this oath, participates in a concursus, this concursus is to be considered as invalid.[71] This note of invalidity, however, is not to be extended to any other duty performed by a synodal examiner, or by a parish priest consultor, who may not have taken an oath of fidelity to duty. The oath is to be taken in the presence of the bishop, or of some other priest delegated by the bishop.[72] The canon does not require that it be taken in the synod.

Canon 364, § 2, 2° prescribes that the curial officials (which includes the synodal examiners and parish priest consultors) shall perform their duties under the authority of the bishop and in accord with the relative laws of the Code. When the Code warns the appointees to do their work in accord with the laws it wishes to im-

[70] Sess. XXIV, *de ref.*, c. 18.

[71] S. C. C., *Bisinianen.*, 12 dec. 1628 et *Illerden.*, 14 mart. 1629—*Pallottini*, X, "examinatores synodales," n. 60; cf. *Militen.*, 21 iulii 1753—*Thes. Resol.*, XVII, pp. 55-57, 64; Rossi, *De Paroecia*, n. 174; d'Angelo, *La Curia Diocesana*, I, p. 40. Opposed to the notion of invalidity is Toso, *Commentaria Minora*, III, pars I, p. 6. d'Angelo, who has been cited in this footnote, does not say explicitly that a concursus held under these circumstances would be invalid, but merely asserts that according to many learned canonists a concursus would be invalid, if only one examiner assisted who had not taken the oath. However, in view of the decisions quoted in this footnote, from the Sacred Congregation of the Council, it seems that the only conclusion that one can come to is the one proposed in the text, namely, that a concursus would be invalid in the event that one of the examiners attending had not taken the oath of fidelity to office.

[72] Mothon, *Institutions Canoniques;* I, n. 665.

press upon these officials the importance of their office, and the serious wrong involved in any act placed contrary to the law. All acts violating the prescriptions of the law are either invalid or illicit. Since the bishop has been placed by the Holy Spirit to rule in the diocese and since the law itself states [73] that the curial officials are appointed as the assistants of the bishop in the administration of the diocese, the command of canon 364, § 2, 2° follows quite logically, namely, that they are to perform their tasks under the authority of the bishop.[74] No oath is required of the synodal examiners and parish priest consultors in this matter.

A further obligation placed by the Code upon the synodal examiners and parish priest consultors at the very beginning of their term of office is that of the secret of office. They must refrain from revealing anything that the law or the bishop decides must be kept secret.[75] The Code does not prescribe any oath in this regard in the canon under discussion, canon 364, § 2, 3°. In canon 2144, § 1, however, there is demanded an oath of secrecy from both the examiners and the consultors, but it has reference only to the matters involved in certain administrative procedures (canons 2142-2185). Of this particular oath more will be said later, in the treatment of the duties of the examiners and consultors in these administrative procedures. Canon 364, § 2, 3° gives to the bishop the right to determine how secrecy must be kept, whenever there is no specific prescription to be found in the law itself: *"secundum modum a iure vel ab episcopo determinatum."* Consequently, the bishop may pass legislation, either synodal or extra-synodal, in this matter, and it is within his right to demand an oath of secrecy.[76]

[73] Canon 363, § 1.

[74] Cf. d'Angelo, *La Curia Diocesana,* I, p. 5.

[75] Canon 364, § 2, 3°.

[76] Cf. d'Angelo, *La Curia Diocesana,* I, pp. 5-6. Toso (*Commentaria Minora,* III, pars I, p. 7) appends in a footnote the formula of an oath required, before the Code, of the synodal examiners and parish priest consultors, by the Sacred Consistorial Congregation (Decr., 15 febr. 1912—*Fontes,* n. 2083). This oath, which had to be taken before each participation in an administrative procedure against a pastor, was threefold. It included an oath to fulfill one's

It must be noted here that the synodal examiners and the parish priest consultors are held to make the Profession of Faith and to take the oath against Modernism. In the *Motu proprio* of Pius X, *Sacrorum Antistitum,* September 1, 1910, it was stated that diocesan curial officials were obliged to take the oath against Modernism and that the taking of this oath was to be preceded by the making of the Profession of Faith.[77] After the promulgation of the Code there arose the question as to whether or not this prescription was still in force. The reasons for doubting the continuance of the obligation were that there was no mention of the oath in the Code, and the fact that canon 6, 6 ° states that when a previous disciplinary law finds neither explicit nor implicit mention in the Code it is to be considered as having lost its force of law. The Holy Office, however, on March 22, 1918, declared that this prescription was not mentioned in the Code because it is of its nature temporary and transitory; but that, since the virus of Modernism has not ceased to spread, this prescription must remain in full force until the Holy See decrees otherwise.[78] The Profession of Faith and oath against Modernism may in particular cases, and provided there is a just cause, be taken before a priest delegated by the bishop.[79]

duties faithfully, an oath of secrecy, and an oath not to receive anything, even as a gift, on the occasion of the exercise of duty. Toso claims that this same oath is to be taken today in virtue of canon 364, § 2, 1°. His statement is, it seems, without foundation, since the Code in canon 364, § 2, 1° refers only to an oath to fulfill one's duties faithfully, and this oath is general, having reference to all the duties of the synodal examiners and parish priest consultors. Another author (Meier, *Adm. Proc. Ag. Neglig. Pastors,* p. 106) also seems to have made an incorrect statement when he refers to canon 364, § 2, 3° as requiring a general oath of secrecy. The Code, in this particular place, merely states that the curial officials must keep secrecy within the bounds and according to the manner determined either by law or by the bishop.

[77] *Fontes,* n. 689: *"Iuramentum hoc" (i. e., antimodernisticum) "praemissa fidei professione . . . antistiti suo dabunt . . . IV . . . officiales in curiis episcopales. . . ."*

[78] *AAS,* X (1918), p. 136; cf. also: Coronata, *Institutiones,* II, n. 970; Beste, *Introductio,* p. 695.

[79] Cf. S. C. Consist., 25 sept. 1910, ad VIII—*Fontes,* n. 2075; Beste, *loc. cit.*

Article 3. Number of Synodal Examiners and Parish Priest Consultors

Canon 385, § 2: Tot eligantur quot Episcopus prudenti suo iudicio necessarios iudicaverit, non tamen infra quattuor, nec ultra duodecim.

It is left to the prudent judgment of the bishop to elect as many synodal examiners and parish priest consultors as he deems necessary. He may not, however, elect less than four, nor more than twelve for either office.

The present law on the number of these curial officials is a change from the law existing before the Code. Previously the bishop was allowed complete freedom and could elect as many as he wished for either office.[80] Now, however, the freedom of the bishop is limited since he must elect at least four and may not elect more than twelve. It seems that a bishop who would violate this law by electing less than four for either office, or more than twelve, would be acting illicitly, but not invalidly, and all those chosen would be true officials of the diocesan curia. Canon 385, § 1 gives the bishop the power to elect these officials, and the second part of the same canon does not contain an express statement, or its equivalent, indicating invalidity in the case of a violation of the law.[81]

In may be remarked that ordinarily the number of parish priest consultors may well be smaller than the number of synodal examiners, for the reason that the former have so few duties to perform.[82]

Aricle 4. Pro-synodal Examiners and Parish Priest Consultors

Canon 386, § 1: Examinatoribus et parochis consultoribus medio tempore inter unam et aliam synodum demortuis vel alia ratione a munere cessantibus, alios

[80] S. C. Consist., decr., *Maxima cura,* 20 aug. 1910, can. 4, § 1—*Fontes,* n. 2074.

[81] Cf. canon 11.

[82] Ferreres, *Institutiones Canonicae,* I, n. 680; Rossi, *De Paroecia,* n. 239, nota n. 8, n. 4.

pro-synodales Episcopus substituat de consilio Capituli cathedralis.

If it should happen that some or all of the synodal examiners or parish priest consultors would die or for some other reason cease to hold their office in the period between one synod and another, the bishop may substitute others in their place, after he has consulted the cathedral chapter (or the diocesan consultors). The substitutes would be known as pro-synodal examiners or pro-synodal parish priest consultors.

With but one very notable change this particular law corresponds almost verbatim to the law in force before the Code.[83] The one change is that whereas the former law required the *consent* of the cathedral chapter (or diocesan consultors) before the bishop might make any substitutions, the new law requires only that the bishop *consult* the cathedral chapter (or diocesan consultors) previous to making substitutions.

In seeking the counsel of the cathedral chapter (or diocesan consultors) the bishop is obliged to call the members of the chapter together. He is not to consult each one individually and at different times and places.[84] The individual members are to speak their mind freely, but must always be motivated in doing so by a spirit of reverence, faith and sincerity.[85]

Canon 386, § 1 gives the bishop the power to elect pro-synodal examiners and parish priest consultors upon the death of one or more of those in office, or whenever one of these officials ceases to hold his office for some reason other than death. These other causes

[83] Cf. S. C. Consist., decr., *Maxima cura,* 20 aug. 1910, can. 4, § 2—*Fontes,* n. 2074.

[84] Canon 105, 2°; Vermeersch-Creusen, *Epitome,* I, n. 230.

[85] Canon 105, 2° and 3°. Cf. Vermeersch-Creusen, *loc. cit.* These brief remarks concerning the manner in which the bishop is to call together the members of the cathedral chapter (or the diocesan consultors) when he is obliged by law to consult them, and concerning the manner in which the members of the cathedral chapter (or the diocesan consultors) are to give their advice must be kept in mind. It would be needless repetition to make note of them over and over again on the many occasions when one is confronted with this necessity on the part of the bishop to seek the advice of others before acting.

or reasons for vacancies may be, for example, resignation, loss of the office of pastor in the case of a parish priest consultor, removal from office as a penalty, or serious illness, etc.[86]

Coronata[87] remarks that there does not seem to be any strict obligation upon the bishop to make substitutions in order that at least four officials might be had for each office. To the contrary, however, there does seem to be an obligation to make substitutions. The Code in the canon under consideration says: *"alios pro-synodales Episcopus substituat."* The force of the word *"substituat"* seems to be that of a command. If a mere permission were intended it seems that the word *"potest"* would have been used. Perhaps it may be conceded that the obligation would not be a very strict one if the bishop still had a sufficient number of officials left in either office, but if the number went below four, then it would seem that the obligation would be grave. This conclusion is reached in the presence of the following considerations: (a) in those places where the law of the concursus still remains in effect there must always be at least three synodal examiners, since the law requires the presence of at least that many for each concursus, and this for the validity of the concursus.[88] (b) Where the law of the concursus is not in effect, the Code requires an examination on doctrine. This examination is given by the bishop and his synodal examiners.[89] The Code does not determine just how many examiners are to take part in this examination, but since it does speak in the plural there must be at least two or three. (c) There must always be at least two parish priest consultors, since two are absolutely required in every instance where the law calls upon the service of these officials. (d) Finally, it is entirely possible that one or more of the synodal examiners or parish priest consultors may, for a very good reason, be impeded from performing their duty at certain times, or may even be rejected from participating in a concursus or administrative procedure as being suspect. The bishop should hardly be forced in such

[86] Toso, *Commentaria Minora,* III, pars I, p. 28.

[87] *Institutiones,* I, n. 432.

[88] Conc. Trident., sess. XXIV, *de ref.,* c. 18; S. C. C., *Cremonen.,—Pallottini,* X, "examinatores synodales," n. 69.

[89] Canon 459, § 3, 3°.

circumstances to postpone a concursus, an examination or an administrative procedure due to a lack of other examiners or consultors.

What must be said of the action of the bishop who would make a substitution without consulting the cathedral chapter (or diocesan consultors)? Is his action invalid? Or is it valid, but illicit? The answer to such a question hinges on the interpretation one gives to the meaning of canon 105, 1° when it states that: if counsel only is required, by words such as: *with the counsel of the consultors, or having heard the Chapter, pastor,* etc., then it is sufficient for a valid act that the Superior hear these persons ("si consilium tantum [requiritur], per verba, ex. gr.: *de consilio consultorum,* vel *audito Capitulo, parocho,* etc., satis est ad valide agendum ut Superior illas personas audiat"). Authors of the highest repute have argued the meaning of this part of canon 105, 1°. Some hold the opinion that, *e. g.*, a bishop would act invalidly if he neglected to seek the counsel of the cathedral chapter, when this was required of him by law. Others, on the other hand, claim that the bishop would act validly, but illicitly. The opinion of the former seems to be the common opinion, at least according to Coronata.[90] The latter opinion, however, is not without strong support from eminent canonists.[91] Without entering into a lengthy discussion of the question, it seems that the first opinion is the correct one. The main reason for this statement is that the meaning of canon 105, 1° appears quite evident from the very text itself. If "it is sufficient" for a valid action that *e. g.*, a bishop hear his diocesan consultors, even though he does not follow their advice, then "it would not be sufficient" for a valid act if he did not hear these consultors.[92]

[90] *Institutiones,* I, n. 153, III, nota 8.

[91] Vermeersch-Creusen, *Epitome,* I, n. 229; Vermeersch, *Periodica de Re Canonica, Morali, Liturgica* (Brugis, 1905—), XII (1923), pp. 6-9; Boudinhon, *Jus Pontificium* (Romae, 1921—), VIII (1928), pp. 29-35; Creusen, *Nouvelle Revue Theologique* (Paris, 1869—), LV (1928), pp. 100-116; Wernz-Vidal, *Ius Canonicum,* II, n. 33, nota n. 3; Cicognani, *Canon Law* (2. ed., *authorized* English version by J. M. O'Hara and Francis Brennan; Philadelphia: Dolphin Press, 1935), p. 560; Bastnagel, *The Appointment of Parochial Adjutants and Assistants,* The Catholic University of America Canon Law Studies, n. 58 (Washington, D. C.: The Catholic University of America, 1930), pp. 227-228.

[92] Cf. canon 18.

What, then, should one conclude, as a norm for action, about the validity of actions placed contrary to this prescription of canon 105, 1°? The answer to this eminently practical question seems to be that there exists a probable doubt that such actions would be invalid. The question has been proposed to the Commission for the Authentic Interpretation of the Code of Canon Law, though as yet no answer has been given.[93] Therefore, in practice there need be no anxiety concerning the validity of acts which have been placed contrary to this prescription of canon 105, 1°. This conclusion must be admitted, it seems, in virtue of canons 15 and 209. Still, it should always be borne in mind that in any instance the act would very definitely be a violation of the law.[94]

Article 5. Elections When No Synod Is Held

Canon 386, § 2: Quae regula servetur quoque in examinatoribus et parochis consultoribus constituendis quoties Synodus non habeatur.

Whenever a synod is not held the bishop is to elect pro-synodal examiners and parish priest consultors. Before the actual appointment he is obliged to consult the cathedral chapter (or diocesan consultors).

According to law [95] diocesan synods should be held every ten years. If it should happen, however, that a synod is not held at the prescribed time, the Code makes special provisions for the election of synodal examiners and parish priest consultors. In such circumstances the bishop is to call together his cathedral chapter (or board of diocesan consultors) and with them he is to discuss the qualifications of the men whom he intends to appoint to the offices of synodal examiner and parish priest consultor. The bishop is not held to follow the majority opinion of the canons (or diocesan consultors), since the Code does not require their consent, but merely

[93] Bastnagel, *op. cit.*, p. 228.

[94] Meier, *Adm. Proc. Ag. Neglig. Pastors*, p. 177.

[95] Canon 356, § 1.

that they be consulted.[96] After having heard the opinions of the members of the cathedral chapter (or the diocesan consultors), the bishop then makes the actual appointment of the new examiners and parish priest consultors. Those elected are known as pro-synodal examiners and parish priest consultors.

There is a real obligation placed upon the bishop to elect these pro-synodal officials whenever a synod is not held. The main reason for this statement is the fact that if he were not obliged to do so, there would arise the possibility of a situation where a diocese would be without synodal examiners and parish priest consultors, since canon 387, § 1 legislates that all such officials automatically lose their office after a period of ten years. Such a situation is certainly not contemplated by the Code. It seems, too, that the very word "*servetur*" of canon 386, § 2 is to be understood in the sense of imposing an obligation: "let this same rule be observed. . . . " If the Code merely wished to give the bishop a right to elect these officials whenever there would be no synod, and not to impose an obligation, it seems that it would have used the words, "servari possit," for the verb "*posse*" is frequently used by the Code to denote a right rather than an obligation. The obligation to elect the officials arises as soon as ten years have elapsed from the last diocesan synod, and recurs every succeeding ten years, unless a synod be held in the meantime.

Article 6. The Term of Office

Canon 387, § 1: Examinatores et parochi consultores, sive in synodo, sive extra Synodum constituti, post decennium ab incepto munere vel etiam prius, adveniente nova Synodo, officio cadunt; possunt tamen negotium iam coeptum ad exitum perducere et, servatis de iure servandis, denuo constitui.

§ 2: Qui loco examinatorum ac parochorum consultorum deficientium constituantur, in officio persistunt dumtaxat quousque perstitissent ii quibus substituti fuerunt.

[96] Cf. canon 386, § 2 together with canon 105, 2°.

The synodal examiners and parish priest consultors, whether appointed in or outside a synod, go out of office after ten years, or even sooner in case a new synod is convened. They may, however, complete any case already begun. Further, they may be re-elected provided the laws regarding appointment be observed. Those who were appointed to take the place of examiners or parish priest consultors who went out of office before the expiration of their full term, are to remain in office only for that period of time necessary to fill out the unexpired terms of their predecessors.

With but one exception canon 387, § 1 corresponds practically word for word with the law in force previous to the Code.[97] Whereas the previous law gave the examiners and parish priest consultors a term of five years in office, the new law gives them twice as long a term, or ten years. The time for the term of office begins to run from the day of their appointment, and it is computed according to canon 33, § 3, n. 3, so that the first day is not taken into account and the term of office ceases at midnight of the same day of the month ten years later. For example, if Titus is appointed examiner on November 3, 1942, he will automatically go out of office at midnight on November 3, 1952.[98]

If an examiner, or parish priest consultor, should find that his term of office has expired while he is still engaged in a particular case, or even in more than one case, he need not feel disturbed about continuing to fulfill the duties of his office on these cases, for the law, in canon 387, § 1, concedes him this right. He may not, however, begin other cases, even though the bishop might happen to overlook the need for the appointment of new officials.

Canon 387, § 2 is a completely new idea in the law on examiners and parish priest consultors, for there is nothing similar to be found in pre-Code legislation. This new law gives to substitute examiners and parish priest consultors less than ten years in office. They continue in office only long enough to fill out the unexpired term of those

[97] Cf. decr., *Maxima cura,* 20 aug. 1910, can. 4, § 4—*Fontes,* n. 2074.

[98] Rossi, *De Paroecia,* n. 174, nota n. 95; cf. also, Dubé, *The General Principles for the Reckoning of Time in Canon Law,* The Catholic University of America Canon Law Studies, n. 144 (Washington, D. C.: The Catholic University of America Press, 1941), pp. 218 ff.

whose place they have taken. Once this period is completed they may, of course, be re-elected, but for this the observance of the laws of canon 385, § 1, or of canon 386, § 2, on elections to these offices must be observed.

ARTICLE 7. REMOVAL FROM OFFICE

Canon 388: Removeri ab Episcopo nequeunt, nisi ex gravi causa et de consilio Capituli cathedralis.

Synodal examiners and parish priest consultors [99] cannot be removed from their office by the bishop, except for a grave cause and after he has taken counsel with the cathedral chapter (or diocesan consultors).

This canon corresponds entirely with the law in existence prior to the Code except in one particular.[100] This one change is the commonly noted substitution in the new law expressed by the words "with the advice of the cathedral chapter" in place of the words "with the consent of the cathedral chapter."

Because of the word *"nequeunt"* ("cannot") in this canon 388 it seems that both a grave cause and the advice of the cathedral chapter (or diocesan consultors) are required for validity. This word appears to be the equivalent of an express statement that an act contrary to this prescription would be invalid.[101] Some authors, however, hold that these conditions are not required for validity, but rather for licitness.[102]

The judgment as to what would constitute a grave cause for removal is left to the prudence of the bishop, though he is certainly aided in making his decision by the counsel obtained from the canons of the cathedral chapter (or from the diocesan consultors). This

[99] Unless the contrary is expressly mentioned, what is said of the synodal examiners and parish priest consultors must always be referred also to pro-synodal examiners and pro-synodal parish priest consultors (*i. e.*, those elected outside a synod).

[100] Cf. decr., *Maxima cura*, 20 aug. 1910, can. 4, § 5—*Fontes*, n. 2074.

[101] Cf. canon 11. Toso, *Commentaria Minora*, III, pars I, p. 28; Coronata, *Institutiones*, I, n. 434 et ad notam n. 8; Cappello, *Summa*, I, n. 408, ad 8.

[102] Augustine, *Commentary*, II, 422-423; Sipos, *Enchiridion*, p. 280, IV, 1, e.

grave cause might be a crime, that is a grave delict on the part of the official, *e. g.*, fraud, simony, violation of secrecy,[103] or again it might be something involuntary and blameless as far as the official is concerned, *e. g.*, a lengthy illness, or prolonged absence from the diocese.[104] The reasons which would justify the removal of a pastor [105] might well be considered as grave causes for the removal of a synodal examiner or parish priest consultor.[106]

Because of the seriousness of a removal from office, the bishop has the right to require of the members of the cathedral chapter (or of the diocesan consultors) that they take an oath of secrecy concerning the discussions held on the question of an official's removal.[107] This oath is especially appropriate when the cause for removal is a crime committed by an official.[108]

It may be suggested that when a bishop is quite certain of the presence of a sufficient cause for removal he might laudably propose to the official that he resign his office.[109] If the official should resign there is no obligation upon the bishop to consult the cathedral chapter (or diocesan consultors) before accepting the resignation.[110]

In connection with the question of removal from office it is necessary to keep in mind the provisions of canon 188. In accord with this canon synodal examiners and parish priest consultors would automatically lose their office: (a) three years after a religious profession; [111] (b) if they accept and take peaceful possession of an office

[103] Cappello, *De Admin. Amotione Parochorum*, p. 79; Augustine, *op. cit.*, 423. Cf. also, canons 1625 and 1666, parallel laws.

[104] Cappello, *loc. cit.*

[105] Cf. canon 2147.

[106] Augustine, *loc. cit.*

[107] Cf. canon 105, 2°.

[108] d'Angelo, *La Curia Diocesana*, I, p. 52.

[109] d'Angelo, *loc. cit.*

[110] Greco, *La rimozione amministrativa dei Parroci*, p. 57—apud d'Angelo, *op. cit.*, I, pp. 52-53.

[111] Cf. also canon 584. (As has been previously mentioned, there is no prohibition against the election of religious to the offices of synodal examiner or parish priest consultor. Nevertheless, if a person were elected to either office while he was a diocesan priest, and subsequently entered a religious community, the provision of canon 188, 1° would have its effect, namely, automatic removal from the office held.)

that is incompatible with the one they hold; (c) if they should be guilty of a public apostasy from the Catholic Faith; (d) if they should attempt to enter marriage, even if only civilly; (e) if they should voluntarily enlist for military service (not, however, if they enlist, with the bishop's permission, in order to be freed more quickly from the obligation);[112] (f) if they should cease wearing the ecclesiastical garb, on their own authority and without just cause, and provided they have not resumed the garb within a month after receiving a warning from their Ordinary. Two of the reasons given in canon 188 for automatic resignation do not apply to the synodal examiners, or to the parish priest consultors: (a) since they do not "take possession" of their office, as a pastor does, there can be no presumed resignation for failure to take possession within a prescribed time; (b) since these officials are not bound, by reason of their office, to any special law of residence, it follows that there can be no automatic abandonment of office for a violation of such a law.

A word should be added here concerning the possibility of penalties against synodal examiners and parish priest consultors for offenses not serious enough to warrant removal from office. The law takes care of such infractions of duty when in canon 2404 it is set down that the abuse of ecclesiastical authority shall be punished at the discretion of the legitimate superior in proportion to the gravity of the guilt, without prejudice to the precepts of the canons which decree a specific penalty for certain abuses.[113] The bishop, therefore, is the judge of the penalty to be imposed. The law merely gives him a norm to determine how severe a penalty should be inflicted: the penalty should be in proportion to the gravity of the offense. There is another canon of the Code, canon 2407, which may appropriately be mentioned in this place. It legislates concerning those who would attempt to bribe curial officials. According to this canon any person who attempts to induce to perform an action or

[112] Cf. also canon 141, § 1.

[113] Cf. canons 1625 and 1666: though these penal canons do not refer specifically to the synodal examiners and parish priest consultors, nevertheless it seems that they may be considered as parallel canons, as norms available for the direction of the bishop in the punishment of certain offenses.

tolerate an omission contrary to the requirements of their office any of the ecclesiastical officials . . . of the Curia, . . . by gifts or promises, shall be punished with appropriate penalties and be forced to repair any damages that may have been caused by his bribery. In this canon 2407 there is an example of an attempted crime constituting an offense to which is attached a penalty. Consequently, in order to apply the penalties spoken of in this canon it is not necessary that the attempt shall have attained its intended effect.[114]

Any synodal examiner or parish priest consultor may, for a just reason, resign his office,[115] but the bishop should not accept a renunciation without this just and proportionate cause.[116] A resignation must be made to the bishop,[117] and to be valid it must be submitted by the resigning official either in writing, or orally before two witnesses. But it may be made by a proxy, to whom a special mandate has been given for this very purpose.[118] The acceptance or rejection of the resignation should be decided upon by the bishop within a month's time.[119] Once the person concerned has received definite notification that the bishop has accepted his resignation, from that moment he ceases to hold his diocesan office, and he may not then retract his resignation.[120]

114 It may be noted here that synodal examiners and parish priest consultors who are at the same time canons are legitimately excused from choir whenever they are engaged in work as curial officials and they do not lose the right to any of the fruits due them as canons because of this absence: canon 420, § 1, 14°. Cf. also "Decrees and Decisions"—*The Jurist* (Washington, D. C., 1941—), III, 2 (1943), p. 331.

115 Canon 184.

116 Canon 189, § 1.

117 Canon 187.

118 Canon 186.

119 Canon 189, § 2.

120 Canons 190; 191, § 1.

CHAPTER V

THE DUTIES OF SYNODAL EXAMINERS IN THE ELECTION OF PASTORS

Introductory Remarks

Canon 459, § 1: Loci Ordinarius, graviter onerata eius conscientia, obligatione tenetur vacantem paroeciam illi conferendi, quem magis idoneum ad eam regendam habuerit, sine ulla personarum acceptione.

§ 2: In hoc iudicio ratio haberi debet non solum doctrinae, sed etiam earum omnium qualitatum, quae ad paroeciam vacantem rite regendam requiruntur.

§ 3: Quare loci Ordinarius:

1. Ne omittat documenta, si qua sint, ex Curiae tabulario desumere quae clericum nominandum respiciunt et notitias, secretas quoque, si opportunum iudicaverit, prudenter exquirere etiam ex locis extra dioecesim;

2. Prae oculis habeat praescriptum can. 130, § 2;

3. Clericum examini super doctrina coram se et examinatoribus synodalibus subiiciat; a quo, de consensu eorundem examinatorum, potest dispensare, si agatur de sacerdote doctrinae theologicae laude commendato.

§ 4: In regionibus in quibus paroeciarum provisio fit per concursum sive specialem ad normam const. Benedicti XIV *Cum illud,* 14 Dec. 1742, sive generalem, haec forma retineatur, donec Sedes Apostolica aliud decreverit.

Canon 459 sets down the norms according to which the Ordinary must proceed when he is conferring a vacant parish. The law is the same whether the parish be irremovable or removable.[1] It will be

[1] Cf. *e.g., AER,* LXXXV (1931), 391.

seen later that there are a certain limited number of exceptions to this law. As is evident, there are two distinct and definitely different methods of procedure mentioned in the canon. The first is found in § 1-§ 3. This method is new and is not found in legislation prior to the Code. The second method is mentioned in § 4. In reality it is twofold, since it admits both the special and the general concursus. This law of the concursus is, of course, not new. The canon states clearly that the concursus, special or general, is to be retained as the law for the conferring of vacant parishes only in those places where it was in force at the time the Code went into effect. It is to remain in force in these places until the Holy See shall have decided otherwise. In all other places the method outlined in § 1-§ 3 must be followed. That these two methods are definitely different one from the other will become abundantly clear from the consideration of them which follows. Since the object of the present work concerns itself here with the duties of the synodal examiners, it will be even more apparent that the work of these officials is quite different in the two methods. It is only indirectly that the question of the manner of appointment to parishes is treated, in other words, only in so far as the methods require the intervention of the synodal examiners.

Before proceeding to a discussion of the duties of the synodal examiners it is appropriate to discuss as briefly as possible two questions: 1. when are parishes conferred by persons other than the local Ordinary? 2. is canon 459 to be followed in the appointment to parishes when someone other than the local Ordinary has the right to present to the latter for appointment, or to elect the person to be appointed pastor? The answers to these questions will help to make clear just what are the exceptions to the rule set down in canon 459 for the conferring of parishes.

In answer to the first question, *i. e.*, when are parishes conferred by persons other than the local Ordinary?, one observes that the local Ordinary has the right to nominate and to institute all pastors within his territory, with the exception of those parishes reserved by law to the Holy See, and excepting those to which is attached the right of election or presentation by another or by others. All contrary customs impairing this right of the local Ordinary are disapproved.[2] The Pope, of course, has the right to confer all parishes,[3] but is not accustomed to do so, except in those cases of reservation mentioned in the law,[4] and in those cases in which the right of bestowal devolves upon the Holy See. This transfer to the Holy See of the right of bestowal of a vacant parish occurs in the following instances: whenever a parish is not conferred within the time allotted,[5] or, in the case of a parish to be conferred by a concursus, whenever the parish was knowingly conferred upon an unworthy person, or whenever there was a substantial defect in the form of the concursus.[6]

The second question which was proposed above is the following: is canon 459 to be followed in the appointment to parishes when someone other than the local Ordinary has the right to present, or to elect the person to be appointed pastor? The answer to this question involves the consideration of a number of distinct cases: (a) Those parishes which are united in full right to a religious house, or to a capitular church, or to any other moral person have as their habitual pastor the moral person, but as their acting pastor a vicar who must be appointed for the actual care of souls. The bishop himself designates the parochial vicar only in cases where he has obtained that right by legitimate privilege or custom, or when the endowment of the vicariate was provided by the bishop with the stipulation that he reserved to himself the right freely to designate the vicar. Aside from these instances it is the religious superior, or the Chapter, or

[2] Canon 455.

[3] Canon 1431.

[4] Canon 1435. Cf. also canon 1434.

[5] Cf. canons 1432, § 3; 155; 458.

[6] Wernz, *Ius Decretalium,* II, nn. 323, 324 et 333, III. The Apostolic Datary (11 nov. 1930—*AAS,* XXII [1930], pp. 525-526 and instructio, 1 ian. 1942—*AAS,* XXXIV [1942], pp. 113-118) has given norms to be observed by Ordinaries in asking the Holy See to confer benefices which are reserved by law to the Holy See, or which, as to appointment, have devolved upon the Holy See. The two documents from the Apostolic Datary give full details as to the method of procedure, when the parish in question is subject to the law of the concursus, and when it is not subject to this law. It is interesting to note that when the parish is subject to the concursus the Ordinary is obliged to hold a concursus and to send to the Apostolic Datary the votes which each candidate has received.

any other moral person to which the parish is attached, who is entitled to nominate the vicar and present him to the bishop, who in turn must appoint him if he finds him qualified. To determine whether or not one is qualified the bishop must follow the norms set down in canon 459.[7] If the parish be united in full right to a religious house, the religious superior is to present a religious of his own Order or Congregation.[8] It follows from what has been said that the examination on doctrine of the religious thus designated as required by canon 459, § 3, 3° must be employed, and the synodal examiners must be called upon to fulfill the duties incumbent upon them in such an examination.[9] (b) When a parish is united to a religious house only as regards temporalities, the religious superior must present to the local Ordinary a secular priest for the care of souls in the parish.[10] The Code does not make any explicit mention of the necessity on the part of the Ordinary to determine that the one presented is fit according to the prescriptions of canon 459, but, arguing from a parallelism with canon 471, § 2, it seems that this would be required.[11] (c) It is possible for a religious to be made pastor of a secular parish, provided permission for this be obtained. Ordinarily this permission must be obtained from the Holy See,[12] but Nuncios, Internuncios and Apostolic Delegates have at present the faculty of granting in particular cases, or temporarily, to diocesan Ordinaries the right to appoint religious to parishes, when there is a deficiency of secular priests. Consent of the superior is necessary, at least two other religious must live with the pastor, and the other

[7] Canons 471, § 1-§ 2; 456. Cf. also Augustine, *Commentary*, II, pp. 525-526; Coronata, *Institutiones*, I, n. 472, 4 et n. 488, 1. Cf. d'Angelo, *Parroco e Parrochia*, pp. 58-59, for a statement concerning the instances in which, by exception, a concursus rather than the simple examination of canon 459, § 1-§ 3 is required in connection with the bestowal of parishes united in full right to a moral person.

[8] Canon 456.

[9] Rossi, *De Paroecia*, n. 144; Fanfani, *De Iure Religiosorum ad Normam Codicis Iuris Canonici* (Taurini: Marietti, 1925), n. 477, B.

[10] Canon 1425, § 1. Cf. also Augustine, *loc. cit.*

[11] Cf. canon 20.

[12] Canons 626, § 1; 1442. Cf. also Coronata, *loc. cit.*

dispositions of the canons must be complied with.[13] It would seem that the prescriptions of canon 459, § 1-§ 3 must be obeyed even in this case. The phrase "and the other dispositions of the canons must be compiled with" seems to imply this conclusion. Therefore the religious to be appointed must, amongst other things, undergo the examination on doctrine before the bishop and the synodal examiners.[14] (d) In regard to parishes to which is attached the right of patronage (whether it be ecclesiastical, lay or mixed), the Code states that presentation of a candidate for appointment must be made to the local Ordinary, who will then judge whether the person presented is fit. In forming his judgment the local Ordinary must diligently seek information concerning the fitness of the person presented. He may even require an examination if he deems this opportune. He is also to obtain secret information, if the case warrants.[15] This, it seems, eliminates the necessity of applying canon 459, § 1-§ 3 to the cases of appointment to parishes subject to the right of patronage. The examination referred to is not that mentioned in canon 459, § 3, 3° but rather the examination spoken of in canon 149. When, however, the parish is one that must be provided for by means of a concursus, the patron may present only a cleric approved in a concursus.[16] (e) Finally, when it is a case of a parish the pastor to which is chosen by means of an election or

[13] Cf. Bouscaren, *The Canon Law Digest* (2 vols. and Supplement, Milwaukee: Bruce, 1934-1941), I, p. 184.

[14] No concursus would be necessary, because the Council of Trent (sess. XXIV, *de ref.*, c. 18) stated that when no one presented himself for a concursus the Ordinary might give the parish without a concursus. This condition would be fulfilled when a religious is put in a secular parish, because, as it seems, the local Ordinary would only appoint a religious to a secular parish when there was a deficiency of secular priests.

[15] Canon 1464, § 1-§ 2. Cf. also canon 1466: if the cleric has been legitimately presented and found qualified and if the presentation has been accepted, he has a right to canonical institution. The right to grant canonical institution or actually to confer the benefice is vested in the local Ordinary; the vicar general may give it by special mandate only (cf., however, canon 429, § 1). If several qualified men were presented, the Ordinary chooses the one whom before God he believes to be better qualified.

[16] Canon 1462.

presentation on the part of the faithful in general, the local Ordinary is first to choose three clerics. The names of these he reports to those having the right of election or presentation. The latter may elect or present only one of these three.[17] Naturally the local Ordinary must designate only fit candidates, but there is nothing in the law which states that in determining the fitness of the candidates he must follow canon 459, § 1-§ 3.

Article 1. Duties of the Synodal Examiners in the Election of Pastors in Places Where No Concursus Is Required

In those places where the law of the concursus was not in force at the time the Code went into effect, the law of the Code prescribes that parishes are to be conferred in accord with the norms set down in canon 459, § 1-§ 3. The only part of this new procedure in which the synodal examiners are concerned is in connection with the examination of the candidate on the matter of doctrine. Canon 459, § 3, 3° states that the local Ordinary shall not neglect to subject the candidate to an examination as to his theological knowledge to be conducted in the presence of himself and the synodal examiners, unless there is question of the candidacy of a priest well known for his theological learning, in which instance he may with the consent of the examiners designated for the case dispense him from the examination.

The present article treats solely of this new method of appointment to parishes. It is only in the succeeding article that the question of the concursus will be considered. It is necessary to keep this in mind, because of the danger of attributing wrongfully certain statements to the other method, when in fact they are made concerning only the particular method under consideration.

[17] Canon 1452. If the parish in question is also under the law of the concursus, the local Ordinary will designate three names from amongst those adjudged fit in a regular concursus. If by custom the names of all those reported fit in a concursus are to be submitted to the electors, this custom is to be continued—S. C. C., *Veronen. et aliarum,* 14 febr. 1920—*AAS,* XII (1920), 163-166.

A. *The Examination on Doctrine Is Not a Competitive Examination*

A close study of canon 459, § 1-§ 3 reveals that the law does not contemplate a competitive examination in § 3, 3°. Rather, the exact interpretation of the canon seems to be that the local Ordinary, after serious consideration in his own mind of the qualifications of the possible candidates, chooses one particular priest as being the most fit for the vacant parish. He then proceeds to investigate in order to determine whether or not the candidate chosen really excels in all the qualifications required by law in a pastor, not excluding the qualification of theological learning. For this purpose he examines all the documents pertaining to the qualifications of the priest which are available in the diocesan curia. He seeks for further information from other sources, even extra-diocesan, and if he thinks it necessary he may also, prudently of course, ask for secret information. He keeps before him the results obtained by the priest in his Junior Clergy examinations. Finally he submits him to an examination on doctrine, before himself and his synodal examiners, though he may exempt the priest from this if the latter is well known for his theological learning. To exempt the priest, however, the local Ordinary needs the consent of the synodal examiners.[18] This consent would be had when a majority of the examiners chosen for the case vote for exemption. If the votes are equal the Ordinary may act either for or against exemption according as he wishes.[18a]

The question may possibly arise as to whether this examination on doctrine may be given to many at the same time, and again, whether it may be held before a parish becomes vacant (as a periodic examination for the office of pastor). An affirmative answer may, it seems, be given to both questions. Such an answer appears to be but a logical deduction from a response from the Pontifical Commission for the Authentic Interpretation of the Code.[19] According to

[18] Cf. "Sunto del Codex Iuris Canonici"—*Monit. Eccl.*, Serie III, Vol. X (1918) (Vol. XXX della intera Collezione), p. 215; "Quistioni"—*Monit. Eccl.*, Serie IV, Vol. III (1921) (Vol. XXXIII della intera Collezione), p. 28.

[18a] Cf. *supra*, p. 61.

[19] 24 nov. 1920, ad V—*AAS*, XII (1920), p. 574.

this response the examination held before the reception of Sacred Orders may be considered as sufficient examination on learning, provided it includes all that would be required in the examination spoken of in canon 459, § 3, 3°. Certain other responses given at the same time [20] give additional indication that the examination may be held before the parish becomes vacant. It must be kept in mind, however, that such an examination for many would not be competitive and would not give the priest who obtained the highest grade any right to a parish that might become vacant. The results obtained would merely afford the local Ordinary the necessary information on the fitness of the various priests with regard to their theological knowledge.[21] It goes without saying that such group examinations would have to be held in the presence of the local Ordinary and of his synodal examiners. Though this "group examination" seems to be admissible, still it would appear to be much more in accord with the exact statement of the law to follow the interpretation which calls for an examination of a single individual whom the local Ordinary considers to be the most fit for the parish, and this after the parish has become vacant.

B. *Scope and Method of This Examination*

What is the matter on which the candidate is to be examined? What form is to be followed by the local Ordinary and his synodal examiners in giving this examination? With regard to the scope of the examination, the Code merely states that the examination is to be on doctrine ("*doctrina*"), or, perhaps more correctly, on theological learning. Since the office in question is that of pastor, it seems to follow quite logically that the Code here means: the examination should cover that theological learning which should be found in a pastor. First, therefore, dogmatic and moral theology and canon law would be included, and, secondly, pastoral theology, that is, the application of the various branches of theological learning to the actual work of a pastor of souls. The administration of the sacraments, preaching, the practical administration of a parish are sub-

[20] *Ibidem*, ad I, II, III.

[21] Cf. *AER*, LXXXV (1931), 390-391.

jects with which the pastor should be acquainted. Briefly, the word "doctrina" seems to include all that knowledge which is necessary for the care of souls. Certainly a pastor should have a greater degree of knowledge in these matters than that required in the ordinary priest who is not a pastor.[22]

Since § 1 of canon 459 speaks of the local Ordinary choosing the priest most fitted *for the vacant parish,* it may be asked if the examination would necessarily vary according to the type of parish which became vacant. Would learning of different types be required in accord with the different types of parishes? Put in such fashion, this question is actually based on a false idea, for there are no different kinds of theological learning, but only one kind. The only difference among the possible appointees would be in the degree of excellence in their grasp of the various branches of doctrine. Ordinarily the examination may be the same for any parish, for when one's knowledge is declared sufficient for one parish, it is generally sufficient for any parish. It would be rather the exception that a special examination, a more difficult examination, on theological knowledge would be required, because of the fact that the particular vacant parish required a greater degree of such knowledge in its pastor.[23] This conclusion that the examination need not ordinarily be different as to the subject matter for different parishes may be inferred from responses of the Pontifical Commission for the Authentic Interpretation of the Code, wherein it is stated that pastors transferred at the will of the local Ordinary are not required to take a new examination for the obtaining of the second parish.[24]

There can no longer be any question as to whether or not the Junior Clergy examination may be considered as a sufficient examination on theological learning. The same Pontifical Commission decided the question in the negative.[25]

[22] Cf. Toso, *Commentaria Minora,* I, p. 88; "Quistioni"—*Monit. Eccl.,* Serie IV, Vol. III (1921) (Vol. XXXIII della intera Collezione), p. 77; Rossi, *De Paroecia,* n. 96; *AER,* LXXXV (1931), 390-391.

[23] Cf. "Quistioni"—*Monit. Eccl.,* Serie IV, Vol. III (1921) (Vol. XXXIII della intera Collezione), p. 28.

[24] *PCI,* 24 nov. 1920, ad I, II, III—*AAS,* XII (1920), 574.

[25] *Ibidem,* ad VI.

As regards the question of the method, or manner of holding this examination on theological learning, the Code makes no further stipulation beyond the statement that it must be held before the local Ordinary and his synodal examiners. One is quite justified, therefore, in concluding that this examination may be oral or written. It seems, too, that the synodal examiners, as well as the local Ordinary, may question the candidate. Or again, the local Ordinary and the synodal examiners may agree beforehand on the questions to be proposed. One point that should be stressed is that the content of the examination should be such that it would be a real test of whether or not the candidate actually possesses sufficient theological learning for the office of pastor.

A difficulty arises from the indefinite statement of the Code: "before himself and the synodal examiners." Must all the synodal examiners be used in each examination? Or may the local Ordinary determine the number to be used in each examination? On the one hand, the law does not state explicitly that "all" must be used. On the other hand the indefinite "the synodal examiners" might seem to imply that all must be used. One thing is certain, that at least more than one must conduct the examination with the local Ordinary. Due to the seeming uncertainty of the law, and since it would appear altogether unnecessary, as well as cumbersome, to have, for example, as many as twelve examiners present, and, finally, in view of the fact that the strict form of the concursus requires only three for validity, one seems justified (*salvo meliori iudicio*) in concluding that the number of synodal examiners may be determined in each instance by the local Ordinary. It might well be suggested that at least three be appointed for each examination, in order that a rather complete judgment may be made on the candidate's theological learning.[26]

There are no specific rules in the Code as to how the synodal examiners are to give their judgment on the candidate's learning, or even on the value of the examiners' report. The local Ordinary is granted complete freedom in the acceptance, or rejection of the

[26] Cf. Augustine, *Rights and Duties of Ordinaries* (St. Louis: Herder, 1924), p. 172.

views of the examiners. Natural justice, however, would demand that he take serious cognizance of the opinions of these examiners. He could not, therefore, justifiably overrule their opinion, without real reason. The law asks for the participation of the synodal examiners, and that not without reason. Consequently, the local Ordinary should give serious consideration to their opinions.

If the local Ordinary should neglect to hold this examination on theological learning before himself and the synodal examiners, the appointment would not thereby be invalidated. There is nothing in canon 459, § 1-§ 3 that would indicate invalidity in the event that the prescription of § 3, 3° of the canon was not complied with.[27]

The synodal examiners are obliged to take part in any examination of this kind to which they may be called by their local Ordinary. Naturally, however, they would be excused if they were legitimately impeded.[28] They may not receive anything in the way of a reward for their services, or as a gift, from the fruits of the parochial benefice which is being conferred. Those accepting such a reward, or gift, would be guilty of simony.[29] It seems but correct to admit that the candidate might object to a synodal examiner before whom he is asked to take the examination. He would, of course, have to show cause why the particular examiner should be barred from examining him. The local Ordinary would be the judge in the matter. There is no specific statement in the law to substantiate this opinion on the admissibility of an objection against a synodal examiner, but natural equity and an argument from parallelism (exceptions of this sort are permitted in the concursus)[30] would appear to make the opinion tenable.

C. *Dispensation from the Examination on Doctrine*

As has been already noted, the local Ordinary may dispense the candidate from the examination on theological learning. This faculty is mentioned in canon 459, § 3, 3°, wherein also are mentioned

[27] Cf. canons 11 and 153, § 3.

[28] Cf. canons 128 and 364, § 2, 1°.

[29] Canon 1441. Cf. also canon 727.

[30] Cf. *supra*, p. 14.

two necessary prerequisites for a dispensation: the candidate in question must be a priest whose theological learning is well known, and the consent of the synodal examiners is required. In consonance with the theory proposed above, namely, that not all the synodal examiners need be present for each examination, but only as many as the local Ordinary may request, it would follow logically that the consent must be had from only those appointed to take part in the particular case. What would be a sufficiency of theological learning to permit of a dispensation? The Code merely states: *"si agatur de sacerdote doctrinae theologicae laude commendato."* Certainly those with the degree of doctorate in dogmatic or moral theology, or in Sacred Scripture, would be considered as possessing a high degree of theological knowledge. So, also, it would seem, would those possessed of the degree of licentiate in any one of these branches of the Sacred Sciences. Professors who teach these subjects in a seminary might well be included. Doctors and those possessing the licentiate in canon law, as well as seminary professors of this subject, would likewise be included, because of the close connection between this subject and the Sacred Sciences, and because of the fact that it would be difficult to imagine a good canonist who did not possess a thorough knowledge of theology.[31] There are still others who might be exempted, those, namely, who although they possess no scholastic degree in the subjects, have nevertheless acquired an outstanding knowledge of the Sacred Sciences. Because of the possibility of a dispensation from the examination, it would be advisable for the local Ordinary, together with the synodal examiners chosen for the case, always to consider first whether or not a dispensation should be granted.[32] It should also be kept in mind that the local Ordinary has the right to dispense from the examination, but that no candidate ever has a right to this dispensation.[33]

The Pontifical Commission for the Authentic Interpretation of the Code has clarified certain doubts concerning the necessity of the examination on theological learning in particular cases. From

[31] Augustine, *Commentary*, II, 530.

[32] "Quistioni"—*Monit. Eccl.*, Serie IV, Vol. III (1921) (Vol. XXXIII della intera Collezione), p. 80.

[33] *Monit. Eccl.*, *loc. cit.*

the solutions given one learns that: (a) a priest, who has already been pastor of a parish and who had already passed an examination for his first parish, need not take a new examination, if the transfer from one parish to another is done at the suggestion and the request of the bishop; if, however, the pastor requests the transfer, he is obliged to undergo a new examination, unless the Ordinary, together with the synodal examiners, judges him qualified for the new parish; [34] (b) a pastor, who is removed from his parish in accordance with canon 2154 (providing for the administrative removal of pastors, whether they be irremovable or movable pastors) and placed in charge of another parish, does not have to undergo the examination; [35] (c) a pastor, who is *ex officio* transferred from one parish to another in accordance with canons 2162-2167, need not undergo the examination;[36] (d) if no priests, whom the Ordinary judges qualified, want to undergo the examination (a not remote possibility when there is question of a parish undesirable for one or another reason), then, unless the Ordinary could find a priest who had already passed an examination for his first parish and who would be willing (without the necessity of a new examination) to accept the parish in question, recourse must be made by the Ordinary to the Sacred Congregation of the Council.[37]

D. *Those Who May Conduct the Examination With the Synodal Examiners*

In a discussion of the duties of the synodal examiners in the examination on theological learning it is important to know just what persons may take part in the examination with them. The canon (459, § 3, 3°) states that the local Ordinary is the one to conduct this examination with the synodal examiners. It is not sufficient, however, merely to refer to canon 198, § 2 where there is given the list of *local Ordinaries,* for the question is more complex than that. In general one may say that the judgment on fitness for

[34] *PCI,* 24 nov. 1920, ad I—*AAS,* XII (1920), 574.
[35] *Ibidem,* ad II.
[36] *Ibidem,* ad III.
[37] *Ibidem,* ad IV.

the parochial office, when it must be made according to canon 459, § 1-§ 3, is to be made by the local Ordinary who possesses the right to confer the parish in title.[38] To determine, then, who may give the examination with the synodal examiners it is necessary to decide just what persons may grant title to the office of pastor according to canon 459, § 1-§ 3. The following have this right: (a) residential bishops; [39] (b) abbots and prelates nullius; [40] (c) permanent apostolic administrators; [41] (d) when the see is vacant or impeded: if the diocese has been vacant for at least a year vicars capitular, diocesan administrators and temporary apostolic administrators may confer parishes of free bestowal; from the moment of their election, or appointment, they may accept presentations to vacant parishes (*e. g.*, in the case of parishes united in full right to a religious house), and they may institute the person presented in the parish. These provisions hold unless the Holy See has decreed otherwise.[42] If by a special provision of the Holy See the Archbishop,

[38] Cf. Maroto, *Institutiones Iuris Canonici ad Normam Novi Codicis,* Vol. I (Matriti, 1919), n. 591. (Hereafter this work will be cited *Institutiones Iuris Canonici.*) The problem here is not concerned with the judgment by the local Ordinary on the fitness: (a) of a candidate who has been elected by others; or (b) of a candidate who has been presented by a patron in a place where the law of the concursus does not hold. In these instances, as has been pointed out above, the local Ordinary is not obliged to follow canon 459, § 1-§3. Another point to note is that in the exceptional cases where someone other than the local Ordinary has the right, by Pontifical privilege, to grant title to a parish, the local Ordinary is still the one to determine the fitness of the person to be appointed—Maroto, *loc. cit.*

[39] Canon 455, § 1. Vicars general have no power to confer parishes as long as the see is occupied, unless they have received a special mandate from the bishop: canon 455, § 3.

[40] Canons 215, § 2; 216, § 1 et § 3; 323, § 1. Quasi-pastors are appointed from the secular clergy by vicars or prefects apostolic with the advice of their council: canon 457. Cf. canon 302.

[41] Canon 315, § 1. Cf., however, canon 314.

[42] Canons 455, § 2, 2°, 3°; 315, § 2, 1°. Cf., however, canon 314. A see would be impeded as to the exercise of jurisdiction if the bishop was in captivity, or was banished, exiled or otherwise inhabilitated, so that he could not even by letter communicate with the people of his diocese—canon 429, § 1. If it should happen that a bishop would come under an excommunication, interdict or suspension, no one is given any power in the diocese till the Holy See makes pro-

or some other bishop, has the right to appoint an administrator to a vacant diocese, this administrator has the same faculties as vicars capitulars with regard to appointment to parishes of free bestowal, acceptation of presentations, and institution of persons presented.[43] Strictly speaking the cathedral chapter (or board of diocesan consultors) would have the right, during the brief period in which they have the right to rule the diocese, to accept presentations, and institute persons presented.[44] According to Jaeger,[45] there is a convincing opinion which holds that when the vicar general administers a see impeded as to jurisdiction, he may confer parishes of free bestowal even within the first year of vacancy. This opinion would not seem to be borne out by canon 455, § 2, 2° which states clearly: the vicar capitular, *or any other who rules the diocese,* etc. Whatever be held on this point, it is certain that he, or any other priest appointed by the bishop to rule the see if the bishop should be impeded, has at least the same powers as the vicar capitular.[46]

In concluding this particular section it is necessary to propose the question of whether the local Ordinary may delegate another to take his place in the examination on theological learning. The Code itself, in canon 455, § 3, expressly mentions the possibility of the vicar general being able to confer parishes, provided he be given a special mandate by the local Ordinary. Without doubt, then, the vicar general may take the place of the local Ordinary in the examination, *i. e.,* whenever he confers the parish by reason of a special mandate

vision—canon 429, § 5. Cf. Jaeger, *The Administration of Vacant and Quasi-Vacant Episcopal Sees in the United States,* The Catholic University of America Canon Law Studies, n. 81 (Washington, D. C.: The Catholic University of America, 1932), pp. 218-221. If a bishop is transferred to another diocese he retains the powers of a vicar capitular in the diocese from which he is being changed until such time as he takes possession of his new diocese. This he must do within four months of the day on which he received notification of the change—canon 430, § 3, 1°.

[43] Canon 431, § 2.

[44] Canons 431, § 1; 435; 455, § 2, 2°. Cf. Jaeger, *op. cit.,* p. 214; Maroto, "De Iuribus Capituli Cathedralis in casu sedis impeditae"—*Jus Pontificium,* II (1929), 210-215.

[45] *Op. cit.,* p. 215.

[46] Canons 429, § 1; 455, § 2, 2°, 3°.

received from the latter. Furthermore, since the right to hold the examination is in virtue of the ordinary jurisdiction of the local Ordinary,[47] it follows that the latter may delegate it to another.[48] Consequently, then, it is possible for another in the place of the local Ordinary to participate in this examination on theological learning with the synodal examiners.

In the United States of America parishes, whether they be irremovable or removable, must be conferred in accord with canon 459, § 1-§ 3. This is the result of a special decree of the Sacred Congregation of the Council, which was approved by His Holiness, Pius XI. The decree was issued on June 24, 1931.[49]

Article 2. Duties of the Synodal Examiners in the Election of Pastors in Places Where the Law of the Concursus Is Still in Effect

Introductory Remarks

Canon 459, § 4 legislates that in those regions where provision of parishes is made by a concursus, whether it be the special concursus according to the norm of the Constitution, *"Cum illud,"* of Dec. 14, 1742, or the general concursus, it is to be retained until the Holy See shall have decreed otherwise.

As a result of this canon the law on the duties of the synodal examiners in a concursus remains the same as in the period previous to the Code. Furthermore, since obviously the old law is restated here, it is necessary, in accord with canon 6, to interpret the law in the same manner as it was interpreted previous to 1918. Variations from the old law are to be admitted only when matters connected with the duties of the synodal examiners are legislated upon differently in the Code than they were in the law previously in effect. An attempt is made to give here only a few further considerations on the functions of the synodal examiners in the concursus and on questions

[47] Canon 459, § 3, 3°.

[48] Canon 199, § 1.

[49] The decree was private and was not published in the *Acta Apostolicae Sedis,* but was transmitted to the Archbishops and Bishops of the United States through His Excellency, the Apostolic Delegate. Cf. Bouscaren, *Canon Law Digest,* I, 249-250.

closely connected with these functions,[50] and in addition to point out what few departures from pre-Code law are required under the Code. The remarks which follow are made in connection with the special concursus. As has been previously stated, the general concursus follows in many respects the same procedure as the special concursus, even though it possesses certain notable distinctive features. What these distinctive features are has already been noted in the previous consideration of the general concursus.[51] There is no further distinction that needs to be added here in conjunction with the duties of the synodal examiners in the general concursus.

A. *The Other Officials in a Concursus*

The officials in a concursus are the presiding official, at least three synodal examiners and the chancellor of the diocesan curia (or another appointed by the bishop in the place of the latter).[52]

The presiding official is the residential bishop, though the law admits also the vicar general if the bishop is impeded.[53] The vicar general does not need a special mandate to preside. If he should be the presiding official, even though the bishop is not impeded, he would act validly, but not licitly.[54] The bishop, since he has ordinary power of jurisdiction in this matter, may also delegate another to be presiding official.[55]

Others who may preside at a concursus are abbots and prelates *nullius* [56] and permanent apostolic administrators.[57] When a see is vacant vicars capitular, diocesan administrators and temporary apos-

[50] For a statement concerning the law still in effect on the duties of the synodal examiners in the special concursus, cf. *supra*, pp. 24-33.

[51] Cf. *supra*, pp. 35-37.

[52] Conc. Trident., sess. XXIV, *de ref.*, c. 18; Bened. XIV, Const., *Cum illud*, 14 dec. 1742, § XVI—*Docum. IV in append. ad Codicem I. C.*

[53] Conc. Trident., *loc. cit.*

[54] Barbosa, *De Off. et Potest. Parochi*, pars I, cap. II, n. 32; d'Angelo, *Parroco e Parrochia*, I, 98, nota 5. Cf. also canon 368, § 1. The vicar general may not, without a special mandate, actually confer a parish of free bestowal, or institute one who is presented—canons 455, § 3; 1432, § 2.

[55] Canon 199, § 1.

[56] Canon 215, § 2.

[57] Canon 315, § 1; cf., however, canon 314.

tolic administrators may preside at a concursus,[58] but they may not in the case of parishes to which appointment belongs to the bishop under the right of free bestowal actually appoint the one whom they have chosen to be the more fit from amongst those reported by the synodal examiners as being fit, unless the diocese has been vacant for at least a year.[59] They may, however, from the time they take office, accept a presentation made by a patron, or by electors, of a person approved in a concursus, and they may institute such an one in the vacant parish in question.[60]

The chancellor, or other appointed by the bishop in his stead, is the official who keeps the acts of the concursus and sees to the carrying out of the minute details of law and order in the concursus.[61]

B. *Scope of the Examination in the Concursus*

It is essential that the synodal examiners know just what the law requires of one who would become a pastor, for it is only when they are aware of what is required that they can really fulfill the duty incumbent upon them, namely, to examine the candidates on the various qualifications necessary for ruling the vacant parish. The Council of Trent,[62] Benedict XIV[63] and the Code[64] all refer to

[58] Canons 435; 315, § 2, 1°. Cf. also canon 314.

[59] Canon 455, § 2, 3°. If one of these superiors should feel that the vacant parish ought to be given a pastor immediately, his only course is to refer the matter to the Holy See, sending on the name of the one whom he has decided is more fit—d'Angelo, *Parroco e Parrochia,* I, 49.

[60] Canon 455, § 2, 2°. Administrators appointed by an archbishop, or by a bishop, when these latter have the right of appointment by a special provision of the Holy See, have the same faculties as vicars capitular—canon 431, § 2; cathedral chapters and boards of diocesan consultors possess the faculties of a vicar capitular for the short space of time in which they rule the vacant diocese—canons 431, § 1; 435, § 2, 2°, 3°; a vicar general, or any other appointed by the bishop to rule the diocese in the event that he should be impeded from personally administering the affairs of his diocese has the same powers as a vicar capitular—canons 439, § 1; 455, §§ 2-3.

[61] d'Angelo, *Parroco e Parrochia,* I, 100.

[62] Sess. XXIV, *de ref.,* c. 18.

[63] Const., *Cum illud,* 14 dec. 1742, § XVI, n. 4—*Docum. IV in append. ad Codicem I. C.*

[64] Canon 453, § 2.

certain fundamental moral requisites, when they require in a candidate for the parochial office good morals, gravity of character, zeal for souls, prudence and such other exceptional virtues as are closely linked to the virtue of faith. Judgment as to the degree in which these moral qualifications should be found in a pastor is left to the prudence of the individual synodal examiners. Allied to these moral qualifications, and to be considered along with them, is that other qualification referred to by Benedict XIV,[65] namely, that based on the services already rendered to the Church and the commendation merited in the other offices one has held. The Council of Trent,[66] Benedict XIV[67] and the Code[68] also demand that the candidate possess a knowledge of the Sacred Sciences and of those other branches of learning which are essential in one having the care of souls, such as ability to preach. Once again it is left to the prudence of the individual synodal examiners to determine just how much of this knowledge is required in a pastor. Besides these requisites there are others which are specifically determined in the law.[69] In reality there is no necessity for the issuance of a judgment on the part of the synodal examiners in regard to these additional qualifications, but merely the necessity to see that they are actually possessed by the individual candidates for the vacant parish. Again, there are certain laws which determine when a person may not be appointed to the parochial office. These latter laws should also be kept in mind by the synodal examiners since they quite definitely affect a candidate's fitness for the office of pastor. The following is a list of the laws which have reference to the fitness of a candidate for the parochial office: (a) only those who have been ordained to the priesthood may validly be appointed pastors;[70] (b) no one may be pastor of more than one parish, unless there is question of two

[65] Const. *Cum illud, loc. cit.*

[66] *Loc. cit.*

[67] Const. *Cum illud,* §§ VII et XVI.

[68] Canon 453, § 2.

[69] Canon 453, § 2: "*sit insuper . . . ceterisque . . . qualitatibus praeditus, quae ad vacantem paroeciam cum laude gubernandam iure . . . communi . . . requiruntur.*"

[70] Canon 453, § 1.

parishes which have been united with equal rights *("aeque principaliter unitae")*;[71] (c) only secular priests may be appointed to secular parishes, and to religious parishes only priests of the particular Order or Congregation that holds the parish;[72] (d) no one may be appointed pastor and at the same time retain an office or benefice which is incompatible with the office of pastor;[73] (e) no one may confer a parochial benefice upon himself;[74] (f) a vicar general should not be appointed pastor except in case of necessity;[75] (g) if a pastorate has become vacant by resignation, or by sentence of privation, the local Ordinary who accepted the resignation, or who pronounced the sentence of privation may not validly confer the office on one of his own relatives, by blood or by marriage, within the second degree inclusively, or on a member of his household; he may not validly confer it, either, on a relative, by blood or marriage, within the second degree inclusively, of the person who resigned the parish;[76] (h) excommunicated priests, when they are *vitandi,* or when a declaratory or condemnatory sentence has been given against them, may not validly be appointed pastors. Other excommunicated priests may not licitly receive the office;[77] (i) priests under a personal interdict, or under suspension, may not validly be appointed to the parochial office, if a declaratory or condemnatory sentence has been pronounced against them; if no sentence has been given they are prohibited from licitly obtaining the office;[78] (j) priests who are infamous in law (*i. e.,* laboring under the penalty *"infamia iuris"*) may not validly obtain the office of pastor; those infamous in fact (*i. e.,* laboring under the penalty *"infamia facti"*) may not licitly be appointed to this office;[79] (k) secularized religious[80] may

[71] Canon 460.

[72] Canons 456; 1442.

[73] Canons 156; 1439.

[74] Canon 1437.

[75] Canon 367, § 3.

[76] Canon 157.

[77] Canon 2265.

[78] Canons 2275; 2283.

[79] Canon 2294.

[80] Cf. *supra,* pp. 84-85, for an interpretation of the meaning of the term "secularized religious."

not be appointed pastors of cathedral parishes;[81] (l) a patron may not present himself. Where several patrons hold the right of patronage to a particular parish they are not forbidden to present one of their number, but in this case the one presented must not have effected the necessary number of votes (a relative majority) for his own presentation with his own personal vote.[82]

C. *Method of Voting on the Fitness of the Candidates*

It is the duty of the synodal examiners to determine which of the candidates are fit and which are unfit to rule the vacant parish for which the concursus is being held.[83] As a basis for their judgment on the fitness of the candidates as regards theological learning they have available the written and oral examination on theological matters as determined by Benedict XIV,[84] while as regards the other qualifications they have the summaries given them by the chancellor of the concursus and composed of the documents presented by the candidates and dealing with their moral life, their qualities, the services they have rendered to the Church, the merit they have won in offices they have held, and with other requisite qualifications.[85] The question arises, though, as to just how the synodal examiners are to make their judgment. How should they rate the different candidates on the various requisites in order that they may be able to make a just judgment?

It must be made clear at the outset that there is no specific method demanded by law. Consequently, the synodal examiners may follow any method they prefer, so long as they render a just judgment. There has been a great amount of diversity in the method

[81] Canon 642, § 1, 1°.

[82] Canons 1461; 1460, § 2. Cf. Woywod, "Law of the Code on Benefices" —*HPR*, XXIX (1929), 506.

[83] Conc. Trident., sess. XXIV, *de ref.*, c. 18: "*Peracto deinde examine renuncientur quotcumque ab his (examinatoribus) idonei iudicati fuerint aetate, moribus, doctrina, prudentia et aliis rebus ad vacantem ecclesiam gubernandam*"; Bened. XIV, Const., *Cum illud*, 14 dec. 1742, § XVI, n. 4—*Docum. IV in Append. ad Codicem I. C.*

[84] Const. *Cum illud*, § XVI, n. 1 et § XVI, n. 4.

[85] Const. *Cum illud*, § XVI, n. 3.

used and even now no uniformity has been reached.[86] A description will be given here of two methods, both of which have much to commend their adoption.

The first method to be described is taken practically in its entirety from Bevilacqua.[87] The voting is divided into two parts, first on the work done by the candidates in their examination on theological learning, and secondly on the various other requisite qualifications of the candidates. The synodal examiners determine at the very beginning of the concursus a number of points which will be considered the maximum that a candidate might receive in either examination, and the exact number of points which will be considered the minimum necessary for a declaration of fitness. For example, ninety points are allotted as the maximum number which a candidate might receive in both the examination on learning and in that on the other qualifications, and it is further determined that forty-five points is the passing grade. Each examiner is then given his quota of the total number of points, which would be thirty points for each voting. (The case assumes that there are but three examiners in the concursus.) Once the examination on theological learning has been completed by the candidates the examiners consider the work of each. One of the examiners, the one best adapted to the duty, is chosen to read the papers of the various candidates. It may be well to keep secret the authors of each paper until after the voting has been completed. To avoid confusion each paper may be given a number for purposes of identification. The sermon may be read first, then the solutions of the cases and the answers to the questions. The examiners should agree beforehand on the correct answers to the questions, though account should always be taken of the arguments a candidate brings forth to substantiate his answers. It would also be of definite value if the examiners would discuss among themselves the merits of each candidate's work before they actually vote. In giving their vote, once the papers have been read, the examiners must remember to take into consideration also the oral explanation

[86] d'Angelo, *Parroco e Parrochia,* I, 111-112.

[87] "Circa il modo di eseguire lo scrutinio, ossia di fare la votazione nei concorsi"—*Monit. Eccl.,* Serie IV, Vol. IV (1932) (Vol. XXXIV della intera Collezione), pp. 277-280.

of the Church's doctrine which each candidate has given.[88] Each examiner then gives to each candidate the number of points that he feels this particular individual deserves. Next the votes of the three examiners are tallied and if the result is forty-five or more the candidate is declared fit in theological learning.

There follows the voting on the other requisite qualifications. Judgment as to these qualifications is most important and must be made prudently and only after serious consideration of the sources of information. This judgment is to be based upon the summaries of the testimonial documents made up by the chancellor of the concursus from the documents presented by each candidate. Naturally, the examiners are not restricted to these documents for information, but they may use still other sources of information, so long as they make certain that the source is trustworthy.[89] They must be especially careful in voting to take into consideration the value of the various qualifications as possessed by each candidate in relation to fitness for governing the actual parish that is vacant. The voting on fitness in regard to these qualifications follows along the same general lines as the voting in the matter of theological learning. Each examiner, after having considered the sources of information, gives to each candidate as many points as he feels the latter deserves. The points given by the examiners on each candidate are then added together, and if the total is half or more of the maximum the candidate is declared fit in regard to the qualifications other than theological learning. Finally, those who have been judged fit on both ballots are reported to the bishop as being fit to rule the vacant parish.

A few additional remarks must be added. First, when the examination on theological matters is extraordinarily difficult, the synodal examiners should, before giving the examination, lower the passing grade. Again, when it is known that a particular individual excels in the requisites other than learning, such an one may be given added consideration if his work in the examination on theological learning is just slightly below what would ordinarily be considered sufficient

[88] d'Angelo, *Parroco e Parrochia,* I, 107-108.

[89] d'Angelo, *op. cit.*, I, 109-110.

for a passing grade. Further, the synodal examiners may not follow that procedure which eliminates the consideration of the other requisites in the case of those candidates who have been judged unfit in the question of theological learning. The reason for this statement is the fact that the Sacred Congregation of the Council and the Constitution, *"Cum illud,"* of Benedict XIV, have time and time again noted that a concursus is invalid if the examiners consider only the question of theological learning.[90] Against such an argument Bevilacqua [91] argues very plausibly that the meaning of the law is that the examiners may not report to the bishop that a candidate is fit when they have only considered the question of learning. On the other hand, however, according to this author, the law surely does not intend to impose as an obligation an examination on the other requisites when this would be useless, a situation which would be verified if a candidate was declared unfit in the matter of learning. The law, Bevilacqua points out, requires that a candidate be declared fit in all the requisites, not merely in some. The present writer, however, bases his argument for the necessity of the second examination in every instance on the fact that a candidate may always appeal against an unjust judgment on the part of the synodal examiners, and when he does the law requires that the complete acts of the original concursus must be transmitted to the bishop of appeal.[92] If the synodal examiners would have omitted the consideration of the requisites other than learning, and if an appeal was made from their judgment the acts sent to the bishop of appeal would definitely be incomplete. Furthermore, what is to be done in this case, if the bishop of appeal should decide that the judgment of the synodal examiners was unjust, and that the appellant should have been declared fit in the matter of learning? The law nowhere speaks of a re-opening of the concursus in order that the examiners

[90] Cf., *e. g.*, Bened. XIV, Const., *Cum illud,* 14 dec. 1742, § X—*Docum. IV in Append. ad Codicem I. C.*

[91] *Ibidem,* pp. 279-280. Bevilacqua is of the opinion that a candidate rejected as unfit in the matter of theological learning need not be examined by the synodal examiners with regard to his fitness in the other requisite qualifications.

[92] Bened. XIV, Const. *Cum illud,* § XVI, n. 6.

may consider the other requisites of the appellant. Briefly, the law precludes the possibility of such difficulties by insisting that in every instance the complete examination be had, so that in case there is an appeal the bishop of appeal may be able to decide the case immediately from the acts of the original concursus.

A second method of voting which may be suggested is taken substantially from d'Angelo.[93] As this author states, this method follows closely the procedure used at Rome.

The synodal examiners consider first the examination which the candidates have undergone on theological learning. Supposing that there are three questions on moral or dogmatic theology, the form would run as follows: each synodal examiner is given one vote for each of the separate parts of the examination on theological learning: the oral explanation of doctrine, the sermon, and each of the questions. In all, therefore, each examiner is given five points for this matter of the candidate's learning. He will give to each candidate as much of the single point as he feels the candidate merits in each of the component parts of the examination on theological learning. Thus, for example, in considering the sermon, he would give the candidate a full point if the sermon was perfect, three-quarters of a point if it was good, a half-point if it was just passing, or if he feels that he does not wish either to pass or reject the candidate on the matter, a quarter-point if the sermon was poor, zero if it was a complete failure. With regard to the other requisite qualifications each of the examiners is likewise given five points, which he will allot as he feels the candidate deserves. He will give the full five points if he feels the candidate is perfect in this matter of the other qualifications, four points if he is very good, etc. Each examiner will keep a chart of his voting, so that at the conclusion he would have before him a chart something like the following:

Identif. No.	Name of Candidate	Oral	Sermon	1st Q.	2nd Q.	3rd Q.	Other Requisites
1	John B.	1	1	1	1	1	5
2	Henry F.	1	½	1	½	1	2
3	Peter C.	0	0	1	1	1	5
4	Edward K.	½	½	½	½	½	2½
5	Philip R.	0	0	½	0	0	4

[93] *Parroco e Parrochia,* I, 112-114.

An examiner who would have voted in this fashion would then declare John B. as fit, Henry F. as unfit,[94] Peter C. as fit, Edward K. as fit (or he might report that he neither approves nor disapproves of this candidate), Philip R. as unfit.

When all the examiners have completed their tabulation and have made their decisions as to which candidates they consider fit, they show their final decision on each candidate to one another. In the case where there are three synodal examiners, all candidates who are declared fit by two or three examiners will then be reported to the bishop as being fit to rule the vacant parish. Candidates who received but one favorable vote are rejected as unfit. If however, one examiner should vote favorably, while a second rejects the candidate, and the third votes neither to reject nor to approve, there is had a case where the bishop (or his vicar general, if he is conducting the examination) is to cast the deciding vote.[95] If there were four examiners and the votes were equally divided as regards the fitness of the candidate, here again there would be a situation which would call for a deciding vote by the bishop.

D. *Practical Observations*

1. Nothing is specified in the law as to who composes the questions to be proposed, and selects the topic on which the sermon is to be given. These matters, however, quite evidently rest with the

[94] d'Angelo, *Parroco e Parrochia,* I, 113, nota 2, states that such an one would be declared fit, but this writer cannot agree, because of the fact that a candidate must be fit in all matters in order that he may be reported as fit to rule the vacant church: S. C. C., *Pistorien.,* 27 ian. 1912—apud d'Angelo, *op. cit.,* I, 157-158. The portent of the decision here referred to is that each candidate must absolutely be declared fit in both the question of learning and in that of the other requisite qualifications, in order that he may definitely be declared as fit to rule the vacant parish. An abundance of votes on learning will not make up for a deficiency of votes on the other qualifications, and vice versa. This decision of the Sacred Congregation of the Council admitted the practice whereby the synodal examiners might add together their individual votes, for example, on theological learning, and then consider as fit in this matter those candidates who received more than half of the total number of votes which the examiners together possessed.

[95] Conc. Trident., sess. XXIV, *de ref.,* c. 18.

bishop, and with those synodal examiners who have been chosen for the case. The questions and the sermon topic to be proposed should by all means be chosen beforehand. It must be remembered that the law demands that they be the same for each candidate.[96]

2. With regard to the oral examination on doctrine,[97] the synodal examiners and the presiding official should determine beforehand the exact topic which is to be discussed orally by the candidates. The candidates are not to know what this topic is until they are called in for the actual oral examination. The topic should be the same for all, and, if questions are to be asked, they too should be identical for all. The candidates are questioned individually, and there must be no possibility of communication between those who have already taken this oral examination and those who are waiting to take it.[98]

3. The synodal examiners, the presiding official and the chancellor are present at the beginning of the concursus. One of the examiners may undertake the dictation of the matter of the written examination. Once the questions and the sermon topic have been proposed to the candidates the synodal examiners and the presiding official leave the place of examination. The chancellor remains, to take care that the candidates do not violate the strict rule of honesty.[99] When all the candidates have completed their work, or, if a definite time limit has been set, once the time allotted has passed, the synodal examiners and the presiding official return. The candidates hand in their papers, affixing their signature to each response and to the sermon. The synodal examiners, the presiding official and the chancellor also affix their signature at this time to each response and to the sermon. The oral examination on doctrine may follow immediately, or it may be postponed till another day.[100]

4. Because of the necessity of not revealing with what success the candidates came through the examination and of not making

[96] Bened. XIV, Const., *Cum illud,* 14 dec. 1742, § VII, n. 1—*Docum. IV in Append. ad Codicem I. C.*

[97] Const. *Cum illud,* § XVI, n. 4.

[98] d'Angelo, *Parroco e Parrochia,* I, 105-106.

[99] d'Angelo, *op. cit.,* I, 100-105.

[100] d'Angelo, *loc. cit.* The signing of the responses and sermon are required by law: Bened. XIV, Const., *Cum illud,* 14 dec. 1742, § VII, n. 6—*Docum. IV in Append. ad Codicem I. C.*

known what was learned of the moral character of the candidates, it is certainly within the right of the bishop to require of the synodal examiners that they take an oath of secrecy in regard to information obtained in the concursus.[101]

5. In places where the law of the concursus holds there is no need for a concursus when a pastor is transferred from one parish to another according to the provisions of canons 2162 ff.,[102] nor is there any need to hold a concursus in the first appointment to a newly erected parish.[103]

Appendix: The Concursus in the Appointment of the Canon Theologian and the Canon Penitentiary

In canons 398-401 the Code of Canon Law treats of the offices and duties of the canon theologian and the canon penitentiary. Canon 398, § 2 states that these two canonries are not to be conferred until after a thorough investigation has been made into the life, morals and doctrine of the candidates. It further states that where the concursus has been the usual form of provision this must be preserved.

It is of interest to know whether the synodal examiners must be used in such a concursus. This is a difficult question, and one can only refer to the particular law of different places to find the answer. In Italy and its adjacent islands, for instance, these canonries must be provided for by means of a concursus, but it is not necessary that the synodal examiners take part in it. Four examiners are chosen by the bishop on the occasion of each election, and they may be the synodal examiners. The actual concursus is the same as that for parishes, except that four questions instead of three must be given, and in the case of the canon theologian the questions must be especially on dogmatic theology and on Sacred Scripture.[104]

[101] Cf. canon 364, § 2, 3°. Cf. also, "Quistioni minori," n. 31—*Monit. Eccl.*, Serie III, Vol. VIII (1916) (Vol. XXVIII della intera Collezione, p. 443).

[102] S. C. C., *Romana et aliarum*, 21 iun. 1919—*AAS*, XI (1919), 318.

[103] *PCI*, 25 iun. 1932—*AAS*, XXIV (1932), 284.

[104] Bened. XIII, Const., *Pastoralis officii*, 19 maii 1725—*Bull. Rom. Taur.*, XXII, § 2, p. 183 et § 5, p. 184. Cf. also, S. C. C., *Aversana*, 21 nov. 1829—*Thes. Resol.*, LXXXIX, p. 235.

In Spain, according to Ferreres,[105] these two canonries are conferred by means of a concursus, but apparently the examiners are others than the synodal examiners. This same author [106] notes that in certain Latin American countries the concursus is also used in selecting appointees for these offices, *e. g.*, in Equador, San Salvador, Costa Rica, Guatemala, Honduras and Nicaragua. One would have to study the particular law of these places, however, in order to determine whether the synodal examiners must be used, whether they might be used, or whether others alone were to be used.

The Apostolic Datary [107] has stated that when these canonries are to be conferred by the Holy See, if the concursus is the usual method of provision, then the concursus as prescribed by Benedict XIII [108] must be held and the acts transmitted to the Apostolic Datary. It further recalls a recent rescript [109] according to which a canon theologian need no longer be possessed of a doctorate or licentiate in Sacred Scripture, though other things being equal one who possesses either degree is to be preferred to one who possesses a doctorate in sacred theology.

[105] *Institutiones Canonicae,* I, n. 691 et n. 694. Cf. also, Simeone, *Lezioni di Dritto Canonico,* I (3. ed., Napoli: Jovene, 1905), 299.

[106] *Op. cit.*, I, n. 696 ter., I, II, III.

[107] 13 apr. 1942, esp. §§ VIII-XII—*AAS,* XXXIV (1942), 113-118.

[108] Cf. *supra,* pp. 24 ff.

[109] Dataria Apostolica, 8 apr. 1940—*AAS,* XXXII (1940), 163.

CHAPTER VI

DUTIES OF SYNODAL EXAMINERS IN OTHER EXAMINATIONS

Introductory Remarks

Canon 389, § 2: Pro experimentis vero habendis ad clericorum ordinationem et approbationem sacerdotum qui petunt facultatem excipiendi sacramentales confessiones aut sacras conciones habendi, et pro examinibus de quibus in can. 130 integrum est Episcopo vel examinatorum synodalium vel aliorum opera uti.

Canon 389, § 2 indicates possible additional duties for the synodal examiners. The canon states that the local Ordinary may either select the synodal examiners, or may pass them over in favor of others, when he makes his choice of examiners for the examinations (a) of candidates for Orders, (b) of priests who petition jurisdiction to hear confessions, (c) of those who seek the faculty to preach, (d) of the Junior Clergy. It is absolutely clear that there is no obligation upon the local Ordinary to choose the synodal examiners. He is left perfectly free to choose others to conduct these examinations, if he should so prefer.

What follows in the succeeding articles of this chapter is a consideration of the matters with which the synodal examiners must be acquainted in the event that they are called upon to conduct the above-mentioned examinations. If the treatment given here of these examinations seems incomplete, it must be remembered that the sole reason for considering them is to study the extent of the work of the examiners, not to give a complete commentary.

Article 1. The Junior Clergy Examinations

Canon 130, § 1: Expleto studiorum curriculo, sacerdotes omnes, etsi beneficium paroeciale aut canonicale consecuti, nisi ab Ordinario loci ob iustam causam

fuerint exempti, examen singulis annis saltem per integrum triennium in diversis sacrarum scientiarum disciplinis, antea opportune designatis, subeant secundum modum ab eodem Ordinario determinandum.

Even though they have a parochial or canon's benefice, all priests for three years after their ordination must undergo an annual examination in various branches of the Sacred Sciences designated a sufficient length of time before the date of the examination. The manner of conducting the examination is to be determined by the Ordinary, who may for a just cause grant exemption from the examinations.[1]

The subject matter of these Junior Clergy examinations is expressed in the canon by the broad term "the different branches of the Sacred Sciences." The Sacred Sciences include Sacred Scripture, dogmatic, moral, pastoral and ascetic theology, canon law, Church history, sacred liturgy, homiletics and catechetics.[2] Some would also include philosophy and the Latin language, on the score that these are implicitly included, since they are a preparation and a foundation for the strictly Sacred Sciences.[3] It does not seem correct, however, to add these subjects to the already lengthy list comprised under the term "Sacred Sciences," first because they are not Sacred Sciences, and secondly, because to add these subjects would be to make the examinations too difficult and thereby possibly to defeat their whole purpose.

[1] Religious priests are not obliged to take this examination, but instead have their own particular Junior Clergy examinations: cf. canon 590. Even if religious are pastors or parochial vicars they are not subject to canon 130—*PCI,* 14 iul. 1922—*AAS,* XIV (1922), 526. Cf. Chartier, "Les obligations des clercs" —*Le Canoniste* (Paris, 1924-1926; originally *Le Canoniste Contemporain,* Paris, 45 vols., 1878-1922), XLII (1926), 337; Schaepman, "De quibusdam examinibus clericalibus"—*Jus Pontificium,* X (1930), 316-317.

[2] Maroto, *Institutiones Iuris Canonici,* I, n. 561; Augustine, *Commentary,* II, pp. 75-76; Ayrinhac, *General Legislation in the New Code of Canon Law* (New York: Benziger, 1923), n. 268. (Hereafter this work will be cited *General Legislation.*) Wernz-Vidal, *Ius Canonicum,* II, n. 134; Coronata, *Institutiones,* I, n. 190.

[3] Maroto, *loc. cit.*; Ayrinhac, *loc. cit.*

Obviously the whole of the Sacred Sciences is not to be the object of each single examination, but, as the canon indicates, the local Ordinary is to determine beforehand, on each occasion, just what parts of the Sacred Sciences will constitute the subject matter of the impending examination.[4] The designation of subjects should, naturally, be made sufficiently in advance of the actual date of the examination to permit the priests time to prepare.[5] It would appear to be ideal if the matter of the examinations was so arranged that, at least in the major subjects, the whole of what was treated in the regular seminary course would be covered within the three years.[6]

Canon 130 does not set down a specific method to be followed in these Junior Clergy examinations, but, rather, leaves this to be determined by the local Ordinary. Similarly, questions of time and place are left to the judgment of the latter. The one thing that the law does require is that there be a real examination.[7] The examiners must, of course, follow any instructions given them by the local Ordinary. Often enough it may happen that the latter will delegate to the examiners the selection of matter, of a method to be followed, and of time and place for the examination.[8] If the Ordinary does not issue any specific rules as to the judgment to be made on the work of the individual priests, the examiners should agree beforehand on an equitable and just method of judging the results of the examination. When they have concluded their scrutiny of the work of the priests they should report their conclusions to the Ordinary.[9]

[4] Cf. Ayrinhac, *loc. cit.*; Augustine, *loc. cit.*; Coronata, *loc. cit.*; Beste, *Introductio*, p. 183.

[5] Cf. Ayrinhac, *loc. cit.*

[6] Cf. Augustine, *loc. cit.*

[7] Wernz-Vidal, *loc. cit.*

[8] Canon 199, § 1.

[9] A Junior Clergy examination may, it seems, be considered by the local Ordinary as sufficing also for the examinations required of those who petition for jurisdiction to hear confessions and the faculty to preach. (Cf. Schaepman, *art. cit.*, p. 319.) If the Ordinary should decide thus, he should be sure that the matter specifically called for in these other examinations is sufficiently included in the actual examination being given. Ordinarily, at least in the United States, such a procedure would be impractical since priests are usually given

Appendix: Junior Clergy Examinations in the United States

The Third Plenary Council of Baltimore decreed [10] that every priest must be examined annually after ordination for a period of five years. The examiners were to be the bishop, or his delegate, and the examiners of the diocesan clergy. The subject matter of the examinations was to include the various parts of ecclesiastical learning, namely, Sacred Scripture, dogmatic and moral theology, canon law, Church history and liturgy. If any priest should fail in one or more of these annual examinations, he was obliged to make up for his failure until he had successfully passed five yearly examinations. The same rule was set for the case wherein a priest, without episcopal dispensation, would miss one or other of the examinations. It mattered not what the cause for the omission might be.

This particular legislation, in so far as it requires the Junior Clergy examinations for five years, since it in no way contradicts the law of canon 130 of the New Code, remains in effect in the United States.[11] Certain parts of this Baltimore legislation, however, must be considered as abolished, since they do conflict with the common law.[12] Thus the scope of the examination is not to be restricted to the subjects enumerated in the Baltimore legislation, for the law of canon 130 states that the bishop may choose from all the Sacred Sciences when he designates the matter of the examination. Furthermore, there is now no need, as there was under the Baltimore legislation, for the bishop, or his delegate, and the *examiners of the diocesan clergy* to conduct the examination, because the Code has

jurisdiction for confessions and the faculty to preach immediately after their ordination to the Sacred Priesthood, whereas the first Junior Clergy examination is ordinarily held at least six months after the latest ordination. The Junior Clergy examination may not be considered as sufficient for appointment to parishes at any time during the entire period in which clerics are obliged to take this examination, even if it was taken before the bishop and his synodal examiners: *PCI,* 24 nov. 1920, ad VI—*AAS,* XII (1920), p. 574.

[10] *Acta et Decreta Conc. Plen. Balt. III,* nn. 187-188.

[11] Canon 6, 6°. Cf. Ayrinhac, *op. cit.,* n. 268; Barrett, *A Comparative Study of the Councils of Baltimore and the Code of Canon Law,* pp. 43-44; Beste, *op. cit.,* p. 183.

[12] Canon 6, 1°.

explicitly given the bishop complete freedom in the choice of examiners.[13]

Article 2. The Examination for Jurisdiction to Hear Confessions

Canon 877, § 1: Tum locorum Ordinarii iurisdictionem, tum Superiores religiosi iurisdictionem aut licentiam audiendarum confessionum ne concedant, nisi iis qui idonei per examen reperti fuerint, nisi agatur de sacerdote cuius theologicam doctrinam aliunde compertam habeant.

§ 2: Si post concessam iurisdictionem aut licentiam prudenter dubitent num probatus a se antea sacerdos pergat adhuc idoneus esse, eum ad novum doctrinae periculum adigant, etsi agatur de parocho aut canonico poenitentiario.

Local Ordinaries as well as religious superiors shall grant jurisdiction or permission to hear confessions only to those priests who have been found qualified by examination, unless the theological knowledge of the priest is well known from other sources. If, after the concession of jurisdiction or permission to hear confessions, a local Ordinary or a religious superior should have a prudent doubt as to whether a priest who has been approved by him is still qualified, he should oblige him to undergo a new examination concerning his knowledge, even though he be a pastor or a canon penitentiary.[14]

[13] Cf. *supra,* pp. 44-45. Cf. Beste, *op. cit.,* Appendix, Allegatum IV, pp. 988-989, where a plan is suggested for the division of subject matter in such a manner that in five years the whole field of dogmatic and moral theology, canon law, liturgy, Sacred Scripture and Church history is completely covered. It should be remarked that questions in the other Sacred Sciences should be added to this list, *i. e.,* in ascetical theology, homiletics and catechetics.

[14] Cf. canon 873 for a list of those who have ordinary jurisdiction to hear confessions. These do not need to undergo any special examination, but receive jurisdiction automatically with the reception of their office. Cf. Cappello, *Tractatus Canonico-Moralis de Sacramentis,* Vol. II, Pars I, *De Poenitentia* (3. ed., Taurinorum Augustae: Marietti, 1938), n. 372. The prescription of canon 877, § 2 gives the local Ordinary the right to subject any priest to an examination, even though he has ordinary jurisdiction, if the Ordinary should prudently doubt that the priest is still qualified.

Synodal examiners are to be found only in dioceses, not in vicariates or prefectures apostolic and not in clerical exempt religious institutes. Consequently, in considering the examinations for jurisdiction to hear confessions, we are not concerned with examinations given by vicars or prefects apostolic, or by superiors in clerical exempt religious institutes, but only with those given by local diocesan Ordinaries.

Whenever a local Ordinary decides upon an examination he is left complete freedom in his choice of examiners, though the law explicitly makes mention of the synodal examiners as a possible selection for the duty.[15]

Canon 877, § 1 speaks of an examination of the fitness of the priest. One might be led to conclude from this that the scope of the examination would be not only the theological learning of the priest, but also his moral fitness to be a confessor, namely, his prudence and sanctity of morals. Indeed, before granting jurisdiction, the local Ordinary must be convinced that the learning, prudence and moral character of the individual are such as are required in a confessor.[16] However, the actual and formal examination which the local Ordinary has the right to require of the candidate and which he commits to others to carry out has as its subject matter solely the question of theological learning. The final clause in § 1 of canon 877 makes this clear. Here it is said that if the local Ordinary knows of the priest's theological learning from other sources, he may omit the examination. Evidently then the examination is restricted to this matter. If it were to extend also to moral fitness, then the canon would have said that the examination might be omitted if the local Ordinary knew of the candidate's fitness in learning and moral

[15] Canon 389, § 2. (Note: In the United States the Third Plenary Council of Baltimore [*Acta et Decreta Conc. Plen. Balt. III*, n. 24] suggested that the *examiners of the diocesan clergy* be used to aid in the approval of those seeking faculty to hear confessions. This suggestion need no longer be given consideration since the Code permits the bishop complete freedom in his choice of examiners to conduct the examination of candidates who seek jurisdiction to hear confessions. Cf. canon 389, § 2.)

[16] Ayrinhac, *The Legislation on the Sacraments* (New York: Longmans, Green & Co., 1928), p. 199; Cappello, *op. cit.*, n. 371.

requisites from other sources.[17] Actually the proof of the possession of the requisite moral qualifications is to be sought by the local Ordinary otherwise than by a formal examination.[18]

The examination on theological learning should concern itself with those ecclesiastical subjects with which every confessor should be acquainted. These would include especially the field of moral theology, and a goodly part of the matter treated in canon law, such as the obligations of the various states of life, the laws on fasting and abstinence, much of the law on the sacraments, the penal law of the Church, etc.[19] The local Ordinary is the one to choose the subject matter of each examination, though he may delegate this choice to the examiners he appoints to conduct the examination.[20]

The law requires no particular method in these examinations, sets no specific time or place for them, and gives no rules to be followed by the examiners when they judge the work of the candidates to see whether or not the results show fitness as regards theological learning. All these details are left to the prudence of the local Ordinary.[21] The latter may himself make regulations on these matters, or he may delegate his power in this regard to the examiners whom he selects.[22] If the examiners are delegated they should, naturally, see that the strict rules of equity are followed in all these details. After they have concluded their judgment on the work of the candidate, or candidates, as the case may be, they are to report their opinions to the local Ordinary.

Article 3. The Examination for the Faculty to Preach

Canon 1340, § 1: Graviter onerata eorum conscientia, loci Ordinarius vel Superior religiosus facultatem vel

[17] Cf. Ayrinhac, *loc. cit.*; Blat, *Commentarium Textus Codicis Iuris Canonici*, lib. III, pars I (2. ed., Romae: ex Typographia Pontificia in Instituto Pii IX, 1924), n. 200.

[18] Blat, *loc. cit.*

[19] Blat, *loc. cit.*

[20] Canon 199, § 1.

[21] Cappello, *Tractatus Canonico-Moralis de Sacramentis,* II, Pars I, *De Poenitentia,* n. 371.

[22] Canon 199, § 1.

licentiam concionandi cuiquam ne concedant, nisi prius constet de eius bonis moribus et de sufficienti doctrina per examen ad normam can. 877, § 1.

§ 2: Si, concessa facultate vel licentia, compererint necessarias dotes in concionatore desiderari, debent eam revocare; in dubio de doctrina, debent certis argumentis dubitationem excutere, novo etiam examine, si opus fuerit.

The local Ordinary and the religious superior are under grave obligation of conscience forbidden to give the faculty or permission to preach [23] to any priest until his good moral standing and sufficiency of knowledge have been first ascertained by examination, as demanded by canon 877.[24] If, after granting the faculty or permission, they find that a preacher lacks the necessary qualifications, they must revoke the faculty or permission; when doubt arises as to the possession of the necessary knowledge, they must dispel this doubt by certain proofs, and even by a new examination, if necessary.

In the consideration of the examination which may be required of one who seeks the faculty to preach,[25] the writer limits himself to

[23] The faculty to preach includes also the right to catechize in a public capacity—Jansen, *Canonical Provisions for Catechetical Instruction,* The Catholic University of America Canon Law Studies, n. 107 (Washington, D. C.: The Catholic University of America, 1937), pp. 43-44.

[24] According to canon 877, which treats of the examination for the granting of jurisdiction to hear confessions, the local Ordinary may dispense with the examination if he knows of the candidate's fitness in learning from other sources. Since the legislation on the examination for the faculty to preach is to follow the norms laid down for the examination for jurisdiction to hear confessions, the local Ordinary may, therefore, also dispense from the examination spoken of in canon 1340, provided he be certain from other sources of the candidate's fitness in learning for the office of preaching. Cf. Sipos, *Enchiridion,* p. 732; Beste, *Introductio,* p. 654; Coronata, *Institutiones,* II, n. 922; McVann, *The Canon Law on Sermon Preaching* (New York: The Paulist Press, 1940), p. 72.

[25] Canon 1340 refers to all secular priests of the diocese, and to all religious who are subjects of the local Ordinary, or who reside in the diocese. Special provision is made in canon 1341 for the granting of the faculty to preach to extra-diocesan priests, whether secular or religious. Canon 1342 admits that deacons, as well as priests, may be given the faculty to preach. Other clerics

a consideration of examinations given by local diocesan Ordinaries, since it is only in dioceses that one finds the synodal examiners. These local Ordinaries are completely free in the choice of examiners to conduct the examination. They may make use of the synodal examiners for this purpose,[26] or they may choose others of the secular clergy, diocesan or even extra-diocesan, or of the regular clergy.[27] According to the Norms for Sacred Preaching laid down by the Sacred Consistorial Congregation,[28] the examiners should be three in number.

The local Ordinary is obliged to reach moral certainty concerning the moral and intellectual fitness of the candidate for the work of preaching, but in attaining this certainty he is required to use the formal examination only in the matter of requisite learning.[29] As to the inquiry into the piety, purity of morals and reputation of the individual, the local Ordinary may make this in whatever manner he desires.

The subject matter of the formal examination on learning is twofold. It comprises, first, doctrinal subjects the knowledge of which is required in a preacher, and secondly, the matter of delivery.[30]

may be given this faculty only in individual cases, and only if the local Ordinary decides that there is a reasonable cause for so doing. All others are absolutely forbidden to preach. Cardinals (canon 239, § 1, 3°), bishops (canon 349, § 1, 1°), pastors (canon 461; S. C. Consist., *Normae, Ut quae,* n. 14, 28 iun. 1917—*AAS,* IX [1917], p. 331 ff. [cited hereafter as *Normae*]) and canon theologians (canon 400; *Normae,* n. 14) have, by reason of their office, the right to preach and need not undergo the special examination of canon 1340. This right, of course, is limited in the case of bishops, pastors and canon theologians. If a bishop at any time should prudently doubt of the continued fitness of a canon theologian or a pastor he may require him to submit to an examination (canon 1340, § 2).

26 Canon 389, § 2; *Normae,* n. 14.

27 Cf. *Normae,* n. 14; Sipos, *op. cit.,* p. 732; Beste, *op. cit.,* p. 654; McVann, *op. cit.,* p. 74.

28 *Normae,* n. 14.

29 *Normae,* n. 14; Beste, *op. cit.,* p. 654; Coronata, *op. cit.,* n. 922.

30 Canon 1340; *Normae,* n. 14; MacCarthy, "The New Regulations on Preaching"—*AER,* LVII (1917), 384; Couly, "La prédication d'aprèz le Code" —*Le Canoniste,* XLVI (1924), p. 218; Beste, *op. cit.,* p. 654; McVann, *op. cit.,* p. 74.

Therefore, this examination should be on such subjects as Sacred Scripture, dogmatic and moral theology, Church history,[31] the composition of sermons and the ability to deliver sermons.[32] It should be both oral and written.[33]

Other regulations, for instance, on method, time, place, and the manner in which the judgment of the examiners is reached, may be made by the local Ordinary, or by the examiners with delegation for this from the local Ordinary.[34] Equity must, of course, prevail in all these matters. At the conclusion of the examination, the examiners will report to the local Ordinary their judgment on the fitness of the candidate for the office of preaching as regards the subject matter of the examination.[35]

Article 4. The Examination Before Ordination

Canon 996, § 1: Quilibet promovendus sive saecularis sive religiosus debet praevium ac diligens examen subire circa ipsum ordinem suscipiendum.

§ 2: Promovendi vero ad sacros ordines in aliis quoque de sacra theologia tractationibus periculum faciant.

§ 3: Episcoporum est statuere qua methodo, coram quibus examinatoribus et quibus in tractationibus sacrae theologiae promovendi periculum facere debeant.

Canon 997, § 1: Hoc examen sive pro clericis saecularibus sive pro religiosis recipit loci Ordinarius qui iure proprio ordinat, aut dat dimissorias litteras; qui tamen

[31] Augustine, *Commentary,* VI, 357-358.

[32] *Normae,* n. 14: "scientia et *actio.*" Cf. also Augustine, *loc. cit.*; McVann, *loc. cit.*

[33] *Normae,* n. 14.

[34] Canon 199, § 1.

[35] It seems quite admissible for the local Ordinary to combine the examination for the faculty to preach with that for the granting of jurisdiction to hear confessions, and thus to have a single examination for the dual purpose. (Beste, *loc. cit.*; Haring—apud Coronata, *op. cit.,* n. 922, nota 4; McVann, *loc. cit.*) When the local Ordinary would follow this procedure he should see to it that the subject matter particular to the individual examinations is included in the single examination.

potest quoque, ex iusta causa, illud Episcopo ordinaturo committere, qui id oneris suscipere velit.

§ 2: Episcopus alienum subditum sive saecularem sive religiosum ordinans cum legitimis litteris dimissoriis, quibus asseritur candidatum examinatum fuisse ad normam § 1, et idoneum repertum, potest huic attestationi acquiescere, sed non tenetur; et si pro sua conscientia censeat candidatum non esse idoneum, eum ne promoveat.

All candidates, both secular and religious, must undergo a careful examination before ordination with reference to the order which they are to receive. Candidates for major orders must also undergo an examination on other tracts of sacred theology. Bishops have the right to determine the method of the examination, to appoint the examiners and to prescribe the subjects of sacred theology in which the examination is to be made. This examination is to be conducted for both seculars and religious under the authority of that local Ordinary, who by law has the right to ordain or to issue dimissorials requesting another bishop to ordain his subjects. If justified by a good reason, this Ordinary may also commit the examination to the ordaining bishop, if the latter is willing to assume that burden. The bishop who ordains non-subjects, either secular or religious, who are sent to him with legitimate dimissorials in which it is stated that the candidates have been duly examined as demanded by § 1 of this canon, and have been judged qualified, may accept this attestation as sufficient, but he is not obliged to do so.[86] If he in conscience believes that a candidate is not suitable, he should not promote him.

Though canon 996 leaves the bishop free in his choice of examiners for the examination of candidates for orders, still canon 389, § 2, makes special mention of the possibility of the use of synodal examiners for the purpose of conducting these examinations. As to the number of examiners, the method to be followed in examining and

[86] The bishop who ordains another's subject may even subject the latter to a new examination if he should conscientiously feel that in this way only would he be satisfied that the candidate is fit—Villien, *Le Canoniste Contemporain*, XLV (1922), pp. 391-392.

in judging the results of the examination, the bishop is free to make whatever regulations he might desire. He may, of course, delegate his power in these particulars to the examiners whom he selects.[37] As is quite evident, when the examiners have concluded their scrutiny and have arrived at a judgment of the work of the candidates, they are to make their report to the bishop as to which of the candidates have proven themselves fit for ordination in the matter of the examination.

The question of the subject matter of the examinations for orders has been expressly noted by the legislation of canon 996. Depending upon whether the candidate aspires to minor or major orders the examination is less or more extensive. In § 1 of the canon it is stated that every candidate, whether he is to be promoted to minor or to major orders, must be examined on the order which he is about to receive. This examination concerns itself solely with the specific order to which one is about to be promoted, its matter and form, the minister, the conditions requisite for the reception of it, the effects in the recipient of the order, and the duties incumbent upon the recipient.[38] Canon 996 in §§ 2-3 legislates that those who are about to receive a major order must also be examined in other matter, namely, on other tracts of sacred theology. What these other tracts will be is left to the judgment of the bishop, or to others whom the bishop may delegate to make the choice.[39]

[37] Canon 199, § 1.

[38] Sipos, *Enchiridion,* p. 483; Cappello, *Tractatus Canonico-Moralis de Sacramentis,* Vol. II, pars III (Taurinorum Augustae: Marietti, 1935), n. 541.

[39] Cappello (*op. cit.,* II, pars III, n. 543) feels that a bishop may consider an examination undergone during the regular theological course in the seminary as sufficient to fulfill the obligation of canon 996, provided that the bishop would see to it that the examination also included the subject matter of the order to be received. This same author (*ibidem,* n. 541) claims that a single examination would suffice for the reception of all the major orders. It must be added that if such would be the case, the subject matter of such a single examination would have to include, besides certain tracts in sacred theology, the three major orders to be received. It seems that one may also admit that a bishop might give a single examination for ordination to the priesthood, for the faculty to preach and for the granting of jurisdiction to hear confessions, provided only that he included in this single examination the subject matter peculiar to each separate examination. According to the Commission for the

Appendix: Examination of Candidates for Orders in the United States

The II Plenary Council of Baltimore, in the chapter on Orders,[40] decreed that in all dioceses four, or at least three, examiners should be appointed by the bishop to examine candidates for promotion to orders. They were to examine the candidates on learning, and were also to pass judgment on the testimonials regarding the quality, person, age and integrity of life of each of the candidates. They were to make a sincere report in writing on all of these matters to the bishop, giving therein their opinion of each candidate, whether he was worthy or not to be admitted to orders. If a bishop had appointed synodal examiners, he could omit the appointment of others and make use of the synodal examiners for this matter of examining candidates for promotion to orders.

The III Plenary Council of Baltimore decreed [41] that the bishops should appoint *examiners of the diocesan clergy,* and suggested that they be used for the examination of candidates for promotion to orders. There was no further mention of the actual examination of candidates for orders, so the provisions of the previous Plenary Council, cited above, continued in effect. As has been previously noted,[42] the *examiners of the diocesan clergy* replaced the synodal examiners wherever the latter may have been introduced, for the II Plenary Council had merely suggested the synodal examiners, while the III Plenary Council actually decreed that bishops should create the *examiners of the diocesan clergy.* Further, the duties suggested by the

Authentic Interpretation of the Code (24 nov. 1920, ad V—*AAS,* XII [1920], 574), the examination on orders as required by canon 996, §§ 2-3 could be considered sufficient examination for appointment to one's first parish, provided it includes questioning on those matters which a cleric should know who wishes to be a pastor. This response of the Commission refers only to the examination spoken of in canon 459, § 3, 3° and should not, it seems, be referred to the examination in a concursus where the latter is required—cf. "Brevi Risposte"—*Monit. Eccl.,* Vol. I, Serie IV (1921) (Vol. XXXI della intera Collezione), p. 93; "Quistioni"—*Monit. Eccl.,* Vol. III, Serie IV (1921) (Vol. XXXIII della intera Collezione), p. 27 sq.

40 *C. Plen. Baltim. II, Acta et Decreta,* n. 316. Cf. also n. 76.

41 *Acta et Decreta Conc. Plen. Balt. III,* n. 24.

42 Cf. above, p. 38.

former Council for the synodal examiners were now suggested for the new officials.[43]

As to the relation between the particular law which has just been cited and the present law of the Code on the matter of the examination of candidates for promotion to orders there are certain points which must be made clear. First of all, there can be no question of any obligation from particular law upon the bishop to use any specific officials to conduct the examination. The Code (canon 389, § 2, and canon 996, § 3) gives the bishop full liberty to choose whatever persons he may prefer. Nor can there be any restriction as to the number of examiners to be used. The Code, in the canons just cited, definitely gives the bishop complete freedom in the matter of examiners, and any particular law which stated just how many examiners should be used would be a restriction of this liberty, and would thereby be contrary to the Code. Furthermore, it is to be noted that the particular law of Baltimore gave to the examiners a duty which the Code does not assign to them, namely, that of examining testimonials on the life and character of the candidates and of passing judgment from such evidence on the worthiness of the candidates. This particular legislation may not, it seems, be considered as still in effect, since it is contrary to the provisions of the present law and not merely over and above present legislation (*praeter Codicem*). The present law on the prerequisites to ordination, as found in the Code,[44] and in an Instruction from the Sacred Congregation of the Sacraments,[45] treats the question of the inquiry into the moral qualifications of the candidates in detail, and the Instruction specifically designates those who are to aid the bishop in the matter of determining the fitness of the candidates for promotion to orders. Consequently, any previous legislation which decrees differently must be considered as abrogated.[46] This is the case with the particular legislation of the Second Council of Baltimore.

[43] There is one duty suggested by the II Plenary Council which is not mentioned by the succeeding Council, namely, the drawing up of testimonial letters. Cf. *C. Plen. Baltim. II, Acta et Decreta*, n. 76.

[44] Canon 992-1000.

[45] Instructio, 27 dec. 1930—*AAS* (1931), XXIII, pp. 120 ff.

[46] Cf. canon 6, 1°.

With regard to *regulars* who were candidates for orders the II Plenary Council of Baltimore required that they be examined by the examiners of the bishop in the matter of learning.[47] The Code, however, is more explicit on the question of the examination for religious. They are required to take the examination on the order which they are about to receive, and if they are to receive a major order they must also undergo an examination on other tracts of Sacred Theology.[48] This examination is to be taken before the examiners designated by that local Ordinary who has the right to ordain or to issue dimissorials.[49]

Article 5. Examinations Required by Particular Law in the United States

A. *Examination for Entrance Into a Major Seminary*

The III Plenary Council of Baltimore decreed [50] that in no place in the United States were students to be admitted to a major seminary unless they were first approved by examiners after an examination on their learning. The Council added that these examiners might be the synodal or pro-synodal examiners of that particular diocese in which the major seminary was situated.

It has been pointed out in another place [51] that although the term *synodal examiners* is here used by the Council, still the Council intended merely to refer to the *examiners of the diocesan clergy*. It seems apparent that this particular legislation on an examination for entrance into a major seminary must be considered as still in effect, for it is not contrary to any law of the Code, but is rather an additional law over and above the common law of the Church.[52]

[47] *C. Plen. Balt. II, Acta et Decret.*, n. 316.

[48] Canon 996.

[49] Canon 997, § 1. Cf. canon 996, § 3.

[50] *Acta et Decreta Conc. Plen. III*, n. 152.

[51] Cf. *supra*, pp. 44-45.

[52] Cf. Barrett, *A Comparative Study of the Councils of Baltimore and the Code of Canon Law*, p. 173.

B. *Examinations of Students in Major Seminaries*

The same III Plenary Council, in its legislation on major seminaries enacted [53] that at the close of each semester, or at least once a year, all the students of the major seminary were required to undergo an examination in the various branches of study before the bishop, or his vicar general, and the *examiners of the clergy.* It added further that others of the diocesan clergy who were outstanding for their learning should also be called upon to participate in conducting these examinations. Since there is no opposition between this particular legislation and any law of the Code it must be concluded that this law of the III Plenary Council of Baltimore is still binding.

It has been concluded that the Baltimore legislation on the semester or annual examinations and on the examination for entrance into a major seminary (spoken of in the preceding section) must be considered as still in effect. What must be said of the *examiners of the clergy* who were suggested to conduct the latter examination, and who were required to conduct the former? Does the office of *examiner of the clergy* still exist? The answer seems rather evident. These officials were created by particular law and since their existence and their duties in these two particular law examinations do not come into conflict with any law of the Code, it follows that according to canon 6, n. 1, this particular law must still be considered as binding. For practical reasons a bishop could easily avoid too numerous examiners in his diocese by making the same persons both synodal examiners and *examiners of the clergy.*[54]

[53] *Acta et Decreta Conc. Plen. III,* n. 175.

[54] It is possible that in many dioceses custom may have abrogated this particular law on the necessity of the *examiners of the clergy* and their use in these two examinations. Note: For the law on the office of *examiner of the clergy, i.e.,* method of appointment, term of office, etc., cf. above, pp. 38-39.

CHAPTER VII

THE DUTIES OF SYNODAL EXAMINERS AND PARISH PRIEST CONSULTORS IN CERTAIN ADMINISTRATIVE PROCEDURES

Introductory Remarks

In the Fourth Book of the Code, which is entitled *De Processibus,* there are three Parts. The first of these, entitled *De Iudiciis,* is concerned with the formal trial. The second deals with the special solemn procedure required for beatification and canonization, and is entitled *De causis beatificationis Servorum Dei et canonizationis Beatorum.* The third Part, under the title *De modo procedendi in nonnullis expediendis negotiis vel sanctionibus poenalibus applicandis,* treats of a number of special procedures which must be followed in certain specific and determined cases which demand a more expeditious and summary solution.[1]

The special processes, or procedures, of Part III have been given various names, such as "administrative," "summary," "economic" and "disciplinary." The term "administrative" is the most common amongst post-Code authors.[2] These administrative procedures of Part III are quite distinct from the process treated in Part I. The obvious difference lies in the absence in the former of a great number of the formalities required in the formal trial.[3] Though the special administrative processes are much less formal and are cer-

[1] Meier, *Adm. Proc. Ag. Neglig. Pastors,* p. 81.

[2] Meier, *op. cit.,* p. 89.

[3] Noval, *Commentarium Codicis Iuris Canonici, Liber IV, De Processibus,* 2 vols., Vol. II (Augustae Taurinorum—Romae: Marietti, 1932), n. 450; (hereafter this work will be cited *De Processibus*). Coronata, *Institutiones,* III, n. 1573; Connor, *Adm. Removal of Pastors,* p. 2; Meier, *op. cit.,* p. 88 ff. Cf. esp. this latter work on this point.

tainly much shorter than the formal trial, nevertheless they do require a certain amount of formality.[4] The formalities which are demanded are the result of positive regulations based on the natural law. They include whatever would be absolutely necessary in any trial. In a word, they are what is necessary for the attainment of the truth and for the solution of the particular question at hand.[5] Certain of these administrative procedures are non-penal in character (Titles XXVII-XXIX) while others have a penal character (Titles XXX-XXXIII). However, the real reason behind all these administrative procedures is not the punishment of a cleric, but rather the "*salus animarum et bonum populi christiani.*" As the decree, "*Maxima cura,*" of the Sacred Consistorial Congregation, upon which these procedures is based, expressed it in referring to the administrative removal of pastors: "*parochi amotio . . . nec parochi poenam propositam habet, sed utilitatem fidelium. Salus enim populi suprema lex est.*" [6] It is precisely because the good of souls demands it that these administrative procedures were formulated. The good of souls demands that such matters as the removal of pastors, their transfer, etc. be taken care of as expeditiously as possible.

The necessary officials in the administrative procedures are few: the Ordinary, a notary,[7] synodal examiners and parish priest consultors. In the following pages consideration will be given to those parts of these administrative procedures which concern the synodal examiners and the parish priest consultors.[8] Obviously the present work must be limited even in its consideration of the duties of these officials, else it would lose all proportion. For example, it is impossible to think of treating here the specific causes for the removal of pastors, for their transfer, etc. At the same time, of course, it must be kept in mind that a thorough knowledge of these causes is abso-

[4] Cf. canons 2147-2194.

[5] Noval, *op. cit.,* II, n. 450; Connor, *op. cit.,* p. 2.

[6] 20 aug. 1910, Proemium—*Fontes,* n. 2074. Cf. also, Coronata, *Institutiones,* III, n. 1573.

[7] Concerning these officials, cf. Meier, *op. cit.,* pp. 94-103.

[8] Since the administrative procedure in inflicting the suspension *ex informata conscientia* does not call for either the examiners or the consultors it will not be considered here.

lutely necessary in these officials if they would perform the duties of their office competently and honestly.[9]

Article 1. General Norms for the Synodal Examiners and Parish Priest Consultors in the Administrative Procedures

In canons 2142-2146 the Code of Canon Law lays down a few general norms which are applicable to all of the administrative procedures treated in the succeeding canons, 2147-2194. Here we take note of those norms only which apply to the synodal examiners and parish priest consultors.

Canon 2142: In processibus de quibus infra, adhibeatur semper notarius, qui scripto consignet acta quae ab omnibus subscribi debent et in archivo servari.

In the procedures to follow a notary should always be used to put into writing the acts of the case. These acts, consigned to writing, must be signed by all and kept in the archives.

The part of this canon which applies to the synodal examiners and parish priest consultors is that which demands the signing of the acts. As will be more evident later, the acts must be signed at the close of each particular stage of the proceeding. Naturally the examiners or consultors will sign only those acts in which they themselves have had a part.[10]

Canon 2144, § 1: Examinatores et consultores ac notarius debent, interposito ab initio processus iureiurando, servare secretum circa omnia quae ratione sui muneris noverint ac praesertim circa documenta occulta, disceptationes in consilio habitas, suffragiorum numerum ac motiva.

[9] For a detailed study of these administrative procedures the following works are suggested: Noval, *De Processibus,* II, n. 442 sq.; Coronata, *Institutiones,* III, n. 1573 sq.; Suarez, *De Remotione Parochorum*; Connor, *Adm. Removal of Pastors*; Meier, *Adm. Proc. Ag. Neglig. Pastors.*

[10] Suarez, *De Remotione Parochorum,* n. 6.

> **§ 2: Si huic praescripto minime paruerint, non solum a munere amoveri debent, sed alia etiam condigna poena ab Ordinario, servatis servandis, plecti poterunt; ac praeterea damna, si qua inde secuta sint, sarcire tenentur.**[11]

The examiners, consultors and notary must at the beginning of the procedure take an oath of secrecy as regards those matters which they shall learn by reason of their office, especially with respect to secret documents, discussions held at meetings, the distribution of votes and the reasons which swayed the officials. If they should fail to obey this precept they are not only to be removed from office, but they may also be punished by the Ordinary with other suitable penalties, *servatis servandis.* Still further, they are bound to repair any harm which may have been caused by their violation of secrecy.

As has been previously noted, when the examiners and consultors enter upon their office, they are obliged by canon 364, § 2, 1° to take an oath to fulfill faithfully their duties. No general oath of secrecy is imposed upon them by the Code. Rather, in this regard the law states in canon 364, § 2, 2°, that these officials are obliged to secrecy within the limits and according to the manner established either by law or by the bishop. In the present canon (2144, § 1) there is presented a general determination by the Common Law of the obligation of secrecy in connection with the administrative procedure of Book IV, Part III of the Code.

First, one should consider the object of this oath of secrecy. The canon says that secrecy must be kept with regard to all those matters which the officials shall learn by reason of their office. It then proceeds to enumerate specifically certain matters which will of necessity be brought up in the process of the case and which, because of their importance, must be the special object of secrecy. Evidently, then, if the examiners or consultors should learn from the proceedings of certain matters connected with the case which they never knew before from other sources, they are bound to the strict-

[11] This law is taken almost word for word from the law set by the decree "*Maxima cura*" (S. C. Consist., 20 aug. 1910, can. 7—*Fontes,* n. 2074). Cf. *supra,* pp. 56-59.

est secrecy. A difficulty arises concerning the object of this obligation of secrecy when there is question of knowledge which the officials possess from a double source, namely, from some source foreign to the actual procedure and from the procedure itself. Some claim that the strict obligation of the law also holds in this case, for the reason that the canon prescinds from the question of whether or not the knowledge may also be derived from other sources. It suffices that the matter has come up in the course of the procedure to make it the object of this official secrecy. The canon makes no distinction, no exception. It does not say that if the official shall have known of the matter already, or if he should come to know of it, from another source, then the obligation ceases. Since the canon does not distinguish, neither should its interpreters.[12] At least one author [13] takes the opposite view, claiming that in strict justice knowledge gained from such a double source is not the object of the oath of secrecy. Quite rightly he adds that prudence, however, would demand silence. This writer is inclined to follow the former opinion because of the reason given. A confirmatory argument for the former opinion is given by Suarez,[14] when he remarks that very often the knowledge obtained from sources outside the procedure is based merely on rumor whereas that obtained in the procedure enjoys authority greater than the knowledge previously had since there is the certitude that it is true. Again, one may hold that the legislator intended to include such knowledge due to the fact that in the event of revelation by an official people might be led to think that he was speaking of matters learned only from the actual procedure. In accord with this opinion it must be concluded, with Noval,[15] that the officials are liable to the penalties of the present canon if they should violate secrecy in regard to knowledge gained even from a double source.

Still another question arises in this matter: does this obligation of secrecy comprise also those matters which are known solely from

[12] Noval, *De Processibus,* II, n. 504; Suarez, *De Remotione Parochorum,* n. 13; Beste, *Introductio,* p. 854; Meier, *Adm. Proc. Ag. Neglig. Pastors,* p. 107.

[13] Coronata, *Institutiones,* III, n. 1576. Cf. also, Connor, *Adm. Removal of Pastors,* p. 89.

[14] *Op. cit.,* n. 13.

[15] *Op. cit.,* II, n. 504.

other sources? Obviously the answer must be in the negative. However, though the oath of secrecy may not demand silence on such information, the natural law, it seems, does make this demand. The reason for this statement is the fact that if officials should speak of matters which are derogatory to the priest in question, or of matters which might appear to be connected with the case, scandals might easily arise. Listeners would be led to feel that such information had been obtained in the fulfillment of their duties of office.[16] People would be inclined to give more than ordinary credence to the statements of an official, coming as they do from one connected with the case.[17] Revelation of such information would not, however, involve the application of the sanctions of the present canon.[18]

Consideration should now be given to the actual taking of the oath. The canon (canon 2144, § 1) states that it is to be taken at the beginning of each procedure. The accepted interpretation of this part of the canon is that the examiners or consultors are obliged to take the oath at such time as they are called into the case. In other words they must fulfill this obligation whenever a procedure begins as far as they themselves are concerned.[19] The oath is to be taken before the Ordinary or his delegate.[20] Since the examiners and consultors are priests they should, it seems, follow the prescription of canon 1622, § 1 and, when taking the oath, place their right hand over their heart, rather than on the Gospel Book.[21]

There is no statement, or its equivalent, in the law to the effect that this oath is required for the validity of subsequent acts. Consequently it must be held that the decree of the Sacred Consistorial Congregation,[22] which held that the oath spoken of in the decree

[16] Noval, *De Processibus*, II, n. 504; Meier, *Adm. Proc. Ag. Neglig. Pastors*, p. 108.

[17] Suarez, *De Remotione Parochorum*, n. 13.

[18] Noval, *op. cit.*, n. 504.

[19] Noval, *op. cit.*, n. 504; Suarez, *op. cit.*, n. 13; Coronata, *Institutiones*, III, n. 1576; Connor, *Adm. Removal of Pastors*, pp. 90-91; Meier, *op. cit.*, p. 105.

[20] Fanfani, *De Iure Parochorum*, n. 139, D; Meier, *op. cit.*, p. 110.

[21] Meier, *op. cit.*, p. 110.

[22] 15 feb. 1912—*AAS*, IV (1912), 141.

from the same Congregation, "*Maxima cura,*" [23] was to be taken under penalty of the invalidity of subsequent acts, is no longer in effect.[24] Coronata seems somewhat uncertain on the matter. He says that the penalty of nullity, at least of nullity which may not be sanated, is not in the present law.[25] There does not appear to be any reason whatsoever to substantiate Coronata's hesitation. Canon 11 of the present law seems to settle the matter quite definitely.

Augustine refers without comment to a formula for taking this oath which was given by the Sacred Consistorial Congregation, in 1912, in connection with the "*Maxima cura*" legislation.[26] That there is no obligation upon the Ordinary to use this formula when requiring the oath seems to be beyond all doubt, for the formula includes not only the oath of secrecy, but also oaths to fulfill one's office faithfully and not to receive anything whatsoever, even under the form of a gift, on the occasion of the performance of one's duties, or even before or after. In the present law the examiners and consultors are obliged at the very beginning of their term of office to take an oath to fulfill the duties of their office faithfully; it would seem superfluous, therefore, to require the same oath on each occasion on which they enter one of the administrative procedures. Furthermore, though these officials should surely refuse to accept all gifts offered them by interested parties on the occasion of the exercise of their office, nevertheless the law nowhere requires an oath to this effect. Consequently, unless an Ordinary might of his own volition require these added oaths, there is not only no obligation to use the formula containing them, but it actually should not be used.[27]

The secret which the examiners and consultors must keep is something more than just a natural secret. The fact that their knowledge comes to them in an official way, that is, because of their office, adds

[23] 20 aug. 1910, can. 7, § 1—*Fontes*, n. 2074.

[24] Canon 11. Cf. Meier, *Adm. Proc. Ag. Neglig. Pastors*, p. 109; Suarez, *De Remotione Parochorum*, n. 13; Connor, *Adm. Removal of Pastors*, pp. 90-91.

[25] *Institutiones*, III, n. 1576.

[26] Decr., 15 feb. 1912—*AAS*, IV (1912), p. 141. Cf. Augustine, *Commentary*, VII, p. 406, footnote n. 3.

[27] Cf. Meier, *Adm. Proc. Ag. Neglig. Pastors*, p. 109; Suarez, *De Remotione Parochorum*, n. 14; Coronata, *Institutiones*, III, n. 1576; Connor, *Adm. Removal of Pastors*, p. 91.

an additional element to the gravity of the matter. Theirs is a *secretum commissum,* and they are bound in virtue of an implied contract to maintain secrecy concerning what they hear as officials. Their obligation to secrecy is most strict because of the nature of the secret. The oath of secrecy adds to this strictness. The penalties threatened for the violation of secrecy are further proof of the seriousness of their obligation.[28]

Canon 2144, § 2 refers to the penalties for a violation of the oath of secrecy. The guilty official must be removed from office, and the Ordinary may also, *servatis servandis,* inflict other fitting penalties. Finally, the guilty one must repair all damages caused by the violation of his oath.

As to removal from office, the canon says that the Ordinary *must* remove the examiner or consultor who would violate his oath of secrecy. Is it necessary to take these words literally? Some authors merely repeat the words of the canon and thereby, possibly, leave the impression that the Ordinary has no alternative but to remove the official.[29] Others,[30] seemingly following a pre-Code author,[31] state quite clearly that the Ordinary has but one course to follow, namely, to remove the offender. More correct, it appears, is the opinion of still other authors. These [32] hold that the present canon contains a vindicative penalty which must be interpreted in the light of the norms set down in Book V of the Code of Canon Law for the interpretation of penalties. They, therefore, refer to canon 2223 for the interpretation of the obligation placed on the Ordinary as regards the delinquent official. From this canon one learns that if a law uses preceptive terminology, then ordinarily the penalty is to be inflicted. However, the same canon admits that under certain circumstances the superior may follow his conscience and his prudent judgment and refrain from imposing the specific penalty mentioned in the law. For

[28] Cf. Ferreres, *Institutiones Canonicae,* II, n. 892; Meier, *op. cit.,* p. 108.

[29] Coronata, *Institutiones,* III, n. 1576; Vermersch-Creusen, *Epitome,* III, n. 344.

[30] Wernz-Vidal, *Ius Canonicum,* VI (Romae: Apud Aedes Universitatis Gregorianae, 1927), n. 740, VI; Augustine, *Commentary,* VII, p. 407.

[31] Cappello, *De Admin. Amotione Parochorum,* pp. 86-87.

[32] Noval, *De Processibus,* II, n. 505; Suarez, *De Remotione Parochorum,* n. 14; Meier, *Adm. Proc. Ag. Neglig. Pastors,* pp. 111-112.

example, if the guilty one has perfectly amended himself and has repaired all scandal the superior may omit the punishment. Again, if there are circumstancs which notably lessen imputability, the superior may impose a less severe penalty, etc.[33] This last interpretation of the matter in question certainly seems to be the more acceptable one. It must be added that removal by the Ordinary, when it takes place, is an administrative act. No formal trial is necessary. Recourse may be taken to the Holy See against the decree of removal, but it would be merely *in devolutivo,* not *in suspensivo.*[34] The advice of the cathedral chapter (or diocesan consultors) must be sought by the Ordinary previous to the removal.[35]

If the Ordinary deems it right he may also impose other fitting penalties upon the guilty official. However, these other penalties may only be inflicted *servatis servandis.* In the present instance this phrase means that it would be necessary for the Ordinary to observe a formal judicial procedure, for such is the procedure to be followed in inflicting penalties, unless the law states otherwise.[36] What these other penalties are to be is left to the prudent judgment of the Ordinary, who should be guided in forming his judgment by the norms set down in canon 2218, § 1.

Finally, if any damage or injury has resulted from the violation of the oath of secrecy, the guilty party is obliged to make fitting reparation. This obligation arises from the natural law itself and exists whether court action is instituted for the recovery of damages or not, unless the silence of the party injured clearly indicates a condoning of the offense.[37] However, if the guilty party does not spontaneously make amends for the damage caused, then court action may be taken. The case may not be settled in an administrative way, but only judicially.[38] It must follow the rules laid down for a criminal procedure in canons 1933 ff. The injured party has the right to

[33] Cf. canon 2223.

[34] Canon 192, § 3.

[35] Canon 388.

[36] Noval, *De Processibus,* II, n. 505.

[37] Noval, *op. cit.,* II, n. 505; Augustine, *Commentary,* VII, 407.

[38] Noval, *op. cit.,* n. 505; Augustine, *op. cit.,* VII, 408; Meier, *Adm. Proc. Ag. Neglig. Pastors,* p. 113.

denounce the guilty official (canon 1935, § 1), or the denunciation may even be made *ex officio,* if there is question of a grave injury or defamation suffered by a cleric or a religious, or caused by a cleric or a religious (canon 1938, § 2). However, it is always the promoter of justice who actually initiates the criminal action or accusation (canon 1934). It is possible for the Ordinary to avoid a criminal trial by persuading the parties concerned to settle the matter by means of a *transactio* (canons 1925-1928), or by a *compromissum in arbitros* (canons 1929-1932).

> **Canon 2145, § 1: In iis processibus summarie procedendum est; at duo vel tres testes, sive ex officio arcessiti sive a parte inducti audiri non prohibentur, nisi Ordinarius, auditis parochis consultoribus seu examinatoribus, existimaverit partes eos inducere ad moras nectendas.**

In these processes the procedure is to be summary. However, two or three witnesses may be heard at the instance of the party concerned, or even *ex officio,* unless the Ordinary, upon consultation with the parish priest consultors or the synodal examiners, should feel that the witnesses are asked for merely to delay matters.[89]

The part of this canon which is of interest here is that which refers to the obligation of the Ordinary to consult the examiners or consultors. There are several difficulties connected with this particular precept of the law which will be taken up in order. The first of these may be expressed as follows: is the Ordinary given freedom to consult either the examiners or the consultors? The solution to this problem is that he must hear those officials, whether examiners or consultors, who have a part in the procedure, when there is question of a procedure which requires the intervention of only examiners, or only consultors. When it is a procedure in which both classes of officials have a part, then the examiners must be heard if the case has not progressed to the stage where the consultors are brought in. But if the consultors have entered the case, then they must be heard,

[89] For the law previous to the Code, cf. *supra,* pp. 64-65.

and not the examiners. Of course, it is only the examiners, or consultors, as the case may be, who have been chosen for the case that are consulted, not any examiners, or any consultors indiscriminately.[40] This answer is verified by the interpretation (which will be studied later) of a similar question. In canon 2154 the law requires that the Ordinary consult the examiners or consultors who had a part in the removal proceedings, when he makes provision for the pastor who has been removed. As will be seen, the more commonly accepted interpretation of this canon is that the examiners are to be consulted if they alone had a part in the procedure, but the consultors are the ones to be heard if they were called into the case.

A second question may be formulated in this fashion: are the examiners, or consultors, as the case may be, to be consulted only if the Ordinary desires to refuse witnesses presented by the accused? Or must he hear them even if he decides to admit the witnesses? There are some who say that the counsel of these officials must be had whenever there is a question of either admitting or rejecting the witnesses.[41] The more common opinion,[42] however, holds that there is no necessity for consultation unless the Ordinary should wish to reject the proposed witnesses. Suarez [43] defends this position with convincing arguments. The first of these looks to the very words of the law: *"at duo vel tres testes . . . audire non prohibentur, nisi Ordinarius, auditis parochis consultoribus seu examinatoribus, existimaverit partes eos inducere ad moras nectendas."* The words following *nisi* indicate the circumstances in which it will be necessary to hear the consultors or examiners. These circumstances are verified

[40] Suarez, *De Remotione Parochorum,* n. 17. Other authors implicitly admit this solution when in their commentaries on relative canons in the various procedures they explicitly state just which of these classes of officials must be heard, *e.g.*, Connor, *Adm. Removal of Pastors,* p. 109 and p. 118; Meier, *Adm. Proc. Ag. Neglig. Pastors,* p. 116.

[41] Vermeersch-Creusen, *Epitome,* III, n. 345; Fanelli, *La Procedura Canonica nei Processi Amministrativi e Penali* (Vicenza: Societá Anonima Tipografica, 1936), p. 19.

[42] Suarez, *De Remotione Parochorum,* n. 61; Woywod, "Procedural Law of the Code"—*HPR,* XXXV (1935), 398; Connor, *Adm. Removal of Pastors,* p. 93; Beste, *Introductio,* p. 854; Meier, *op. cit.,* pp. 116-117.

[43] *Op. cit.,* n. 61.

when the Ordinary has a suspicion that the witnesses were introduced merely to cause delay. In such circumstances he must call the examiners or consultors together and hear them on the question. Then according to his conviction he should, or should not, reject the witnesses. Suarez adds that there is definitely a difference in the two situations, which would explain the consulting of the examiners or consultors in one instance and the omission of any consultation in the other. In the instance where the Ordinary feels that witnesses should be admitted there is no harm done to the pastor in question, nor is there any special favor being granted him. Therefore there is no special reason why the Ordinary should consult others. On the other hand, however, if the witnesses proposed are rejected, without any consultation of others, it is possible that the Ordinary is doing an injustice to the party concerned, for example, a pastor who is being deprived of the means to prove that his ministry has not been harmful or inefficacious. Consequently, in order to preclude any injustice, the law orders that others should be heard before the Ordinary rejects any or all of the witnesses proposed by the accused.

The Code refers in canon 2145 to witnesses in the strict sense, that is, witnesses who give testimony on some matter they know by some external sense, not to mere character witnesses. Experts are included under the classification of witnesses. These latter are required at times, for example, to prove the permanency of a pastor's infirmity.[44] Canons 1756-1758 may well be consulted as a norm for the admission of witnesses, though there is no obligation upon the Ordinary to follow them.[45] The number "two or three" which the Code speaks of should not be interpreted strictly. More may be admitted if the Ordinary feels they are necessary. The desire of the law is that there be no more witnesses than are necessary, first because these procedures should be as expeditious as possible, and secondly because the very matter of these procedures may give rise to scandal. As to the possibility of scandal, if there were admitted more witnesses than necessary the danger would be unnecessarily increased

[44] Noval, *De Processibus,* II, n. 507; Connor, *Adm. Removal of Pastors,* p. 94; Meier, *Adm. Proc. Ag. Neglig. Pastors,* p. 115.

[45] Augustine, *Commentary,* VII, 408; Meier, *op. cit.,* pp. 114-115.

of a revelation of matters pertaining to the procedure. Such a revelation would frequently be the source of scandal.[46]

Canon 2145 states that witnesses are to be rejected by the Ordinary, after consultation with the consultors or examiners, if the Ordinary should consider that they have been introduced merely to cause delays. This is the only reason why the Ordinary may refuse to admit witnesses, otherwise an injustice might be done to the person trying to defend himself. If the reasons, *e. g.*, for the removal of a pastor, are so notorious that they need no proof, if the publicity and notoriety of the facts are so perfectly well-known and proved that no further proof is needed, then the Ordinary may, after the required consultation, refuse to admit the witnesses. In such circumstances witnesses would merely cause an unnecessary delay in the proceedings.[47]

Still another question arises in connection with this canon, a question, indeed, which comes up very frequently in connection with the law on administrative procedures. It is the question of whether, or not, the consulting of the examiners or parish priest consultors is necessary for validity. The answer to this question involves the interpretation which one gives to canon 105, 1°. This question has already been treated elsewhere in this work,[48] and the conclusion advanced, in accord with the common, or at least far more probable, opinion, is that the consultation is necessary for validity. However, as has been pointed out, there does exist a probable opinion to the contrary which makes for the existence of a doubt of law, *dubium iuris*. Therefore, in accord with canons 15 and 209 there need be no anxiety about the validity of acts placed contrary to canon 105, 1° (*i. e.*, when no consultation was had). As regards the future placing of acts the strict interpretation should be followed, but it cannot be forced upon anyone in view of the probability of the opposite opinion.

There are some canons (2152, 2153, 2159, 2165) which actually

[46] Cf. *supra*, p. 65; Noval, *op. cit.*, II, n. 583; Suarez, *De Remotione Parochorum*, n. 17; Connor, *op. cit.*, p. 93; Vermeersch-Creusen, *Epitome*, III, n. 345; Meier, *op. cit.*, pp. 115-116.

[47] Woywod, "Procedural Law of the Code"—*HPR*, XXXV (1935), 161.

[48] Cf. *supra*, pp. 92-93.

add an express phrase to the effect that the Ordinary must hear the examiners, or consultors as the case may be, *for valid action.* Vermeersch-Creusen [49] use this as a proof of their contention that where an express statement to this effect is missing, the hearing of others is required only for licitness, not for validity. This contention, however, need not necessarily be accepted, and in fact is not convincing. The meaning of canon 105, 1° seems perfectly clear, and it may be held that the Code adds the express statement in the few canons referred to merely *claritatis sensu* or *ad maiorem firmitatem praescriptis tribuendam.*[50] There is, however, one important conclusion which must be noted when there is present in a canon an express nullifying clause. There can be no question whatsoever concerning the invalidity of actions placed contrary to such a canon. In canons 2159 and 2165 there is definitely present such a nullifying clause regarding the consultation. In canons 2152 and 2153, however, it is not certain whether the nullifying clause refers to the consultation or not. The present writer thinks that it does because of parallelism with canons 2159 and 2165.[51]

Whatever may be the correct interpretation of this much debated question of the validity of acts placed contrary to the prescriptions of canon 105, 1°, it is certain that the Ordinary is not obliged to follow the opinion of his counsellors, even though it be unanimous. Still, he should not differ from their unanimous opinion without reason. This is the warning of the law itself in canon 105, 2°.

Article 2. Duties of the Synodal Examiners and Parish Priest Consultors in the Administrative Removal of Irremovable Pastors

Title XXVII of the Code of Canon Law (canons 2147-2156) treats of the removal of irremovable pastors. Besides the legislation on the actual removal, it includes also legislation on the provision for pastors who are removed (canons 2154-2155). The concern of

[49] *Epitome,* III, nn. 350; 352, 3; 353, 4; 359, 2; 363, 3.

[50] Suarez, *De Remotione Parochorum,* n. 64.

[51] Suarez, *op. cit.,* nn. 64; 70; 100; 120.

this study is only with those parts of this legislation which have to do with either the synodal examiners or the parish priest consultors.[52]

> Canon 2148, § 1: Quoties, prudenti Ordinarii iudicio, in unam ex causis de quibus in can. 2147 parochus incidisse videatur, ipsemet Ordinarius, auditis duobus examinatoribus et veritate gravitateque causae cum eis discussa, parochum scripto vel oretenus ad paroeciae renuntiationem intra certum tempus faciendam invitet, nisi agatur de parocho vitio mentis laborante.
>
> § 2: Invitatio ut acta valeant, continere debet causam quae Ordinarium movet et argumenta quibus ipsa innititur.

Whenever the Ordinary prudently judges that there is present in regard to a particular pastor a cause for removal (*cf.* canon 2147) he must, after hearing two synodal examiners and discussing with them the truth and the gravity of the cause, invite the pastor to resign his parish within a certain specified time. No invitation is necessary if the pastor is mentally unsound. The invitation may be given in writing or orally. In order that the acts may be valid, this invitation must contain the cause which moves the Ordinary to take this step, and the arguments which have convinced him of the existence of the cause.

Once the Ordinary feels that one of the causes for removal mentioned in canon 2147 is present in regard to a pastor he must first of all call in two examiners to discuss the matter. This is required even if the cause be insanity.[53] The former legislation required that he take the two examiners who enjoyed seniority,[54] but in the present

[52] For a very complete study in English of this particular administrative procedure, as well as of the succeeding procedure, cf. Connor, *Adm. Removal of Pastors.*

[53] Coronata, *Institutiones,* III, n. 1585. Whereas in the new law mere consultation is required, the old law required that the Ordinary have the consent of the examiners before he might proceed to the invitation. Cf. *supra,* pp. 62-63.

[54] S. C. Consist., decr., *Maxima cura,* 20 aug. 1910, can. 5, § 1—*Fontes,* n. 2074. Cf. *supra,* p. 54.

law the Ordinary is free to choose any two of the synodal examiners whom he may desire.[55] The number to be chosen is two. Neither more nor less are permitted.[56] The Ordinary should, of course, avoid selecting as examiners those who may be considered as under suspicion because of friendship or enmity, or those who might have a personal interest in the removal or non-removal of the pastor. The decree, *"Maxima cura,"* [57] gave the pastor the right to take exception to an examiner whom the Ordinary had chosen. This should still be considered as an existent right, for, as it seems, it is really a right given by the natural law. Any man should be permitted to take exception to one who is to have a part in a judgment which will possibly be rendered against him, even if the part be only a consultive one, and if he can prove that his exception is founded on good reasons, the official should be removed. Consequently, though the law does not make explicit mention of this right of exception, it should be considered as still enjoyed by the pastor.[58]

When the examiners are called by the Ordinary they should take the oath of secrecy before entering upon any of their duties. This oath is to be taken before the Ordinary, and the notary should also be present to record the fact in the acts.[59]

For the discussion on the existence and the gravity of the cause the examiners are to be called not singly, but together. This is evident from canon 105, 2°. The Ordinary then reveals to them all the pertinent facts in the case. He should conceal nothing which has a bearing on the case. All writings and every argument which prove, or appear to prove, the existence of a sufficient cause for removal should be brought forth. This is an evident requisite of the law, for otherwise how could they give the advice that the law

[55] Noval, *De Processibus,* II, n. 564; Suarez, *De Remotione Parochorum,* n. 46; Connor, *Adm. Removal of Pastors,* p. 96.

[56] Fanfani, *De Iure Parochorum,* n. 139, A. The old law was the same, cf. above, p. 62.

[57] S. C. Consist., 20 aug. 1910, can. 5, § 2—*Fontes,* n. 2074. Cf. *supra,* pp. 55-56.

[58] Muñiz, *Procedimientos Eclesiásticos* (2. ed., 3 vols. Sevilla: Lib. de. Sobrino de Izquierdo), I, n. 640. In disagreement with this opinion are Wernz-Vidal, *Ius Canonicum,* VI, n. 749.

[59] Suarez, *De Remotione Parochorum,* n. 46.

demands? [60] As is quite logical, if the Ordinary is to reveal the facts to the examiners, he must beforehand have made a careful investigation of the whole matter. In this way only would he have sufficient reason even to take up the case.[61]

Great care must be taken by the Ordinary that he leave the examiners complete freedom to express their opinion. To this end, therefore, he should not so express himself that these officials know full well that his mind is absolutely set on what he is going to do. Briefly, he should so set forth the case and so act that the examiners are given but one impression, namely, that the Ordinary really is seeking their counsel on the matter, that he wishes to have their help in order that he may be better able to make up his mind.[62] Indeed this should in all truth be the real mind of the Ordinary. The Code itself warns him that he should not disagree, without strong reason, from the unanimous opinion of his counsellors.[63]

The object of the discussion is to see whether the cause for removal, as alleged by the Ordinary, really does exist and whether it is grave enough, sufficiently serious, to warrant removal from the parochial office. After the discussion the examiners will give their vote, which is, of course, consultive, not decisive. According to the opinion expressed above,[64] the hearing of the examiners is necessary for validity.

It is possible that the examiners may feel that the proofs for the existence of a grave cause are not sufficient. In such a case they may ask the Ordinary to gather further evidence. The Ordinary is not held to follow such advice, but if he does it would be necessary to recall the examiners for a second consultation when the new evidence has been obtained. This recalling would be required even if the Ordinary himself, and not the examiners, concluded that more proof was necessary.[65]

[60] Noval, *De Processibus,* II, n. 565; Suarez, *op. cit.,* n. 46; Connor, *Adm. Removal of Pastors,* p. 96.

[61] Woywod, "Procedural Law of the Code"—*HPR,* XXXV (1935), 391-392; Beste, *Introductio,* p. 858.

[62] Noval, *op. cit.,* n. 565; Suarez, *op. cit.,* n. 46; Connor, *op. cit.,* p. 96.

[63] Canon 105, 1°.

[64] Cf. *supra,* pp. 157-158.

[65] Suarez, *De Remotione Parochorum,* n. 47.

In canon 10, § 3, of the decree, "*Maxima cura,*" it was stated[66] that if there was question of an occult crime the invitation to resign, if made in writing, should allege only some general cause as being the reason for removal. Later when the pastor appeared in person, the Ordinary was to make known to him orally and in the presence of an examiner, who was to act as notary, the specific cause and the specific proofs that this cause was really present. This prescript of the former law may, according to some authors,[67] be considered as not contrary to the Code, and as still applicable. As Connor remarks,[68] an unscrupulous pastor might on the strength of a document which contains mention of an occult crime prosecute the Ordinary in a civil court for defamation of character. It should, it seems, be remarked that even if this point of legislation is to be considered as still in effect, nevertheless it is no longer necessary that an examiner should act as notary, since the procedure itself now calls for a notary to record the acts of the case. This point is not made by those who refer to the matter. They leave the impression that even now the Ordinary should select one of the examiners for the purpose.

Once the consultation has been concluded the examiners must sign the acts which the notary has drawn up as a record of the consultation.[69]

Canon 2152, § 1: Rationes a parocho contra invitationem adductas Ordinarius, ut valide agat, auditis iisdem examinatoribus de quibus in can. 2148, § 1, perpendat, approbet aut reiiciat.

If the pastor should give reasons why he should not resign, the Ordinary, in order to act validly, must, after taking counsel with the same examiners as those mentioned in canon 2148, § 1, consider, approve or reject the pastor's reasons.

At times a pastor will feel that the cause alleged by the Ordinary

[66] Cf. *supra,* p. 63.

[67] Ferreres, *Institutiones Canonicae,* II, n. 901; Augustine, *Commentary,* VII, 421-422.

[68] *Adm. Removal of Pastors,* p. 99.

[69] Cf. canon 2142. Also, cf. *supra,* p. 147.

in the invitation is not true, or he will be convinced that it is not sufficiently grave to warrant his removal from office. In such a case he has the right to refuse the invitation to resign and instead to defend himself by presenting arguments to prove his own convictions. The arguments he will give either in writing or orally,[70] and he may also present documentary evidence.[71] He is even allowed to present witnesses, though the Ordinary may, after consulting the examiners, reject these as being proposed merely to cause delays.[72]

In connection with an oral defense, or with oral testimony by witnesses, there arises a question as to whether or not the examiners have a right to be present during these oral depositions, or again whether they may be present. Augustine answers in a rather vague manner saying that "the examiners should, or at least may, be present when the oral defense is made." [73] However, it does not seem that such a procedure is either ordered or contemplated in the present law. Canon 2152, § 1, merely states that the Ordinary is to hear the examiners on the reasons which have been brought forth (*"allatas"*). Other authors who write on this subject make no mention whatsoever of the examiners being present at the oral depositions.[74] Woywod, in fact, writes: [75] "After the closing of the defense presented by the pastor and his witnesses, the Ordinary is to call the two examiners. . . ." Suarez [76] speaks of the pastor giving his arguments orally before the Ordinary and the notary, of the witnesses being heard, of documents being presented, and then he adds: *"his omnibus iam habitis, Ordinarius iterum audiat examinatores prius in invitatione iam auditos."* In view of the fact that more should not be added to the law than is actually there, and because of the silence of authors of note (when they would hardly be silent if the opposite

[70] Suarez, *De Remotione Parochorum,* n. 63.

[71] Connor, *Adm. Removal of Pastors,* p. 111.

[72] Canon 2145, § 1. Cf. *supra,* pp. 155-157.

[73] *Commentary,* VII, 427. Coronata (*Institutiones,* III, n. 1588) makes the very same statement, giving Augustine as his reference.

[74] Noval, *De Processibus,* II, n. 580; Suarez, *op. cit.,* n. 63; Woywod, "Procedural Law of the Code"—*HPR,* XXXV (1935), 398; Connor, *op. cit.,* pp. 110-111.

[75] *Ibidem,* p. 398.

[76] *Op. cit.,* n. 63.

opinion was correct), it should be concluded that the examiners need not and should not be present at the oral defense of the pastor, or at the giving of testimony by witnesses.

Suarez [77] maintains that according to the wording of the canon, the Ordinary would, strictly speaking, be obliged to consult the examiners only on the defense made by the pastor, and not on depositions by witnesses or on other proofs when these were gotten *ex officio*. This author, however, then goes on to say that nevertheless the prudent thing for the Ordinary to do is to submit all the evidence in the case to the examiners, first of all in order that the latter may be able to reach a complete judgment as the basis of their counsel to the Ordinary, and secondly because even *ex officio* evidence may be considered as having been adduced at least indirectly by the pastor himself. It seems that when one considers the quite evident mind of the legislator, namely, that the examiners give their counsel to the Ordinary, and when one adds the reasons alleged by Suarez for the prudent procedure of the Ordinary, one is rather led to the conclusion that the law itself demands that all the evidence be submitted to the examiners. If one were to hold the view of Suarez it would be equivalent to an admission that the strict sense of the law is that the examiners must give their counsel to the Ordinary on the question of whether the cause may still be considered as existent and as sufficiently serious to warrant the removal of the pastor, even though the Ordinary is not bound to reveal to them all the facts in the case. The correct conclusion, therefore, is that the Ordinary must reveal all the evidence to the examiners. This he will do, not by a mere oral explanation of the facts in the case, but by submitting the acts of the case which have been drawn up by the notary.

The examiners whom the Ordinary must consult are the same two as were previously consulted in the case.[78] However, it may occur at times that the same examiners cannot be heard, because, for example, one or both are dead, sick, have been called away, etc. What is to be done in such an instance? No one is held to the im-

[77] *Op. cit.*, n. 63. Coronata, quoting Suarez, holds the same opinion—*op. cit.*, n. 1588.

[78] Canon 2152, § 1.

possible, and consequently the Ordinary will make a substitution.[79] Still, this law should be considered as very strict and no Ordinary should consider that substitutions may be made for any slight reason. The law has a reason for demanding the same two examiners, which is the fact that they are already acquainted with the case and are therefore better able to counsel the Ordinary. This purpose of the law is not to be contemned.

The examiners will consider whether or not the reasons alleged by the pastor (including documentary evidence and testimony from witnesses) are sufficient to prove that the cause for removal is either non-existent or is not sufficiently serious (*i. e.,* whether it renders the pastor's ministry in the parish harmful or inefficacious) to warrant removal from office. According to their opinion they will advise the Ordinary.[80] At times the examiners may suggest the gathering of further evidence, or the Ordinary himself may determine on this procedure. In such a case, the examiners are to be recalled when the new evidence has been obtained. Once the Ordinary has received the consultive vote of the officials the notary will record the fact and the nature of the vote. The acts will then be signed by the Ordinary, the examiners and the notary.[81]

It has already been pointed out sufficiently what opinion is held in this work in regard to the necessity of the consultation for the validity of the procedure.[82]

Canon 2153, § 1: Contra decretum amotionis potest parochus intra decem dies recursum interponere apud eundem Ordinarium, qui, ne invalide agat, debet, auditis duobus parochis consultoribus, novas allegationes ab eodem parocho intra decem dies ab interposito recursu producendas, simul cum rationibus primo allatis, examinare, approbare aut reiicere.

[79] Coronata, *Institutiones,* III, n. 1588.

[80] In the law of the decree, "*Maxima cura,*" the examiners had a decisive vote. Now, however, they possess merely a consultive vote. Cf. *supra,* p. 67.

[81] Coronata, *op. cit.,* n. 1588; Suarez, *De Remotione Parochorum,* n. 65. Cf. also *supra,* p. 147.

[82] Cf. *supra,* pp. 157-158.

Within ten days after the decree of removal, the pastor may have recourse to the same Ordinary against the decision. For the validity of the proceedings, the Ordinary must, in consultation with two of the parish priest consultors, examine, approve or reject the new allegations made by the pastor together with the reasons he advanced in the first stage of the procedure. The pastor must produce the new proofs within ten days after recourse.

An irremovable pastor has the right to lodge a recourse against the decree of removal which followed the rejection of his first defense.[83] The law grants him a period of ten days within which he may bring forth new proofs against the truth of the cause alleged for removal, or against the seriousness of this cause.[84] It is not necessary, however, that the pastor adduce new proofs, or that he present witnesses who could not have been called upon previously.[85] He may simply ask that the reasons which he formerly brought forth be again examined.[86] Indeed he may even allege that there was some substantial defect in the previous acts of the procedure.[87] It will avail the pastor little to have recourse if his only complaint is against a defect in form, because the Ordinary can very simply remedy such a defect.[88] In fact, even when recourse is taken to the Holy See because of a defect in form, if a sufficiently grave cause is proved from the acts, the Holy See is accustomed to sanate any defects of form and to refuse to sustain the recourse.[89]

When the new defense of the pastor has been completed, the Ordinary must select two parish consultors to discuss the case with him. He is perfectly free in his choice of officials, but may not select more or less than two.[90]

[83] Cf. canons 2152; 2153, § 1.

[84] Canon 2153, § 1. In the law before the Code the pastor was granted recourse against the decree of removal, but this recourse differed considerably from the recourse of the present law. Cf. *supra*, pp. 69-71.

[85] Coronata, *Institutiones*, III, n. 1589.

[86] Suarez, *De Remotione Parochorum*, n. 69; Connor, *Adm. Removal of Pastors*, p. 117.

[87] Suarez, *op. cit.*, n. 69; Beste, *Introductio*, p. 861.

[88] Beste, *op. cit.*, p. 861.

[89] Cf. Suarez, *op. cit.*, n. 24.

[90] Cf. *supra*, pp. 159-160.

The law, in requiring these particular officials, really does provide well for the protection of the pastor. They themselves are pastors and as such may be considered to be most competent to judge another pastor, to say whether or not his ministry has become harmful or inefficacious in his parish and to give counsel to the Ordinary.[91] These parish priest consultors are given a consultive vote, not a decisive one. Following the opinion already expressed in this work, it is necessary for validity that the Ordinary consult these officials.[92]

The Ordinary must make known all the facts in the case to the consultors. He must acquaint them with the facts not only of the pastor's second defense, but also with those of the first defense.[93] It is not sufficient that the consultors hear the facts from the Ordinary. Rather, they should read them for themselves in the acts of the case.[94] As always in cases of necessary consultation, the Ordinary must leave the officials complete freedom to express their opinion.[95] It is possible that the consultors may suggest the gathering of further evidence. If the Ordinary should accept this suggestion, or if he should do so of his own accord, it will be necessary to have another discussion of the whole matter.[96] When the consultation is completed the Ordinary, the consultors and the notary will sign the acts concerning this meeting which the latter has drawn up.[97]

Canon 2154, § 1: Amoto parocho Ordinarius, examinatoribus vel parochis consultoribus, qui partem habuerunt in amotione decernenda, in consilium adscitis, pro viribus consulat sive translatione ad aliam paroeciam vel assignatione alius officii aut beneficii, si ad haec idoneus sit, sive pensione, prout casus ferat et adiuncta permittant.

[91] Noval, *De Processibus,* II, n. 582; Suarez, *De Remotione Parochorum,* n. 70.

[92] Cf. *supra,* pp. 157-158.

[93] Canon 2153, § 1. Cf. Connor, *Adm. Removal of Pastors,* p. 117. Cf. also above, p. 164.

[94] Noval, *op. cit.,* n. 582; cf. *supra,* p. 164.

[95] Cf. *supra,* p. 161.

[96] Cf. *supra,* p. 161.

[97] Cf. canon 2142; also *supra,* p. 147.

§ 2: Ceteris paribus, in provisione favendum magis renuntianti quam amoto.

After a pastor has been removed, the Ordinary shall consult the examiners or the parish priest consultors who took part in the proceedings of removal, and carefully decide what provision should be made for the pastor. According to the facts and circumstances of the case, the provision will take the form of a transfer to another parish, or of an assignment to some other office or benefice, if the priest be fitted for these, or finally of a pension. All other things being equal, a pastor who resigns is to receive more favorable consideration in this provision than a pastor who was removed.[98]

The first reading of this canon might lead one to think that the Ordinary is left free to choose either the examiners or the consultors, as his counsellors, in the matter of the provision for the pastor who is removed. Evidently this is not the case if the pastor accepted the invitation to resign, or if he refused or neglected to make a recourse, for in such circumstances only the two examiners would have had *partem . . . in amotione decernenda.* But there are some authors who give this freedom of choice to the Ordinary in their interpretation of the canon in the event that both types of officials have entered the case.[99] Most authors,[100] however, hold that the new law should be interpreted in the light of the pre-Code law of the decree, "*Maxima cura,*"[101] and that therefore the consultors must be heard if they had any part in the procedure. Otherwise it is the examiners who must be consulted. Since there is a doubt whether the old law is the same as the new, and since this doubt is founded on the words

[98] This canon 2154, § 1, is taken almost verbatim from the law of the "*Maxima cura.*" Cf. *supra,* p. 68.

[99] Coronata, *Institutiones,* III, n. 1593; Vermeersch-Creusen, *Epitome,* III, n. 345.

[100] Ferreres, *Institutiones Canonicae,* II, n. 911; Noval, *De Processibus,* II, n. 585; Suarez, *De Remotione Parochorum,* n. 76; Augustine, *Commentary,* VII, 430; Woywod, "Procedural Law of the Code"—*HPR,* XXXV (1935), 400; Beste, *Introductio,* p. 861; Connor, *Adm. Removal of Pastors,* pp. 126-127.

[101] Canon 26, § 2: *In provisionis assignatione Ordinarius examinatores, vel parochos consultores si usque ad eos causa pervenerit, audire ne omittat.* Cf. *supra,* p. 68.

of the canon itself of the new law, it follows according to canon 6, 4° that the old law is to be the accepted interpretation of the new law. In reality this seems the only justifiable solution, because if the consultors have been called into the procedure they would know more about the case than the examiners and thus would be better qualified to give counsel in the question of provision for the pastor who has been removed. Usually more evidence is brought forth in the recourse.[102]

The examiners or consultors whom the Ordinary is to consult must be the same ones who had taken part in previous proceedings in the case.[103] If it is impossible to have the same ones, then it is obviously necessary that the Ordinary substitute other examiners or consultors, and in this case he should acquaint the substitutes with the facts in the case.[104] It is not necessary that the business of providing for the pastor should take place at the same time as the final decree of removal is given, but at the same time it should not be delayed any longer than necessary. In fact, canon 2155 states that if it is not taken care of at the time of removal, it should be completed as soon as possible. It is hardly necessary to repeat again that counsel only is required, not the consent of the examiners, or consultors. This consultation, though, is necessary for validity, according to the more accepted opinion.[105]

As to the actual consultation, the Ordinary is obliged to seek the advice of the examiners or consultors merely in reference to the general character of the provision that should be made for the priest who has been removed from his parish.[106] Thus, the discussion will center about such questions as whether the pastor would be capable, or not, of exercising a fruitful and beneficial ministry in another parish, whether he would be at least suited for some other office, such as that of assistant pastor, or chaplain, or professor, or for some other benefice, or finally whether it would be best to provide for him by

102 Cf. Suarez, *op. cit.*, n. 76.

103 Canon 2145, § 1: *"qui partem habuerunt in amotione decernenda."*

104 Suarez, *op. cit.*, n. 76; cf. also *supra*, pp. 164-165.

105 Cf. *supra*, pp. 157-158.

106 Suarez, *op. cit.*, n. 76; Coronata, *op. cit.*, III, n. 1593; Connor, *op. cit.*, p. 127.

means of a pension.[107] The usual procedure is for the Ordinary to suggest some provision and then the counsellors give their opinion on this suggestion.[108]

Article 3. Duties of the Synodal Examiners in the Administrative Removal of Removable Pastors

A removable pastor may be removed from his parish for a just and grave reason as explained in canon 2147 [109] (*i. e.*, for a reason which, even though the pastor be blameless, renders his ministry in the parish harmful or at least inefficacious). The causes for the removal of removable pastors must be grave and the proofs sufficient, but still they need not be quite as grave and serious as for the removal of irremovable pastors.[110] It is interesting to note that in the administrative procedure for the removal of removable pastors there is a canon somewhat similar to canon 2148, § 1, of the preceding process, yet one that is quite different as far as the synodal examiners are concerned, for it eliminates the obligation on the part of the Ordinary to consult two synodal examiners before he may issue an invitation to the pastor to resign.[111]

Canon 2159: Firmo praescripto can. 2149, si parochus renuat, rationes in scriptis reddat, quas Ordinarius, ut valide procedat, perpendere debet una cum duobus examinatoribus.

If the pastor does not answer the invitation within the time fixed by the Ordinary, canon 2149 applies. If he replies that he refuses to resign, he shall state his reasons in writing, and these, for the

[107] Cf. Connor, *op. cit.*, p. 127.

[108] Suarez, *op. cit.*, n. 76.

[109] Canon 2157, § 1. There is no necessity to use this administrative procedure in the removal of *parochi amovibiles ad nutum*—Suarez, *De Remotione Parochorum*, n. 89. In the case of the removal of religious pastors canon 454, § 5 is to be followed, not this administrative procedure—canon 2157, § 2.

[110] Noval, *De Processibus*, II, n. 596; cf. also Coronata, *Institutiones*, III, n. 1595.

[111] Cf. canon 2158.

validity of the proceedings, the Ordinary must discuss with two synodal examiners.

When a removable pastor has received an invitation to resign he has the right in law to offer reasons in writing why he should not be removed. He may even offer witnesses in his defense.[112] The whole object of the pastor's defense is to refute the reasons alleged in the invitation, to show that the cause for removal either does not exist or is not serious enough to warrant removal from office.[113] Once this defense has been made the Ordinary is obliged to call in two synodal examiners for the purpose of discussing with them the reasons and arguments which constitute the defense of the pastor and of seeking their advice as to whether the cause may still be considered as proved and as sufficiently serious to warrant removal.[114]

It would be quite superfluous to repeat here what has already been said in connection with canons 2148 and 2152 as regards such questions as the freedom of the Ordinary in his choice of examiners, the right of the pastor to take exception to an appointee of the Ordinary, the necessity of a complete revelation of the facts in the case to the examiners, the nature and necessity of the vote of the examiners, etc. For a treatment of these questions the reader is referred to what has already been written.[115] It will be abundantly clear just what part of the comments made with regard to canons 2148 and 2152 should be applied to the present canon, *i. e.*, canon 2159. As to the oath which the examiners must take, the reader is referred to the commentary on canon 2144.[116]

A removable pastor is allowed but a single defense, whereas the irremovable pastor, as has been noted in treating of the preceding procedure, is always allowed a second opportunity to defend himself. Because of this fact there is required but one consultation of other officials by the Ordinary when the procedure is for the removal of a removable pastor. The officials to be consulted are two synodal

[112] Connor, *Adm. Removal of Pastors*, p. 122. Cf. *supra*, pp. 154 ff.

[113] Connor, *op. cit.*, p. 122.

[114] Canon 2159. Cf. Connor, *op. cit.*, p. 122.

[115] Cf. *supra*, pp. 159 ff. and pp. 162 ff.

[116] Cf. *supra*, pp. 147 ff.

examiners.[117] In this particular procedure the parish priest consultors are never to be used by the Ordinary.

Canon 2161, § 2: Parocho autem renuntianti aut amoto providere tenetur ad normam can. 2154-2156.

The Ordinary is obliged to provide for the resigning or removed pastor according to canons 2154-2156.

The duties of the synodal examiners in connection with the provision for the removed pastor (for it is the synodal examiners and not parish priest consultors who must be consulted) [118] have already been discussed.[119]

Article 4. Duties of the Parish Priest Consultors in the Administrative Transfer of Pastors

Title XXIX of Book IV in the Code of Canon Law sets forth the procedure to be followed in the transfer of pastors. This procedure, new with the Code,[120] is administrative, just as all the other procedures treated in Part III of Book IV, and its nature is non-penal.[121] Its object is the transfer to another parish of a pastor who is administering his parish satisfactorily when the good souls necessitates this.[122] There is no question here of a pastor whose ministry has become harmful or inefficacious. The pastor has, in fact, exercised a useful ministry in his parish. Now, however, the good of souls requires that he be moved to another parish where his ministry will prove even more useful. Briefly, it is the good of the parish to which the pastor is to be moved, not that of the parish from which he will be moved, which is considered.[123] The transfer considered in this

[117] Canon 2159.

[118] Suarez, *op. cit.*, n. 105. Cf. *supra*, pp. 168-169.

[119] Cf. *supra*, pp. 168-169.

[120] Ferreres, *Institutiones Canonicae*, II, nn. 925-926; Rossi, *De Paroecia*, n. 274; Coronata, *Institutiones*, III, n. 1600.

[121] Meier, *Adm. Proc. Ag. Neglig. Pastors*, p. 90.

[122] Canon 2162.

[123] Ferreres, *op. cit.*, II, n. 927; Rossi, *op. cit.*, n. 276; Noval, *De Processibus*, II, n. 606 et n. 610; Suarez, *De Remotione Parochorum*, n. 106; Augustine, *Commentary*, VII, 446; Coronata, *op. cit.*, n. 1600.

Title XXIX should not be confused with a voluntary exchange of benefices, concerning which canon 1487 treats. Nor should it be confused with a transfer made at the request of the pastor (cf. canons 193-195). The present procedure regards only instances where the transfer is made at the instance of the Ordinary, even though the pastor may willingly accept.[124]

Whenever it would be necessary or very useful for the good of souls that a pastor be changed, the law requires of the Ordinary who would make the transfer that he propose it to the pastor and that he persuade the pastor to consent to the change out of love for God and for souls.[125] An irremovable pastor not only has the right to refuse such an invitation but if he does refuse the Ordinary has no power to proceed to his transfer, unless he has obtained special faculties from the Holy See.[126] In the case of a removable pastor, however, the pastor may indeed refuse the Ordinary's invitation, but if he does he must explain in writing his reasons for refusal, for even though he be unwilling he may still be transferred so long as the parish to which he is being moved is not of too inferior a rank.[127]

Canon 2165: Ordinarius, si, non obstantibus allatis causis, iudicet a proposito non esse recedendum, debet, ut valide agat, super eisdem causis audire duos parochos consultores, et cum eisdem perpendere adiuncta in quibus versatur tum paroecia *a qua* tum paroecia *ad quam*, et rationes quae translationis utilitatem aut necessitatem suadent.

If, notwithstanding the reasons stated by the removable pastor, the Ordinary still intends to make the transfer, he must for valid action hear two parish priest consultors on the reasons advanced by the pastor, and discuss with them the circumstances of both the parish from which the pastor is to be moved and the parish to which

[124] Noval, *op. cit.*, n. 606; Suarez, *op. cit.*, n. 106.
[125] Canon 2162.
[126] Canon 2163, § 1.
[127] Canons 2163, § 2; 2164.

he is to be moved, and also the reasons which make the transfer of the pastor either useful or necessary.

The removable pastor who is unwilling to accept the invitation of the Ordinary should submit in writing to the Ordinary his reasons for not wanting to be transferred.[128] These reasons are then given consideration by the Ordinary. If it so happens that the latter, even after having considered the reasons of the pastor, should still feel convinced that the transfer ought to be made, he must call in two parish priest consultors. The synodal examiners take no part whatsoever in this procedure for the transfer of removable pastors. To these consultors he is obliged to make known (a) the reasons brought forth by the pastor, (b) the condition or state of both parishes, namely, the one now held by the pastor and the one to which he would be transferred, and (c) the reasons which seem to make the transfer either necessary or useful.[129] The parish priest consultors will then study these matters and give their advice, according to their judgment, as to whether they feel the transfer should or should not be made. Though the Ordinary is obliged *ad validitatem* to hear these consultors,[130] he is not bound to follow their advice, for canon 2165 requires the counsel of these officials, not their consent.

The consultors, in order to fulfill their task well, must study the reasons adduced by the pastor. These written reasons of the pastor are to be shown to the consultors, not merely explained orally by the Ordinary.[131] Do they prove that the pastor would not be able to exercise a more fruitful ministry for souls in the parish to which the Ordinary wishes to move him?[132] Again, the consultors must consider well the condition of the two parishes in question, for if the parish to which the pastor would be moved is too much inferior to the parish which he now holds, the consultors must point this out to the Ordinary and they must advise against the transfer. Canon 2163 clearly states that the removable pastor may be removed, even though he be unwilling, *"si paroecia ad quam non sit ordinis nimio inferi-*

[128] Canon 2164.

[129] Noval, *De Processibus*, II, n. 614.

[130] Cf. *supra*, pp. 157-158.

[131] Suarez, *op. cit.*, n. 120.

[132] Cf. Augustine, *Commentary*, VII, 447; Noval, *op. cit.*, n. 2164.

oris."[133] Finally, these officials are obliged to ponder well the reasons which the Ordinary himself proposes why the transfer should be made. These reasons must give evidence that the pastor would exercise a more useful ministry in the new parish, even though his ministry in his present parish has always been successful.[134]

Once the parish priest consultors have considered the abovementioned matters and once they have given their advice to the Ordinary their duties in this particular procedure cease. They are not called into the case again.

There are, of course, many other remarks which could be added here in connection with canon 2165, but it seems quite sufficient for a complete understanding of this canon to refer to what has already been written in commentary on parallel canons in the procedure for the removal of irremovable pastors. Under canon 2148 will be found statements on the freedom that the Ordinary enjoys in his choice of consultors, on the right of the pastor to take exception to a consultor chosen by the Ordinary, on the complete freedom to be given the consultors when their advice is asked, and, finally, on the possibility of these officials requesting further information.[135] On the question of the oath of secrecy to be taken by the consultors as soon as they enter the procedure reference should be had to the commentary on canon 2144,[136] while the question of the necessity on the part of the consultors to sign the acts of this stage of the procedure may be understood from the treatment of canon 2152.[137]

Article 5. Duties of the Synodal Examiners in the Penal Administrative Procedure Against Non-resident Clerics

Title XXX of Book IV of the Code of Canon Law gives the procedure to be followed in the application of penalties for the violation of the law of residence. It is a penal administrative procedure.[188] Residence is considered as merely material when the

[133] Augustine, *op. cit.*, VII, 447; Coronata, *Institutiones*, III, n. 1602.

[134] Noval, *op. cit.*, n. 2165.

[135] Cf. *supra*, pp. 159 ff.

[136] Cf. *supra*, pp. 147 ff.

[137] Cf. *supra*, p. 147.

[188] Wernz-Vidal, *Ius Canonicum*, VI, n. 777; Meier, *Adm. Proc. Ag. Neglig. Pastors*, p. 90.

beneficiary is present corporeally, but does not perform the duties incumbent upon him by reason of his benefice. It is formal when the beneficiary is not only actually present but also performs his duties. The present procedure looks to the punishment of the violation of material residence. The neglect of parochial duties is punishable according to the procedure in Title XXXII of Book IV.[139] With a few exceptions, all clerics who possess an office, benefice or dignity to which is attached an obligation of residence are subject to the procedure against non-resident clerics if they violate the law of residence.[140] Bishops and Cardinals are excepted from this procedure, for they are to be punished solely according to canon 1557. Those clerics who possess an office, dignity or benefice from which they may be removed *ad nutum* are also excluded.[141]

The first step in the procedure is a warning from the Ordinary to the cleric who has violated the law of residence. Any pastor, canon, or other cleric who violates the law of residence to which he is bound by reason of his benefice, shall be admonished by the Ordinary, who shall meanwhile, if there is question of a pastor, make provision at the expense of the pastor to prevent any detriment to the welfare of souls. In the admonition the Ordinary shall remind the offender of the penalties which clerics incur who do not comply with the law of residence, and also of the precept of canon 188, 8°, in accordance with which the benefice shall become vacant *ipso facto,* if he does not obey or answer the admonition; the Ordinary shall specify the period of time within which the cleric must resume residence.[142] If a cleric does not resume his residence within the specified time or give reasons for his absence, the Ordinary shall declare the parish or other benefice vacant; before issuing the declaration, he must,

[139] Noval, *De Processibus,* II, n. 619; Muñiz, *Procedimientos Eclesiásticos,* n. 663; Suarez, *De Remotione Parochorum,* n. 132; Reilly, *Residence of Pastors,* The Catholic University of America Canon Law Studies, n. 97 (Washington, D. C.: The Catholic University of America, 1935), p. 48. Wernz-Vidal (*op. cit.,* VI, n. 775) hold that the punishment of a violation of formal residence is the object of this penal administrative procedure.

[140] Cf. canons 2381; 2168, § 1.

[141] Noval, *op. cit.,* II, n. 619.

[142] Canon 2168.

however, observe the formalities of canon 2149.[143] If the cleric resumes residence, and if his absence has been illegitimate, the Ordinary is bound not only to punish him with deprivation of the income of the benefice for the time of his absence (as canon 2381 requires), but he may also, if the case calls for it, punish him with other penalties in proportion to his guilt.[144]

Canon 2171: Si clericus residentiam non instauret, sed absentiae causas afferat, Ordinarius, accitis duobus examinatoribus et institutis, si opus fuerit, opportunis investigationibus, videre debet num causae sint legitimae.

If the cleric does not resume residence but gives reasons for his absence, the Ordinary, after having called in two examiners and after having instituted any opportune investigations which may be necessary, shall consider whether the reasons are legitimate.

This is the first step in the procedure which calls for the use of the synodal examiners. The parish priest consultors have no part in the procedure. The cleric who is absent from his benefice or office has the right to offer to the Ordinary his reasons for his absence. If he does, the Ordinary may not immediately declare the parish, or benefice, vacant. He must first of all take cognizance of the excuses or reasons offered by the cleric, and he must also call in two synodal examiners in order to discuss with them these allegations of the cleric and to receive their advice as to whether these reasons prove that the cleric has a legitimate cause for his absence. The cleric may allege, for instance, that his absence is justified because the grave illness of a parent required his leaving without obtaining permission. Or again, he may send on testimony of a doctor as proof that his absence was necessitated by serious personal sickness.[145]

In their examination of the excuses offered by the cleric the synodal examiners must study whether the cause adduced is really

[143] Canon 2169.

[144] Canon 2170.

[145] Noval, *De Processibus,* II, n. 632; Suarez, *De Remotione Parochorum,* n. 151; Reilly, *Residence of Pastors,* p. 56.

sufficient to justify the absence. They must be careful to note whether the cleric could have asked for permission before leaving, because if this were possible then the absence certainly was illegitimate; and to learn whether the cleric neglected to notify the Ordinary of his absence as soon as he was able to do this.[146] At times it will be necessary for the Ordinary to make investigations in order that he may obtain confirmation of the truth of the cleric's statements. Canon 2171 gives the Ordinary the right to make any necessary investigations, for example, to inform himself on the health of the pastor.[147] If such investigations are made, the examiners must be notified of the results. Otherwise they would be giving counsel to the Ordinary without knowing the full facts in the case.[148] The cleric may also propose witnesses for his defense, or these may be called in *ex officio* by the Ordinary.[149] Evidence from such sources also should be made known to the examiners.

After they have considered the reasons of the cleric and all confirmatory evidence, the examiners give their opinion to the Ordinary as to whether they feel the reasons brought forth by the cleric are legitimate or not. The Ordinary, though bound *ad validitatem* to hear the examiners, is not held to follow their advice.[150]

Other considerations which are applicable to this canon have already been treated, such as, the Ordinary's freedom to choose whichever two examiners he may prefer, the right of the pastor to take exception to an appointee of the Ordinary, the complete freedom of discussion to be given the examiners by the Ordinary, the possibility of a request by the examiners for further investigation, the signing of the acts by the examiners.[151] The oath of secrecy to be taken by the examiners upon their entrance into the case has been considered in connection with canon 2144.[152]

[146] Suarez, *op. cit.*, n. 151.

[147] Wernz-Vidal, *Ius Canonicum*, VI, n. 778, nota 18; Suarez, *op. cit.*, n. 152.

[148] Wernz-Vidal, *op. cit.*, VI, n. 778; Suarez, *op. cit.*, n. 153. Noval, *op. cit.*, II, n. 629, and Reilly, *op. cit.*, p. 56, hold that the Ordinary is not obliged to hear the examiners on the results of these investigations.

[149] Suarez, *op. cit.*, n. 152. Cf. also *supra*, pp. 154 ff.

[150] Cf. *supra*, pp. 157-158.

[151] Cf. *supra*, pp. 159 ff.

[152] Cf. *supra*, pp. 147 ff.

Canon 2174, § 1: Si clericus, qui beneficium inamovibile obtinet, residentiam non instauret, sed novas alleget deductiones, Ordinarius eas cum eisdem examinatoribus ad examen revocet ad normam can. 2171.

If a cleric who holds an irremovable benefice does not resume residence, but alleges new reasons, the Ordinary shall examine these with the same examiners, according to the norm of canon 2171.

The two canons which intervene between canons 2171 and 2174 must be given here for an understanding of the new step in which the examiners participate. Canon 2172 states that if, after consultation with the examiners, the Ordinary judges that the reasons are not legitimate, he shall again give the cleric a specified interval within which he must return. Since his absence is declared illegitimate, he must be deprived of the income of his benefice for the time of his illegal absence. According to canon 2173, if a removable pastor [153] does not return to his parish within the prescribed time, the Ordinary may at once proceed to deprive him of the parish. If he returns, the Ordinary shall give him a precept not to leave his parish again without written permission under penalty of deprivation of the parish to be incurred *ipso facto*. From these canons, taken together with the present canon 2174, it is evident that a removable pastor is allowed but a single opportunity to prove the legitimacy of his absence, whereas a cleric who possesses an irremovable benefice, may propose new reasons, even though his first defense has been rejected.

The new reasons which the cleric may allege, for example, personal illness which has become worse, the necessity of remaining absent for a while longer due to the grave sickness of a parent, etc.[154] are to be discussed by the Ordinary with the same two examiners as were previously consulted in the procedure. It would, of course, be useless

[153] Canon 2173, in this part, refers also to all clerics who are bound by the law of residence, *ratione officii, beneficii vel dignitatis*. If, however, the benefice be an irremovable one, this canon is not applicable, but the Ordinary must proceed according to the following canon, *i. e.*, canon 2174. Cf. Suarez, *De Remotione Parochorum*, n. 157.

[154] Suarez, *op. cit.*, n. 160; Coronata, *Institutiones*, III, n. 1613; Reilly, *Residence of Pastors*, p. 61.

for the cleric to give the same reasons as he had previously brought forth.[155] As to the discussion, its object, the precise duties of the examiners, etc., canon 2174, § 1 itself states that canon 2171 is to be followed as a norm. Therefore what has been said above in commentary on canon 2171 in regard to the duties of the examiners applies also here.

Canon 2175: Neutro in casu Ordinarius beneficium vacans declaret, nisi postquam, perpensis una cum examinatoribus discessus rationibus quas clericus forte allegaverit, eiusdem Ordinarii licentiam in scriptis ab eodem clerico peti potuisse constiterit.

In neither case shall the Ordinary declare a benefice vacant, until he has discussed with the examiners the reasons which the cleric may have alleged for leaving the benefice, and has established the fact that the cleric could have asked the written permission of the same Ordinary.

This canon has reference to canon 2173 and to canon 2174 § 3. In the former it is stated that if the pastor *(amovibilis)* returns after receiving the warning from the Ordinary that his reasons have been rejected, the Ordinary will impose upon him the precept of not leaving his place of necessary residence without written permission, under threat of *ipso facto* loss of his parish. Canon 2174, § 3 demands that the same precept be given to a cleric who possesses an irremovable parish or benefice, in the case where the cleric returns after he has received word that his second presentation of excuse has been rejected. Canon 2175, therefore, means that if a cleric who has received such a precept should nevertheless leave his place of necessary residence without permission, the Ordinary should not immediately declare the benefice to be vacant; this he should do only after investigating with the examiners the reasons which the cleric may offer in his own defense for having left without first obtaining written permission, and further, even if the cleric offers no excuses, after discussing with the examiners the results of his own investigations, in order that he may judge, with their advice, that the cleric

[155] Cf. the same sources as in previous footnote.

actually could have obtained written permission before leaving.[156] It may very easily happen that the cleric had to leave suddenly for some reason or other.[157] In the case where the cleric himself offers no excuses the Ordinary will have to make his own investigations, for it may be that the cleric had no means of communication with the Ordinary, or that his letter was lost, or misplaced.[158] On the result of these investigations the Ordinary must consult the examiners. Perhaps the strict letter of the law would not require the Ordinary to consult the examiners on the results of these investigations, but certainly the sense of the law seems to impose this obligation. There is no reason why consultation should be required in the matter of the cleric's allegations and should not be required in this other matter. The same reason seems to demand consultation in both instances, namely, to help avert any possible mistake on the part of the Ordinary. What the law intends in this canon is that the Ordinary should consult the examiners before he proceeds to the serious matter of a declaration of vacancy.[159]

If the Ordinary should consider the reasons offered by the cleric to be legitimate, and should not intend to proceed to the declaration that the benefice, office or dignity is vacant, it appears that he is not held to hear the examiners. In other words, it would be only when he himself feels that the declaration of vacancy should be made that he would be obliged to hear the examiners.[160]

The examiners to be heard should be the same ones who had previously taken part in the proceedings.[161] The law does not explicitly say that they should be the same, but this may be deduced from the fact that in these administrative procedures the law usually requires the intervention of the same persons when the same type of official has discharged a previous duty in the proceedings.[162] Again,

[156] Augustine, *Commentary,* VII, 455-456; Suarez, *op. cit.,* n. 164; Coronata, *Institutiones,* III, n. 1613.

[157] Augustine, *op. cit.,* VII, 456; Suarez, *op. cit.,* n. 164.

[158] Augustine, *op. cit.,* VII, 456; Coronata, *op. cit.,* III, n. 1613.

[159] Cf. Suarez, *op. cit.,* n. 164; Coronata, III, *op. cit.,* n. 1613.

[160] Suarez, *op. cit.,* n. 164.

[161] Suarez, *op. cit.,* n. 164.

[162] Cf. canons 2152; 2154; 2174.

if the same examiners are consulted, the Ordinary will have as his counsellors men who are already well acquainted with the case, whereas if new examiners were introduced into the procedure at this stage they would have no knowledge whatsoever of the proceedings.

Article 6. Duties of the Synodal Examiners in the Penal Administrative Procedure Against *Clerici Concubinarii.*

In Title XXXI of Book IV of the Code of Canon Law there is provided the penal administrative procedure against *clerici concubinarii.* Concubinage may be either real, or presumed, and both are punishable by this particular procedure.[163] A cleric is living in real concubinage when he habitually has carnal relations with a woman or women, whom he keeps in his house, or when he habitually has such relations with a woman or women outside his own house. A cleric is presumed to be living in concubinage when he lives with one or more women who are suspected *(suspectae de incontinentia vel lascivia),* or when considering all the circumstances he fosters by frequent visits a suspicious company-keeping or familiarity outside his own house with one or more such women.[164] Canon 133 gives the norm for determining just which women are to be considered as suspect.[165] The passive subject of this procedure is any cleric in major orders, exclusive of bishops and Cardinals.[166]

[163] Canons 2176; 2359.

[164] Noval, *De Processibus,* II, n. 638; Wernz-Vidal, *Ius Canonicum,* VI, n. 782.

[165] Canon 2176: *Ordinarius clericum qui contra praescriptum can. 133 mulierem suspectam secum habeat aut quoquo modo frequentet, moneat, etc.*

Canon 133, § 1: Caveant clerici ne mulieres, de quibus suspicio esse possit, apud se retineant aut quoquo modo frequentent.

§ 2: Eisdem licet cum illis tantum mulieribus cohabitare in quibus naturale foedus nihil mali permittit suspicari, quales sunt mater, sorer, amita et huiusmodi, aut a quibus spectata morum honestas, cum provectiore aetate coniuncta, omnem suspicionem amoveat.

§ 3: Iudicium an retinere vel frequentare mulieres, etiam illas in quas communiter suspicio non cadit, in peculiari aliquo casu scandalo esse possit aut incontinentiae afferre periculum, ad Ordinarium loci pertinet, cuius est clericos ab hac retentione vel frequentatione prohibere.

§ 4: Contumaces praesumuntur concubinarii.

[166] Bishops and Cardinals are tried in accordance with canon 1557, § 1.

Once an Ordinary is convinced that a cleric is guilty of either real or presumed concubinage he will begin the procedure. As is quite evident, the Ordinary should not proceed until he is convinced of the facts in the case. If it is impossible to obtain direct proofs of concubinage, there may be available strong presumptions, *e. g.*, the testimony of many concerning the character of a woman whom the cleric habitually visits. As already stated, canon 133 supplies a means of determining presumed concubinage, because there the law determines just which women may be considered as suspect.[167] The law requires a retaining, or frequenting of a suspected woman. Consequently the living with, or the visiting, must be more or less habitual.[168] Other delicts against the sixth commandment committed by clerics are punishable according to canon 2359, § 2-§ 3.

Canon 2176 sets down the first step in the procedure: the cleric who, contrary to the law of canon 133 keeps under his roof or in any manner associates with a woman of suspicious character, shall be admonished by the Ordinary to send her away, or not to associate with her further, under pain of incurring the penalties which canon 2359 decrees against clerics living in concubinage. Canon 2177 gives the next step in the procedure: if the cleric neither obeys the precept nor answers, the Ordinary, after having ascertained that he could have obeyed the orders or given an answer, shall 1. suspend him *a divinis;* 2. deprive him at once of the parish, if he is a pastor; 3. deprive a cleric who holds a benefice without care of souls of one-half of the income of his benefice, if within two months from the suspension he has not amended; after three more months, of all the income of his benefice, and after another three months of the benefice itself.

Clerics in minor orders are punishable according to canon 2358. Religious in major orders are subject to this administrative procedure, though if they belong to a clerical exempt Order or Congregation they are to be punished by their major superior, since he also is an Ordinary (canon 198, § 1). Cf. Suarez, *De Remotione Parochorum*, nn. 167-168.

[167] Cf. Wernz-Vidal, *Ius Canonicum*, VI, n. 785 cum nota 4; Beste, *Introductio*, p. 866; Augustine, *Commentary*, VII, 459.

[168] Suarez, *De Remotione Parochorum*, n. 172.

Canon 2178: Si clericus non obediat, sed causas excusationis adducat, Ordinarius debet super eisdem audire duos examinatores.

If the cleric does not obey the precept of the Ordinary but gives reasons of excuse, the Ordinary must consult two examiners regarding the reasons advanced.

The cleric may feel that there is no reason why he should, for example, dismiss a certain woman who lives in the same house as he does and who does the work of a housekeeper. He is permitted to offer to the Ordinary his reasons to justify himself, namely, that the woman is a good-living person, that there are a number of priests living in the same house who can testify that nothing out of the way ever occurs,[169] that the accusation came from a person who acted maliciously, etc.[170] It would do the cleric no good to claim that he never sinned with the woman, because, it must be remembered, this procedure is not only against real concubinage but also against presumed concubinage. In other words, a cleric may be punished just for having in his house, or frequenting the company of, a woman whom the law, or the Ordinary, judges to be suspect.[171] When the Ordinary receives a cleric's reasons of excuse he is to call in two synodal examiners in order to discuss with them whether these excuses are valid. After the discussion the examiners will give their advice to the Ordinary, who, even though he is obliged *ad validitatem* to hear these officials, is not bound to follow their advice.[172] Because they are required to give their advice, it follows that the Ordinary should reveal to the examiners not only the acts containing the cleric's statements, but also the evidence on which he justified his initiation of proceedings against the cleric, and all evidence gained from witnesses, whether these were introduced *ex officio* or at the instance of the cleric.[173]

[169] Suarez, *De Remotione Parochorum*, n. 180.

[170] Coronata, *Institutiones*, III, n. 1619.

[171] Coronata, *op. cit.*, n. 1619.

[172] Cf. *supra*, pp. 157-158.

[173] Cf. *supra*, p. 164. Cf. also Augustine, *Commentary*, VII, 462; Wernz-Vidal, *Ius Canonicum*, VI, n. 785.

Here reference is made to what has been written in connection with previous canons for the interpretation, applicable to this canon, of the following points: the freedom of choice which the Ordinary possesses in regard to which examiners are to be called in for consultation, the right of the pastor to take exception to an appointee of the Ordinary, the complete freedom which the Ordinary must allow the examiners in offering their counsel, the nature of the vote possessed by the examiners, the possibility that the examiners may request further evidence,[174] the fact that the examiners need not be present at any oral deposition by the cleric or by witnesses, and the requirement that the examiners sign the acts.[175] The question of the oath of secrecy [176] and of the consultation of examiners which is required when the Ordinary would reject witnesses offered by the cleric [177] have also been treated sufficiently in connection with canons 2144 and 2145 respectively.

An interesting question presents itself in the event that the cleric would petition the Ordinary to delay proceedings. He has received the warning, spoken of in canon 2176, and does not obey it, but at the same time he is not simply offering the defense spoken of in canon 2178. He merely asks for an extension of the time within which he must obey the warning. For example, the Ordinary warns a priest to dismiss a woman of thirty years of age, who has been working for the priest as a housekeeper and who has been living in the priest's house. The priest instead of obeying asks the Ordinary that he be permitted to retain this person until he may obtain a suitable substitute. The question which presents itself in connection with such an eventuality is whether or not the Ordinary is obliged to consult two examiners before granting the request. If the priest has requested for a good reason that he be permitted to delay for a short time the dismissal of the woman, there would be no need for any consultation. The case would not seem to come under canon 2178. However, if the delay were to be lengthy, or if the reason offered was considered by the Ordinary to be of doubtful value, then there would be had

[174] Cf. *supra*, pp. 159 ff.

[175] Cf. *supra*, pp. 162 ff. and 147.

[176] Cf. *supra*, pp. 147 ff.

[177] Cf. *supra*, pp. 154 ff.

the equivalent of the case contemplated in canon 2178. In other words, the cleric is really offering excuses for cohabitating with the woman, or for visiting her. And since canon 2178 requires consultation in all cases which come under it, the Ordinary would be required to consult the examiners before granting the petition.[178]

> Canon 2180: Parochum amovibilem inobedientem Ordinarius statim ad normam can. 2177 coercere potest; si vero agatur de clerico qui, beneficium inamovibile obtinens, non paret, sed novas allegat deductiones, Ordinarius eas ad examen revocet ad normam can. 2178.

If the cleric is a removable pastor and he does not obey within the time fixed in the precept, the Ordinary may at once coerce him by the penalties stated in canon 2177. If a cleric holding an irremovable benefice does not obey but alleges new reasons, the Ordinary shall consider these in accordance with the norm set down by canon 2178.

If the Ordinary, after consulting the examiners on the reasons adduced by the cleric against the first warning, should judge that the excuses are not sufficient, he is obliged to inform the cleric of his decision as soon as possible, and he should give him another formal precept to obey within a specified brief period of time.[179] In the next step in the procedure the law once again introduces the distinction between the holder of a removable benefice and the one possessing an irremovable benefice. Canon 2180 legislates that if a removable pastor (or any cleric who does not possess an irremovable benefice, office or dignity)[180] should disobey this second precept the Ordinary may immediately apply the penalties of canon 2177, according to the norms of that canon. If, however, a cleric who holds an irremovable benefice (office or dignity)[181] should disobey and at the same time offer new reasons in his own defense, the Ordinary

[178] Noval, *De Processibus,* II, n. 649; Suarez, *op. cit.,* n. 180.

[179] Canon 2179.

[180] Suarez, *De Remotione Parochorum,* n. 185.

[181] Suarez, *op. cit.,* n. 186.

must call in the same two examiners[182] and discuss with them the new reasons offered by the cleric. The examiners will give their advice to the Ordinary as to whether or not they feel that these reasons of the cleric are legitimate. Canon 2180 itself states that the consultation is to proceed according to the norm of canon 2178. Therefore it suffices to refer to what was said in commentary on this latter canon for an understanding of the duties of the examiners in this new stage of the proceedings. If it should happen that the cleric not only refuses to obey but does not even offer new reasons, there will be no consultation and the Ordinary may immediately proceed to the punishments of canon 2177.[183]

The examiners are given no further duties in this procedure. The parish priest consultors have no part in this procedure at any time. The procedure itself has but one final step after the one just considered: if the Ordinary does not consider the new reasons as a legitimate excuse for evading his precept, he shall again command the irremovable cleric to obey within a specified time. If this time elapses without obedience to the precept, the Ordinary is to proceed against the cleric according to canon 2177.[184]

Article 7. Duties of the Synodal Examiners in the Penal Administrative Procedure Against Negligent Pastors

The last of the administrative procedures in which the synodal examiners have a part is that outlined in Title XXXII, Book IV of the Code of Canon Law. This is the penal administrative procedure against negligent pastors.[185] Parish priest consultors have no part in this process. As is evident from the very title, this procedure is solely against pastors, not against other beneficiaries or against other clerics.

[182] The same examiners are to be used. The reasons for this conclusion are the same as those given for a similar deduction in connection with canon 2175. Cf. *supra,* pp. 181-182.

[183] Suarez, *op. cit.,* nn. 185-186.

[184] Canon 2181.

[185] For an excellent study of this process, cf. Meier, *Adm. Proc. Ag. Neglig. Pastors.*

In order that the procedure may be instituted against a pastor there must be on the part of the pastor a real delict, a certain, grave and more or less habitual neglect or violation of one of the parochial duties mentioned in canons 2182 and 2382. This list is exhaustive, so that the procedure may not be instituted for the violation or neglect of some other parochial duty.[186]

In canon 2182 it is stated that if a pastor should have gravely neglected or violated the parochial duties mentioned in canons 467, § 1, 468, § 1, 1178, 1330-1332, 1344 the bishop shall admonish him, reminding him of his strict obligation in conscience and of the penalties which the law decrees against these delicts. Before issuing this canonical admonition the Ordinary should be morally certain that the pastor has gravely, more or less habitually, and culpably violated or neglected one of the parochial duties mentioned in this canon 2182, or in canon 2382. In order to obtain this moral certitude he should investigate the matter, for instance by questioning the vicar forane of the pastor, neighboring pastors, curates of the pastor, and even reputable laymen. The results of such an investigation are to be committed to writing and placed in the acts of the case. Though the opinions of approved canonists, moral theologians and the jurisprudence of the Holy See may be looked upon as norms to determine the gravity of the neglect or violation, still in the final analysis the prudent judgment of the Ordinary determines the question of the gravity of the offense. However, in making his judgment the Ordinary should consider not only the nature of the duty neglected or violated, but also attendant circumstances, such as, the amount of work which the pastor has to do, the effect of the neglect or violation upon the parishioners, the nature of the parish, etc. Individual acts of negligence or violation are not the object of this procedure; the neglect of violation must be something more or less habitual.[187]

[186] Noval, *De Processibus,* II, n. 663; Suarez, *De Remotione Parochorum,* n. 191; Meier, *op. cit.,* pp. 123, 126 and 129.

[187] Wernz-Vidal, *Ius Canonicum,* VI, n. 789; Suarez, *op. cit.,* n. 194; Coronata, *Institutiones,* III, n. 1622; McVann, *The Canon Law on Sermon Preaching,* p. 124; Meier, *op. cit.,* pp. 155-156.

Canon 2183: Si parochus sese non emendaverit, Episcopus eum corripiat et aliqua congrua poena pro gravitate culpae puniat, postquam, auditis duobus examinatoribus et facta parocho sese defendendi facultate, probatum iudicaverit praedicta paroecialia officia etiam atque etiam per notabile tempus in re gravis momenti praetermissa aut violata fuisse et eorundem omissiones aut violationes nulla iusta causa excusari.

If the pastor does not amend, the bishop is to correct him, and he is to impose on him an appropriate penalty in proportion to his guilt, if, after having consulted two of the examiners and after having given the pastor an opportunity to defend himself, he has judged that the above-mentioned parochial duties have been neglected or violated in a serious matter again and again for a notable period of time without any just excuse.

The wording of this canon is not too clear. However, a close study seems to reveal that the following is prescribed by the canon: if the bishop judges that the pastor has not shown amendment, he is to correct him (*eum corripiat*). Then, if the pastor, in the judgment of the bishop, should still continue in his neglect or violation, he is to be given an opportunity to defend himself. After the defense the bishop is to consult two synodal examiners, and then he is to judge whether or not the continuance in neglect or violation is proved. If it is proved he is to punish the pastor.

The reason for the interpretation that the consultation with the synodal examiners is to follow the defense of the pastor is quite obvious. The examiners are to give counsel to the Ordinary, and they can only give a counsel based on complete knowledge of the facts if they know what the pastor has to say in his own defense. Parallel canons in the preceding administrative processes always call for the hearing of the examiners or consultors after the pastor or cleric has made his defense.[188]

When the Ordinary feels that there is sufficient evidence that the pastor has not amended his ways after the *correptio* spoken of in the first part of canon 2183 but continues to neglect or violate the

[188] Cf. canons 2160; 2165; 2171; 2178.

same duty he may proceed to the next step in the process. The continued neglect or violation must be in regard to the same parochial duty in order that the procedure may be taken up in this new stage. Neglect in or violation of another species of duty would necessitate the beginning of a new process.[189] When the Ordinary decides to proceed against the pastor, he must first allow the latter to make his defense. This defense will be made either orally or in writing. The pastor may attack the truth of the charge that he has neglected or violated his duty, or he may try to show that the neglect or violation was not serious, or not habitual. He may attempt to prove that his accusers are his enemies and were moved in their accusations against him by unworthy motives. Finally, he might offer reasons of excuse for his apparent neglect or violation. Witnesses may be offered by the pastor, or may be introduced *ex officio.* The defense of the pastor, if given orally, and all other evidence obtained must be put in writing and kept in the acts of the case.[190]

Once the pastor has concluded his defense and all the other evidence has been gathered the Ordinary must call in two synodal examiners for consultation to receive their advice on whether or not the pastor has failed to amend himself. Canon 2183 says that the Ordinary may inflict penalties on the pastor *"postquam, auditis duobus examinatoribus . . . , probatum iudicaverit praedicta paroecialia officia etiam atque etiam per notabile tempus in re gravis momenti praetermissa aut violata fuisse et eorundem omissiones aut violationes nulla iusta causa excusari."* Therefore it is the part of the examiners to discuss with the Ordinary and to give their counsel on whether or not there is proof that the parochial duties were omitted or violated again and again for a long period of time, and without there being present any just excusing reason. The examiners should, of course, keep in mind what was mentioned above, that the omission or violation spoken of must constitute a real delict on the part of the

[189] Cf. Meier, *op. cit.*, p. 170; Suarez, *op. cit.*, n. 198. The opposite opinion, namely, that the neglect or violation may be even in another species of duty is held by Noval, *op. cit.*, n. 664, and by Beste, *Introductio,* p. 867.

[190] Suarez, *op. cit.*, n. 199; Coronata, *op. cit.*, III, n. 1623; Jansen, *op. cit.*, p. 71; Meier, *op. cit.*, p. 173. On the question of witnesses introduced by the pastor, cf. *supra,* pp. 154 ff.

pastor. In order that the examiners may know the facts in the case the Ordinary must show to them all the acts of the process, the evidence on which the original admonition was based, the evidence gathered to show a lack of amendment both before and after the *correptio*, the defense of the pastor, the depositions of witnesses.[191]

It is quite clear that the examiners should know just what canon 2183 means when it speaks of a lack of amendment on the part of the pastor. Does the canon in using the phrase *"etiam atque etiam per notabile tempus"* means that it must be proved that even after the *correptio* the pastor has for a long time continued to neglect or violate the same duty? Some authors reply in the affirmative,[192] but it seems that such an answer can hardly be correct. Rather, the correct interpretation seems to be that if the pastor continues to commit the same violation of duty or to omit the same pastoral duty, even if by a single act, then he has indeed been guilty of neglecting or violating his duty for a long period of time, and has not shown amendment.[193] As Meier expresses it, the support of the opposite view "amounts to allowing the negligence to continue in order to accumulate instances for this canonical step. This, of course, if it were tenable, would militate against the spirit of the Code, the spiritual interests of the parishioners and the beneficial administration of the parish."[194]

Another point which must be considered by the examiners in order that they may give good advice to the Ordinary concerns the length of time which would be considered sufficient to show that a neglect or violation no longer constitutes a continuation of the former neglect or violation. In other words, how long must a pastor refrain from his neglect or violation in order that he may be considered as having amended his ways? Extremes must be avoided in replying to this question. A few days of obedience to duty does

[191] Cf. Wernz-Vidal, *Ius Canonicum,* VI, n. 789; Suarez, *De Remotione Parochorum,* n. 199; Meier, *Adm. Proc. Ag. Neglig. Pastors,* pp. 174-175.

[192] Vermeersch-Creusen, *Epitome,* III, n. 371; Blat, *Commentarium,* IV, n. 788, Cocchi, *Commentarium,* VII, n. 398.

[193] Suarez, *op. cit.,* n. 198; Coronata, *Institutiones,* III, n. 1623; McVann, *The Canon Law on Sermon Preaching,* p. 125; Meier, *op. cit.,* pp. 169-170.

[194] Meier, *op. cit.,* p. 170.

not prove amendment, nor may a single omission after a few years be looked upon as a continuance of a former habit. In the last analysis, of course, the Ordinary is the judge, but the examiners may use the norms of canonists to offer their advice. According to canonists a three year period of fulfillment of duty would show sufficient amendment, so that in the event of a relapse afterwards into the old neglect or violation, the Ordinary should begin the procedure anew.[195]

After they have carefully considered all the evidence the examiners will give their advice to the Ordinary. This advice of the examiners is not on the matter of what particular penalty or penalties the Ordinary should inflict, but solely on whether or not a lack of emendation is proved from the acts. This conclusion is drawn from parallel canons in the preceding administrative processes of Part III, Book IV of the Code of Canon Law.[196]

Reference is here made to what has been written in commentary on previous canons for other considerations which are necessary for a complete understanding of the present canon in so far as it regards the synodal examiners: the freedom of choice which the Ordinary enjoys in the selection of examiners, the right of the pastor to take exception to a choice of the Ordinary, the complete freedom which must be given to the examiners in their consideration of the case and in their offering of their counsel, the consultive nature of their vote, the necessity of the consultation for validity, the possibility of a request by the examiners for further evidence,[197] the fact that there is no law requiring that the examiners be present at an oral defense by the pastor, or at other depositions of testimony, the necessity that the examiners sign the acts of that part of the procedure in which they intervened.[198] The oath of secrecy which the examiners must take when they are first called into the process has also been treated sufficiently, in connection with canon 2144.[199]

[195] Suarez, *op. cit.*, n. 198; McVann, *op. cit.*, p. 125; Jansen, *Canonical Provisions for Catechetical Instruction*, pp. 71-72.

[196] Cf. *e.g.*, canons 2171; 2174, § 1; 2175; 2178; 2181. Meier (*op. cit.*, p. 171) appears to be wrong when he makes the statement that the examiners also "suggest the kind and mode of punishment."

[197] Cf. *supra*, pp. 159 ff.

[198] Cf. *supra*, pp. 162 ff. and 147.

[199] Cf. *supra*, pp. 147 ff.

If the pastor should make no defense the Ordinary may, *without consulting the examiners,* proceed to the punishments of canon 2183, provided he is convinced that the pastor was not impeded from presenting his defense. This situation in which the pastor makes no defense is not contemplated in the canons on this procedure, and therefore one turns to a parallel canon, 2159, in confirmation of his position. The pastor is presumed to have made no defense because he has none to make. Meier,[200] appears to be wrong in requiring the consulting of the examiners even in this instance, for certainly there is no such requisite in the parallel canon, 2159. Coronata,[201] in commenting on the following canon, 2184, refers to canon 2149 in defense of a statement that the examiners are to be called in even if the pastor makes no defense. Canon 2149, however, in no way calls for the presence of the examiners, so Coronata's statement must be rejected. Not only must it be rejected, but it even proves the position taken here. It is preferred to refer, in proof of the contention asserted, to canon 2159 (which in turn refers to canon 2149) because canon 2159 is a canon more nearly parallel to the one under present consideration, canon 2183.

Canon 2184: Si et correptio et punitio in irritum cesserint, Ordinarius, probata, ad normam can. 2183, perseverante ac culpabili officiorum paroecialium omissione vel violatione in re gravi, parochum amovibilem sua paroecia statim privare potest; parochum vero inamovibilem beneficii fructibus, pauperibus ab Ordinario distribuendis, pro gravitate culpae in totum vel ex parte privet.

If both the rebuke and the punishment prove unavailing, the Ordinary, after having proved according to canon 2183 the pastor's culpable perseverance in the neglect or violation of the pastoral duties in a grave matter, may at once deprive a removable pastor of his parish; he may deprive an irremovable pastor of the income of

200 *Op. cit.*, p. 174 and p. 188.
201 *Op. cit.*, III, n. 1624.

his benefice, either in whole or in part in proportion to the gravity of his guilt, and distribute it among the poor.

Since the canon itself states that in this further step in the procedure the persisting and culpable omission or violation in a serious matter of the parochial duties is to be proved according to the norm set down in canon 2183, it follows that the duties of the examiners are precisely the same as explained in the previous canon. Of course, the object of the new consideration by the examiners on which they give their advice to the Ordinary is the continuance of the serious and culpable neglect or violation. Those acts of the case which contain the evidence obtained by the Ordinary to prove this continued neglect or violation of duty, together with the pastor's new defense and all other new testimony obtained from witnesses are to be submitted to the examiners. The reader is referred to the commentary on the previous canon for an interpretation of the duties of the examiners in this stage of the proceedings.

An interesting question arises in connection with canon 2184. Must the examiners be the same ones as those who were previously engaged in the case? The same problem was discussed in connection with canon 2180, in the administrative procedure against *clerici concubinarii.* There the answer given was that the same examiners must be used, unless, of course, this be morally impossible or unless a very good reason would necessitate a substitution.[202] The same answer must be given here, and for the same reasons. Parallel canons in certain of the preceding procedures explicitly require that the same examiners be heard.[203] The identical reasons which may be alleged for the requirement imposed in these parallel canons that the same examiners must be used, seem also to be present in connection with canon 2184. Consequently, if the same reasons are present, then in the absence of an explicit regulation one should certainly follow the precept of the parallel canons. The reasons why the same examiners should be used are quite obvious. They know the case very well and would, as a result, be best suited to participate in this further stage of proceedings.[204]

[202] Cf. *supra,* pp. 181-182 and 186-187.

[203] Cf. canons 2152, § 1; 2174; 2175.

[204] Wernz-Vidal, *Ius Canonicum,* VI, n. 789; Suarez, *De Remotione Paro-*

Canon 2185: Mala voluntate persistente ac probata, ut supra, Ordinarius etiam parochum inamovibilem e sua paroecia removeat.

If the bad will of the irremovable pastor continues and is proved in the manner described above, the Ordinary shall remove even an irremovable pastor from his parish.

This final stage in the procedure has regard solely to an irremovable pastor. If the Ordinary has established proof that an irremovable pastor has continued in his neglect or violation of the same parochial duty for which he has already been admonished, reprimanded, punished and deprived of the fruits of his benefice, then the Ordinary may proceed to this final step, the removal of the pastor. However, before he may actually give the decree of privation, the Ordinary must consult the same examiners as to whether or not the bad will of the pastor quite definitely still persists. In other words, is it proved that the pastor has continued in his omission or neglect of the same parochial duty?[205] As canon 2185 itself states, the whole question of the consultation at this stage of the proceedings follows the pattern set down in canon 2183. For the necessary commentary on the examiners and their duties the reader is referred to what has already been written in connection with canons 2183 and 2184.

chorum, n. 202; McVann, *The Canon Law on Sermon Preaching*, p. 125; Meier, *Adm. Proc. Ag. Neglig. Pastors*, p. 184. Some few authors allow the Ordinary freedom to appoint different examiners if he should so prefer: Blat, *Commentarium*, lib. IV, n. 789; Coronata, *Institutiones*, III, n. 1624.

[205] Suarez, *op. cit.*, n. 205; Coronata, *op. cit.*, III, n. 1624; Meier, *op. cit.*, p. 192.

CONCLUSIONS

1. Though the II Plenary Council of Baltimore (1866) had suggested the election of true synodal examiners, the III Plenary Council of Baltimore (1884) prescribed instead the election of *examiners of the clergy*. The latter were not true synodal examiners, though their duties in the particular law concursus for vacant irremovable rectorships were quite similar to those of synodal examiners in the concursus provided by the Common Law for vacant parishes.

2. The legislation of the II and III Plenary Councils of Baltimore with regard to the *examiners of the diocesan clergy* in the examinations of the Junior Clergy, of priests seeking faculties to hear confessions, of candidates for Orders must be considered as abrogated for the Code law gives to the bishop complete freedom in his choice of examiners for these examinations.

3. When it was declared by the Sacred Consistorial Congregation, February 28, March 13, 1911, that the decree *"Maxima cura"* applied to the removal of irremovable rectors in the United States, there arose an obligation for the bishops of the United States to elect true synodal examiners and parish priest consultors.

4. Synodal examiners and parish priest consultors possess a true ecclesiastical office, but only in the wide sense of the term, not in the strict sense.

5. It is not expedient that a vicar general, an *officialis* or a chancellor be chosen for the office of synodal examiner, nor is it expedient that a vicar general, an *officialis,* a chancellor or a diocesan consultor be given the office of parish priest consultor.

6. There appears to be a strict obligation for bishops to substitute pro-synodal examiners and parish priest consultors if the number of either class of officials drops below four at any time during the ten year period in which these officials remain in office. There is also a strict obligation for them to elect new officials, or to re-elect the same officials, once the ten year term of office is completed.

7. The more acceptable interpretation of canon 105, 1°, is the one which regards the required seeking of counsel as a law which binds under penalty of nullity. However, since a probable doubt of

law exists, acts placed without the required counsel are illicit, but not invalid, except in those cases wherein an express nullifying clause is present in a specific canon.

8. It is not required that all the synodal examiners be employed on each occasion to conduct with the Ordinary the examination on theological learning of which canon 459, § 3, 3° speaks, but it is suggested that at least three be appointed for each examination.

9. When the synodal examiners or the parish priest consultors are called upon to give their counsel in an administrative procedure subsequent to the defense of a cleric, the Ordinary should reveal to these counsellors from the acts not merely the actual defense of the cleric, but also all other evidence gathered in connection with this defense, even though it was obtained *ex officio*.

10. When the canons in an administrative procedure require that synodal examiners should be consulted more than once, the Ordinary should use the same examiners.

BIBLIOGRAPHY

Sources

Acta Apostolicae Sedis, Commentarium Officiale, Romae, 1909—

Acta Sanctae Sedis, 41 vols., Romae, 1865-1908.

Acta et Decreta Concilii Plenarii Baltimorensis Tertii, A. D. MDCCCLXXXIV, Baltimorae, John Murphy, 1886.

Acta et Decreta Sacrorum Conciliorum Recentiorum, Collectio Lacensis, 7 vols., Friburgi Brisgoviae: Herder & Co., 1870-1890.

Bouscaren, T. Lincoln, *Canon Law Digest*, 2 vols. and Supplement—1941, Milwaukee: Bruce, 1934-1941.

Bullarum Diplomatum et Privilegiorum Sanctorum Romanorum Pontificum Taurinensis Editio, 24 vols. et Appendix, Augustae Taurinorum-Neapoli, 1857-1872.

Canones et Decreta Concilii Tridentini, ed. Richter-Schulte, Lipsiae, 1853.

Codex Iuris Canonici Pii X Pontificis Maximi iussu digestus Benedicti Papae XV auctoritate promulgatus, Praefatione, Fontium annotatione et Indice Analytico-Alphabetico ab Emo. Petro Card. Gasparri Auctus, Romae, Typis Polyglottis Vaticanis, 1917. Reimpressio, 1934.

Codicis Iuris Canonici Fontes cura Emi. Petri Card. Gasparri editi, 9 vols., Romae (Civitate Vaticana): Typis Polyglottis Vaticanis, 1923-1939. (Vols. VII-IX ed. cura et studio Emi. Justiniani Card. Serédi.)

Concilii Plenarii Baltimorensis II, in Ecclesia Metropolitana Baltimorensi, a die VII ad diem XXI Octobris, A. D. MDCCCLXVI, et a Sede Apostolica Recogniti, Acta et Decreta, ed. altera, Baltimorae: Ioannes Murphy, 1894.

Corpus Iuris Canonici, 2. ed., Lipsiensis (Friedberg), 2 vols., Lipsiae, 1879-1881.

Pallottini, Salvator, *Collectio Omnium Conclusionum et Resolutionum Quae in Causis apud Sacram Congregationem Cardinalium S. Concilii Tridentini Interpretum Prodierunt ab eius institutione anno MDLXIX ad annum MDCCCLX, distinctis titulis alphabetico ordine per materias digesta*, 17 vols., Romae, 1868-1893.

Schroeder, H. J., *Canons and Decrees of the Council of Trent*, St. Louis: B. Herder, 1941.

Thesaurus Resolutionum Sacrae Congregationis Concilii, 167 vols., Romae, 1718-1908.

Waterworth, J., *The Canons and Decrees of the Sacred and Oecumenical Council of Trent*, London, 1848.

Reference Works

Ayrinhac, H. A., *General Legislation in the New Code of Canon Law*, New York: Benziger, 1923.

———, *Constitution of the Church in the New Code of Canon Law,* New York: Benziger, 1925.

———, *The Legislation on the Sacraments,* New York: Longmans, 1928.

[Bachofen], Charles Augustine, *A Commentary on the New Code of Canon Law,* 8 vols. (Vol. II, 5. ed., 1928; Vol. VI, 2. ed., 1923; Vol. VII, 3. ed., 1930), St. Louis, London: Herder.

———, *Rights and Duties of Ordinaries,* St. Louis: Herder, 1924.

Barbosa, Augustinus, *Collectanea Doctorum in varia Concilii Tridentini, Decreta et Canones,* Lugduni, 1657.

———, *De Officio et Potestate Parochi,* Lugduni, 1665.

———, *De Officio et Potestate Parochi,* Animadversiones et Additamenta, Ubaldo Giraldi, Romae, 1831.

Barrett, John D., *A Comparative Study of the Councils of Baltimore and the Code of Canon Law,* The Catholic University of America Canon Law Studies, n. 83, Washington, D. C.: The Catholic University of America, 1932.

Bastnagel, Clement V., *The Appointment of Parochial Adjutants and Assistants,* The Catholic University of America Canon Law Studies, n. 58, Washington, D. C.: The Catholic University of America, 1930.

Benedictus XIV, *De Synodo Dioecesana,* 2 vols., Romae, 1806.

Beste, U., *Introductio in Codicem,* Collegeville, Minnesota: St. John's Abbey Press, 1938.

Bevilaqua, Americo, *De Episcopi seu Ordinarii ex Novo Codice Canonico Iuribus ac Obligationibus,* Romae, Ratisbonae, Coloniae Agrippinae, Neo Eboracei, Cincinnati: Pustet, 1921.

Blat, Albertus, *Commentarium Textus Codicis Iuris Canonici,* 5 vols. in 6, Romae: Ex Typographia Pontificia in Instituto Pii IX, 1921-1927. Lib. II, 2. ed., 1921; lib. III, pars I, 2. ed., 1924; lib. IV, 1927.

Bouuaert, F. Claeys, *Selecta Capita Codicis Iuris Canonici Analytice Proposita, et Brevi Commentario Adaucta,* Gandae, 1919.

Cappello, Felix, *De Administrativa Amotione Parochorum seu Commentarium in Decretum "Maxima cura,"* Romae, 1911.

———, *Tractatus Canonico-Moralis de Sacramentis,* 3 vols. in 6, Taurinorum Augustae: Marietti, 1932-1939. Vol. II, pars I, 3. ed., 1938; Vol. II, pars III, 1935.

———, *Summa Iuris Canonici,* 3 vols., Romae: Apud Aedes Universitatis Gregorianae. Vol. I, 3. ed., 1938.

Chelodi, Joannes, *Ius de Personis,* ed. altera a Sac. Ernesto Bertagnolli Tridenti: Libr. Edit. Tridentum, 1927.

Cicognani, Amleto, *Canon Law,* 2. ed., authorized English version by J. M. O'Hara and Francis Brennan, Philadelphia: Dolphin Press, 1935.

Coady, John J., *The Appointment of Pastors,* The Catholic University of America Canon Law Studies, n. 52, Washington, D. C.: The Catholic University of America, 1929.

Cocchi, Guidus, *Commentarium in Codicem Iuris Canonici,* 8 vols., Taurinorum Augustae: Marietti. Vol. II, 3. ed., 1930; Vol. III, 3. ed., 1931; Vol. VII, 1930.

Connor, Maurice, *The Administrative Removal of Pastors,* The Catholic University of America Canon Law Studies, n. 104, Washington, D. C.: The Catholic University of America, 1937.

Coronata, Matthaeus Conte a, *Institutiones Iuris Canonici,* 5 vols., Taurini: Marietti. Vols. I-II, 2. ed., 1939; Vols. III-V, 1933-1936.

d'Angelo, Sosio, *La Curia Diocesana a norma del Codice di Diritto Canonico,* Giarre (Sicilia): Lisi, 1922.

———, *Parroco e Parrochia nel Codice di Diritto Canonico, Nomina del Parroco, Esame, Concorso,* Giarre (Sicilia): Lisi, 1921.

de Luca, Joannes Baptista Card., *Theatrum Veritatis et Iustitiae,* 16 vols. in 9, tom. III, pars V, *Annotationes Practicae ad Conc. Tridentinum,* Coloniae Agrippinae, 1706.

Dubé, Arthur J., *The General Principles for the Reckoning of Time in Canon Law,* The Catholic University of America Canon Law Studies, n. 144, Washington, D. C.: The Catholic University of America Press, 1941.

Dugan, Henry F., *The Judiciary Department of the Diocesan Curia,* The Catholic University of America Canon Law Studies, n. 26, Washington, D. C.: The Catholic University of America, 1925.

Fagnanus, Prosper, *Commentaria in Libros Decretalium, Commentarium in Tertium Librum Decretalium,* Venetiis, 1696.

Fanelli, Nicola, *La Procedura Canonica nei Processi Amministrativi e Penali,* Vicenza: Società Anonima Tipografica, 1936.

Fanfani, Ludovicus, *De Iure Parochorum ad Normam Codicis Iuris Canonici,* Taurini: Marietti, 1924.

———, *De Iure Religiosorum ad Normam Codicis Iuris Canonici,* Taurini, Marietti, 1925.

Ferraris, Lucius, *Prompta Biblioteca, Canonica, Iuridica, Moralis, Theologica necnon Ascetica, Polemica, Rubricistica, Historica,* 9 vols., Romae, 1885-1899.

Ferreres, Joannes B., *Institutiones Canonicae,* 2 vols., Barcinone: Subirana. Vol. I, 2. ed., 1920; Vol. II, 1918.

Garcia, Nicolaus, *Tractatus de Beneficiis Ecclesiasticis,* Coloniae Allobrogum, 1636.

Jaeger, Leo, *The Administration of Vacant and Quasi-Vacant Dioceses in the United States,* The Catholic University of America Canon Law Studies, n. 81, Washington, D. C.: The Catholic University of America, 1932.

Jansen, R. J., *Canonical Provisions for Catechetical Instruction,* The Catholic University of America Canon Law Studies, n. 107, Washington, D. C.: The Catholic University of America, 1937.

Leurenius, Petrus, *Forum Beneficiale,* 2 vols., Venetiis, 1742.

Maroto, Philippus, *Institutiones Iuris Canonici ad Normam Novi Codicis,* 2 vols., Matriti. Vol. I, 1919.

McVann, James, *The Canon Law on Sermon Preaching,* New York: The Paulist Press, 1940.

Meier, Carl Anthony, *Penal Administrative Procedure Against Negligent Pastors,* The Catholic University of America Canon Law Studies, n. 140, Washington, D. C.: The Catholic University of America Press, 1941.

Mothon, Jos. Pie, *Institutiones Canoniques,* 3 vols., Paris: Desclée, de Brouwer et Cie., 1922-1924. Vol. I, 1922.

Munerati, Dantes M., *Iuris Ecclesiastici Publici et Privati Elementa,* 4. ed., Romae: ex schola typographica Salesiana, 1926.

Muñiz, T., *Procedimientos Eclesiásticos,* 2. ed., 3 vols., Sevilla: Lib. de Sobrino de Izquierdo.

Noval, Joseph, *Commentarium Codicis Iuris Canonici, Lib. IV, De Processibus,* 2 vols.; Vol. II, Augustae Taurinorum—Romae: Marietti, 1932.

Oesterle, Gerardus, *Praelectiones Iuris Canonici,* Vol. I, Romae: Collegio S. Anselmi, 1931.

Pax Iordanus, *Opera Omnia,* 3 vols., Coloniae Allobrogum et Lugduni, 1729.

Prümmer, Dominicus M., *Manuale Iuris Canonici,* 4. et 5. ed., Friburgi Brisgoviae: Herder, 1927.

Reclusio, Franciscus, *Tractatus de Concursibus, Collationibus, et Vacationibus Parochiarum Aliorumque Beneficiorum,* Romae, 1774.

Reilly, P., *Residence of Pastors,* The Catholic University of America Canon Law Studies, n. 97, Washington, D. C.: The Catholic University of America, 1935.

Rossi, J., *De Paroecia,* Romae: Pustet, 1923.

Schäfer, Timotheus, *De Religiosis ad Normam Codicis Iuris Canonici,* 3. ed., Romae: Herder, 1940.

Simeone, Gennaro, *Lezioni di Diritto Canonico,* 2 vols.; Vol. I, 3. ed., Napoli: Jovene, 1905.

Sipos, Stephanus, *Enchiridion Iuris Canonici,* 3. ed., Pécs: Haladás R. T., 1936.

Soglia, Joannes, *Institutiones Iuris Publici Ecclesiastici,* 2. ed., 2 Vols., Paris: Courcier, sine anno.

Suarez, Emmanuel, *De Remotione Parochorum Aliisque Processibus Tertiae Partis Lib. IV C. I. C.,* Romae: Pontificium Internationale Institutum Angelicum de Urbe, 1931.

Toso, Albertus, *Ad Codicem Iuris Canonici Commentaria Minora,* 5 vols., Romae: Jus Pontificium; lib. II, *De Personis,* pars I, tom. III, 1925.

Vecchiotti, S. M., *Institutiones Canonicae,* 19. ed., 3 vols., Augustae Taurinorum, 1886.

Ventriglia, J., *Praxis Rerum Notabilium Praesertim Fori Ecclesiastici,* 2 vols., Venetiis, 1694.

Vermeersch, A.-Creusen, J., *Epitome Iuris Canonici,* 3 vols., Mechliniae: H. Dessain, 1934-1937. Vol. I, 6. ed., 1937; Vol. II, 5. ed., 1934; Vol. III, 5. ed., 1936.

Wernz, F. X., *Ius Decretalium,* 6 vols., Romae: ex typographia Polyglotta S. C. P. F. Vol. II, 1899; Vol. V, 1914. Prati, ex officina Libraria Giachetti, Filii et Soc., 1914.

Wernz, F. X.-Vidal, P., *Ius Canonicum,* 7 toms. in 8 vols., Romae: Apud Aedes Universitatis Gregorianae. Tom. II, 2. ed., 1928; tom. VI, 1927.

Woywod, S., *A Practical Commentary on the Code of Canon Law,* 5. ed., 2 vols., New York: Wagner, 1939.

Periodicals

Apollinaris, Romae, 1928—

Archiv für katholisches Kirchenrecht, Innsbruck, 1857-1861; Mainz, 1862—

Canoniste, Le, Paris, 1924-1926 (originally *Le Canoniste Contemporain,* Paris, 45 vols., 1878-1922).

Ecclesiastical Review, The (originally *The American Ecclesiastical Review*), Philadelphia, 1889—

Homiletic and Pastoral Review, The, New York, 1900—

Irish Ecclesiastical Record, The, Dublin, 1864—

Jurist, The, Washington, D. C., 1941—

Jus Pontificium, Romae, 1921—

Monitore Ecclesiastico, Il, Romae, 1876—

Nouvelle Revue Théologique, Paris, 1869—

Perfice Munus, Augustae Taurinorum, 1926—

Periodica de Re Canonica et Morali, Brugis, 1905—; ab anno 1927: *Periodica de Re Canonica, Morali, Liturgica.*

Principal Articles

Bevilacqua, "Circa il modo di eseguire lo scrutinio, ossia di fare la votazione nei concorsi"—*Il Monitore Ecclesiastico,* Serie IV, Vol. IV (1932) (Vol. XXXIV della intera Collezione), pp. 274-280.

d'Angelo, S., De Examinatoribus Synodalibus"—*Apollinaris,* III (1930), p. 140.

Gennari, "Sulla Rimozione dall'Officio e dal Beneficio Curato. Breve Commento del Decreto *Maxima cura"*—*Il Monitore Ecclesiastico,* Serie III, Vol. II (1910) (Vol. XXII della intera Collezione), pp. 445-454; 492-502; 535-550.

ABBREVIATIONS

AAS—Acta Apostolicae Sedis.
AER—American Ecclesiastical Review.
ASS—Acta Sanctae Sedis.
PCI—Pontifical Commission for the Authentic Interpretation of the Code.
Fontes—Codicis Iuris Canonici Fontes cura . . . Gasparri editi.
HPR—Homiletic and Pastoral Review.
Monit. Eccl.—Il Monitore Ecclesiastico.
S. C. C.—Sacred Congregation of the Council.
S. C. Consist.—Sacred Congregation of the Consistory.
S. C. Ep. et Reg.—Sacred Congregation of Bishops and Regulars.
Thes. Resol.—Sacrae Congregationis Concilii Resolutiones (1718-1908).

ALPHABETICAL INDEX

BIOGRAPHICAL NOTE

John Patrick Connolly was born April 10, 1911, at San Francisco, California. His grammar school education was completed at St. Mary's Parochial School in Oakland, California. He spent six years at St. Joseph's Junior Seminary, Mountain View, California. He took his Philosophy course at St. Patrick's Seminary, Menlo Park, California. In October, 1935, he was appointed to the North American College, Rome, Italy, where he received the Baccalaureate in Theology in 1937 and the Licentiate in Theology in 1939. He was ordained to the sacred priesthood at Rome on December 8, 1938. In September of 1940 he entered the Catholic University of America to pursue a graduate course of studies in Canon Law. From this institution he received the degree of Baccalaureate in Canon Law in June, 1941, and the degree of Licentiate in Canon Law in May, 1942.

CANON LAW STUDIES *

1. Freriks, Rev. Celestine A., C.PP.S., J.C.D., Religious Congregations in Their External Relations, 121 pp., 1916.
2. Galliher, Rev. Daniel M., O.P., J.C.D., Canonical Elections, 117 pp., 1917.
3. Borkowski, Rev. Aurelius L., O.F.M., J.C.D., De Confraternitatibus Ecclesiasticis, 136 pp., 1918.
4. Castillo, Rev. Cayo, J.C.D., Disertacion Historico-Canonica sobre la Potestad del Cabildo en Sede Vacante o Impedida del Vicario Capitular, 99 pp., 1919 (1918).
5. Kubelbeck, Rev. William J., S.T.B., J.C.D., The Sacred Penitentiaria and Its Relation to Faculties of Ordinaries and Priests, 129 pp., 1918.
6. Petrovits, Rev. Joseph, J.C., S.T.D., J.C.D., The New Church Law on Matrimony, X-461 pp., 1919.
7. Hickey, Rev. John J., S.T.B., J.C.D., Irregularities and Simple Impediments in the New Code of Canon Law, 100 pp., 1920.
8. Klekotka, Rev. Peter J., S.T.B., J.C.D., Diocesan Consultors, 179 pp., 1920.
9. Wanenmacher, Rev. Francis, J.C.D., The Evidence in Ecclesiastical Procedure Affecting the Marriage Bond, 1920 (Printed 1935).
10. Golden, Rev. Henry Francis, J.C.D., Parochial Benefices in the New Code, IV-119 pp., 1921 (Printed 1925).
11. Koudelka, Rev. Charles J., J.C.D., Pastors, Their Rights and Duties According to the New Code of Canon Law, 211 pp., 1921.
12. Melo, Rev. Antonius, O.F.M., J.C.D., De Exemptione Regularium, X-188 pp., 1921.
13 Schaaf, Rev. Valentine Theodore, O.F.M., S.T.B., J.C.D., The Cloister, X-180 pp., 1921.
14. Burke, Rev. Thomas Joseph, S.T.D., J.C.D., Competence in Ecclesiastical Tribunals, IV-117 pp., 1922.
15. Leech, Rev. George Leo, J.C.D., A Comparative Study of the Constitution "Apostolicae Sedis" and the "Codex Juris Canonici," 179 pp., 1922.
16. Motry, Rev. Hubert Louis, S.T.D., J.C.D., Diocesan Faculties According to the Code of Canon Law, II-167 pp., 1922.
17. Murphy, Rev. George Lawrence, J.C.D., Delinquencies and Penalties in the Administration and the Reception of the Sacraments, IV-121 pp., 1923.
18. O'Reilly, Rev. John Anthony, S.T.B., J.C.D., Ecclesiastical Sepulture in the New Code of Canon Law, II-129 pp., 1923.

---

* Below n. 100 only the following numbers are still available: Nn. 3, 4, 9, 25, 34, 57 and 75. Beginning with n. 100 only the following are unavailable: Nn. 100, 101, 102, 104, 105, 107, 108, 109, 111 and 113.

19. Michalicka, Rev. Wenceslas Cyrill, O.S.B., J.C.D., Judicial Procedure in Dismissal of Clerical Exempt Religious, 107 pp., 1923.
20. Dargin, Rev. Edward Vincent, S.T.B., J.C.D., Reserved Cases According to the Code of Canon Law, IV-103 pp., 1924.
21. Godfrey, Rev. John A., S.T.B., J.C.D., The Right of Patronage According to the Code of Canon Law, 153 pp., 1924.
22. Hagedorn, Rev. Francis Edward, J.C.D., General Legislation on Indulgences, II-154 pp., 1924.
23. King, Rev. James Ignatius, J.C.D., The Administration of the Sacraments to Dying Non-Catholics, V-141 pp., 1924.
24. Winslow, Rev. Francis Joseph, O.F.M., J.C.D., Vicars and Prefects Apostolic, IV-149 pp., 1924.
25. Correa, Rev. Jose Servelion, S.T.L., J.C.D., La Potestad Legislativa de la Iglesia Catolica, IV-127 pp., 1925.
26. Dugan, Rev. Henry Francis, A.M., J.C.D., The Judiciary Department of the Diocesan Curia, 87 pp., 1925.
27. Keller, Rev. Charles Frederick, S.T.B., J.C.D., Mass Stipends, 167 pp., 1925.
28. Paschang, Rev. John Linus, J.C.D., The Sacramentals According to the Code of Canon Law, 129 pp., 1925.
29. Piontek, Rev. Cyrillus, O.F.M., S.T.B., J.C.D., De Indulto Exclaustrationis necnon Saecularizationis, XIII-289 pp., 1925.
30. Kearney, Rev. Richard Joseph, S.T.B., J.C.D., Sponsors at Baptism According to the Code of Canon Law, IV-127 pp., 1925.
31. Bartlett, Rev. Chester Joseph, A.M., LL.B., J.C.D., The Tenure of Parochial Property in the United States of America, V-108 pp., 1926.
32. Kilker, Rev. Adrian Jerome, J.C.D., Extreme Unction, V-425 pp., 1926.
33. McCormick, Rev. Robert Emmett, J.C.D., Confessors of Religious, VIII-266 pp., 1926.
34. Miller, Rev. Newton Thomas, J.C.D., Founded Masses According to the Code of Canon Law, VII-93 pp., 1926.
35. Roelker, Rev. Edward G., S.T.D., J.C.D., Principles of Privilege According to the Code of Canon Law, XI-166 pp., 1926.
36. Bakalarczyk, Rev. Richardus, M.I.C., J.U.D., De Novitiatu, VIII-208 pp., 1927.
37. Pizzuti, Rev. Lawrence, O.F.M., J.U.L., De Parochis Religiosis, 1927. (Not Printed.)
38. Bliley, Rev. Nicholas Martin, O.S.B., J.C.D., Altars According to the Code of Canon Law, XIX-132 pp., 1927.
39. Brown, Mr. Brendan Francis, A.B., LL.M., J.U.D., The Canonical Juristic Personality with Special Reference to its Status in the United States of America, V-212 pp., 1927.
40. Cavanaugh, Rev. William Thomas, C.P., J.U.D., The Reservation of the Blessed Sacrament, VIII-101 pp., 1927.

41. Doheny, Rev. William J., C.S.C., A.B., J.U.D., Church Property: Modes of Acquisition, X-118 pp., 1927.
42. Feldhaus, Rev. Aloysius H., C.PP.S., J.C.D., Oratories, IX-141 pp., 1927.
43. Kelly, Rev. James Patrick, A.B., J.C.D., The Jurisdiction of the Simple Confessor, X-208 pp., 1927.
44. Neuberger, Rev. Nicholas J., J.C.D., Canon 6 or the Relation of the Codex Juris Canonici to the Preceding Legislation, V-95 pp., 1927.
45. O'Keefe, Rev. Gerald Michael, J.C.D., Matrimonial Dispensations, Powers of Bishops, Priests, and Confessors, VIII-232 pp., 1927.
46. Quigley, Rev. Joseph A. M., A.B., J.C.D., Condemned Societies, 139 pp., 1927.
47. Zaplotnik, Rev. Johannes Leo, J.C.D., De Vicariis Foraneis, X-142 pp., 1927.
48. Duskie, Rev. John Aloysius, A.B., J.C.D., The Canonical Status of the Orientals in the United States, VIII-196 pp., 1928.
49. Hyland, Rev. Francis Edward, J.C.D., Excommunication, Its Nature, Historical Development and Effects, VIII-181 pp., 1928.
50. Reinmann, Rev. Gerald Joseph, O.M.C., J.C.D., The Third Order Secular of Saint Francis, 201 pp., .1928.
51. Schenk, Rev. Francis J., J.C.D., The Matrimonial Impediments of Mixed Religion and Disparity of Cult, XVI-318 pp., 1929.
52. Coady, Rev. John Joseph, S.T.D., J.U.D., A.M., The Appointment of Pastors, VIII-150 pp., 1929.
53. Kay, Rev. Thomas Henry, J.C.D., Competence in Matrimonial Procedure, VIII-164 pp., 1929.
54. Turner, Rev. Sidney Joseph, C.P., J.U.D., The Vow of Poverty, XLIX-217 pp., 1929.
55. Kearney, Rev. Raymond A., A.B., S.T.D., J.C.D., The Principles of Delegation, VII-149 pp., 1929.
56. Conran, Rev. Edward James, A.B., J.C.D., The Interdict,, V-163 pp., 1930.
57. O'Neill, Rev. William H., J.C.D., Papal Rescripts of Favor, VII-218 pp., 1930.
58. Bastnagel, Rev. Clement Vincent, J.U.D., The Appointment of Parochial Adjutants and Assistants, XV-257 pp., 1930.
59. Ferry, Rev. William A., A.B., J.C.D., Stole Fees, V-136 pp., 1930.
60. Costello, Rev. John Michael, A.B., J.C.D., Domicile and Quasi-Domicile, VII-201 pp., 1930.
61. Kremer, Rev. Michael Nicholas, A.B., S.T.B., J.C.D., Church Support in the United States, VI-136 pp., 1930.
62. Angulo, Rev. Luis, C.M., J.C.D., Legislation de la Iglesia sobre la intencion en la application de la Santa Misa, VII-104 pp., 1931.
63. Frey, Rev. Wolfgang Norbert, O.S.B., A.B., J.C.D., The Act of Religious Profession, VIII-174 pp., 1931.

64. ROBERTS, REV. JAMES BRENDAN, A.B., J.C.D., The Banns of Marriage, XIV-140 pp., 1931.
65. RYDER, REV. RAYMOND ALOYSIUS, A.B., J.C.D., Simony, IX-151 pp., 1931.
66. CAMPAGNA, REV. ANGELO, PH.D., J.U.D., Il Vicario Generale del Vescovo, VII-205 pp., 1931.
67. COX, REV. JOSEPH GODFREY, A.B., J.C.D., The Administration of Seminaries, VI-124 pp., 1931.
68. GREGORY, REV. DONALD J., J.U.D., The Pauline Privilege, XV-165 pp., 1931.
69. DONOHUE, REV. JOHN F., J.C.D., The Impediment of Crime, VII-110 pp., 1931.
70. DOOLEY, REV. EUGENE A., O.M.I., J.C.D., Church Law on Sacred Relics, IX-143 pp., 1931.
71. ORTH, REV. CLEMENT RAYMOND, O.M.C., J.C.D., The Approbation of Religious Institutes, 171 pp., 1931.
72. PERNICONE, REV. JOSEPH M., A.B., J.C.D., The Ecclesiastical Prohibition of Books, XII-267 pp., 1932.
73. CLINTON, REV. CONNELL, A.B., J.C.D., The Paschal Precept, IX-108 pp., 1932.
74. DONNELLY, REV. FRANCIS B., A.M., S.T.L., J.C.D., The Diocesan Synod, VIII-125 pp., 1932.
75. TORRENTE, REV. CAMILO, C.M.F., J.C.D., Las Processiones Sagradas, V-145 pp., 1932.
76. MURPHY, REV. EDWIN J., C.PP.S., J.C.D., Suspension Ex Informata Conscientia, XI-122 pp., 1932.
77. MACKENZIE, REV. ERIC F., A.M., S.T.L., J.C.D., The Delict of Heresy in its Commission, Penalization, Absolution, VII-124 pp., 1932.
78. LYONS, REV. AVITUS E., S.T.B., J.C.D., The Collegiate Tribunal of First Instance, XI-147 pp., 1932.
79. CONNOLLY, REV. THOMAS A., J.C.D., Appeals, XI-195 pp., 1932.
80. SANGMEISTER, REV. JOSEPH V., A.B., J.C.D., Force and Fear as Precluding Matrimonial Consent, V-211 pp., 1932.
81. JAEGER, REV. LEO A., A.B., J.C.D., The Administration of Vacant and Quasi-Vacant Episcopal Sees in the United States, IX-229 pp., 1932.
82. RIMLINGER, REV. HERBERT T., J.C.D., Error Invalidating Matrimonial Consent, VII-79 pp., 1932.
83. BARRETT, REV. JOHN D. M., S.S., J.C.D., A Comparative Study of the Third Plenary Council of Baltimore and the Code, IX-221 pp., 1932.
84. CARBERRY, REV. JOHN J., PH.D., S.T.D., J.C.D., The Juridical Form of Marriage, X-177 pp., 1934.
85. DOLAN, REV. JOHN L., A.B., J.C.D., The Defensor Vinculi, XII-157 pp., 1934.
86. HANNAN, REV. JEROME D., A.M., S.T.D., LL.B., J.C.D., The Canon Law of Wills, IX-517 pp., 1934.

87. LEMIEUX, REV. DELISE A., A.M., J.C.D., The Sentence in Ecclesiastical Procedure, IX-131 pp., 1934.
88. O'ROURKE, REV. JAMES J., A.B., J.C.D., Parish Registers, VII-109 pp., 1934.
89. TIMLIN, REV. BARTHOLOMEW, O.F.M., A.M., J.C.D., Conditional Matrimonial Consent, X-381 pp., 1934.
90. WAHL, REV. FRANCIS X., A.B., J.C.D., The Matrimonial Impediments of Consanguinity and Affinity, VI-125 pp., 1934.
91. WHITE, REV. ROBERT J., A.B., LL.B., S.T.B., J.C.D., Canonical Ante-Nuptial Promises and the Civil Law, VI-152 pp., 1934.
92. HERRERA, REV. ANTONIO PARRA, O.C.D., J.C.D., Legislacion Ecclesiastica sobra el Ayuno y la Abstinencia, XI-191 pp., 1935.
93. KENNEDY, REV. EDWIN J., J.C.D., The Special Matrimonial Process in Cases of Evident Nullity, X-165 pp., 1935.
94. MANNING, REV. JOHN J., A.B., J.C.D., Presumption of Law in Matri monial Procedure, XI-111 pp., 1935.
95. MOEDER, REV. JOHN M., J.C.D., The Proper Bishop for Ordination and Dimissorial Letters, VII-135 pp., 1935.
96. O'MARA, REV. WILLIAM A., A.B., J.C.D., Canonical Causes for Matrimonial Dispensations, IX-155 pp., 1935.
97. REILLY, REV. PETER, J.C.D., Residence of Pastors, IX-81 pp., 1935.
98. SMITH, REV. MARINER T., O.P., S.T.Lr., J.C.D., The Penal Law for Religious, VIII-169 pp., 1935.
99. WHALEN, REV. DONALD W., A.M., J.C.D., The Value of Testimonial Evidence in Matrimonial Procedure, XIII-297 pp., 1935.
100. CLEARY, REV. JOSEPH F., J.C.D., Canonical Limitations on the Alienation of Church Property, VIII-141 pp., 1936.
101. GLYNN, REV. JOHN C., J.C.D., The Promoter of Justice, XX-337 pp., 1936.
102. BRENNAN, REV. JAMES H., S.S., M.A., S.T.B., J.C.D., The Simple Convalidation of Marriage, VI-135 pp., 1937.
103. BRUNINI, REV. JOSEPH BERNARD, J.C.D., The Clerical Obligations of Canons 139 and 142, X-121 pp., 137.
104. CONNOR, REV. MAURICE, A.B., J.C.D., The Administrative Removal of Pastors, VIII-159 pp., 1937.
105. GUILFOYLE, REV. MERLIN JOSEPH, J.C.D., Custom, XI-144 pp., 1937.
106. HUGHES, REV. JAMES AUSTIN, A.B., A.M., J.C.D., Witnesses in Criminal Trials of Clerics, IX-140 pp., 1937.
107. JANSEN, REV. RAYMOND J., A.B., S.T.L., J.C.D., Canonical Provisions for Catechetical Instruction, VII-153 pp., 1937.
108. KEALY, REV. JOHN JAMES, A.B., J.C.D., The Introductory Libellus in Church Court Procedure, XI-121 pp., 1937.
109. MCMANUS, REV. JAMES EDWARD, C.SS.R., J.C.D., The Administration of Temporal Goods in Religious Institutes, XVI-196 pp., 1937.

110. Moriarty, Rev. Eugene James, J.C.D., Oaths in Ecclesiastical Courts, X-115 pp., 1937.
111. Rainier, Rev. Eligius George, C.SS.R., J.C.D., Suspension of Clerics, XVII-249 pp., 1937.
112. Reilly, Rev. Thomas F., C.SS.R., J.C.D., Visitation of Religious, VI-195 pp., 1938.
113. Moriarty, Rev. Francis E., C.SS.R., J.C.D., The Extraordinary Absolution from Censures, XV-334 pp., 1938.
114. Connolly, Rev. Nicholas P., J.C.D., The Canonical Erection of Parishes, X-132 pp., 1938.
115. Donovan, Rev. James Joseph, J.C.D., The Pastor's Obligation in Prenuptial Investigation, XII-322 pp., 1938.
116. Harrigan, Rev. Robert J., M.A., S.T.B., J.C.D., The Radical Sanation of Invalid Marriages, VIII-208 pp., 1938.
117. Boffa, Rev. Conrad Humbert, J.C.D., Canonical Provisions for Catholic Schools, VII-211 pp., 1939.
118. Parsons, Rev. Anscar John, O.M.Cap., J.C.D., Canonical Elections, XII-236 pp., 1939.
119. Reilly, Rev. Edward Michael, A.B., J.C.D., The General Norms of Dispensation, XII-156 pp., 1939.
120. Ryan, Rev. Gerald Aloysius, A.B., J.C.D., Principles of Episcopal Jurisdiction, XII-172 pp., 1939.
121. Burton, Rev. Francis James, C.S.C., A.B., J.C.D., A Commentary on Canon 1125, X-222 pp., 1940.
122. Miaskiewicz, Rev. Francis Sigismund, J.C.D., Supplied Jurisdiction According to Canon 209, XII-340 pp., 1940.
123. Rice, Rev. Patrick William, A.B., J.C.D., Proof of Death in Prenuptial Investigation, VIII-156 pp., 1940.
124. Anglin, Rev. Thomas Francis, M.S., J.C.D., The Eucharistic Fast, VIII-183 pp., 1941.
125. Coleman, Rev. John Jerome, J.C.D., The Minister of Confirmation, VI-153 pp., 1941.
126. Downs, Rev. Joseph Emmanuel, A.B., J.C.D., The Concept of Clerical Immunity, XI-163 pp., 1941.
127. Esswein, Rev. Anthony Albert, J.C.D., Extrajudicial Penal Powers of Ecclesiastical Superiors, X-144 pp., 1941.
128. Farrell, Rev. Benjamin Francis, M.A., S.T.L., J.C.D., The Rights and Duties of the Local Ordinary Regarding Congregations of Women Religious of Pontifical Approval, V-195 pp., 1941.
129. Feeney, Rev. Thomas John, A.B., S.T.L., J.C.D., Restitutio in Integrum, VI-169 pp., 1941.
130. Findlay, Rev. Stephen William, O.S.B., A.B., J.C.D., Canonical Norms Governing the Deposition and Degradation of Clerics, XVII-279 pp., 1941.

131. GOODWINE, REV. JOHN, A.B., S.T.L., J.C.D., The Right of the Church to Acquire Property, VIII-119 pp., 1941.
132. HESTON, REV. EDWARD LOUIS, C.S.C., Ph.D., S.T.D., J.C.D., The Alienation of Church Property in the United States, XII-222 pp., 1941.
133. HOGAN, REV. JAMES JOHN, A.B., S.T.L., J.C.D., Judicial Advocates and Procurators, XIII-200 pp., 1941.
134. KEALY, REV. THOMAS M., A.B., Litt.B., J.C.D., Dowry of Women Religious, IX-152 pp., 1941.
135. KEENE, REV. MICHAEL JAMES, O.S.B., J.C.D., Religious Ordinaries and Canon 198, V-164 pp., 1942.
136. KERIN, REV. CHARLES A., S.S., M.A., S.T.B., J.C.D., The Privation of Christian Burial, XVI-279 pp., 1941.
137. LOUIS, REV. WILLIAM FRANCIS, M.A., J.C.D., Diocesan Archives, X-101 pp., 1941.
138. MCDEVITT, REV. GILBERT JOSEPH, A.B., J.C.D., Legitimacy and Legitimation, X-247 pp., 1941.
139. MCDONOUGH, REV. THOMAS JOSEPH, A.B., J.C.D., Apostolic Administrators, X-217 pp., 1941.
140. MEIER, REV. CARL ANTHONY, A.B., J.C.D., Penal Administrative Procedure Against Negligent Pastors, XI-240 pp., 1941.
141. SCHMIDT, REV. JOHN ROGG, A.B., J.C.D., The Principles of Authentic Interpretation in Canon 17 of the Code of Canon Law, XII-331 pp., 1941.
142. SLAFKOSKY, REV. ANDREW LEONARD, A.B., J.C.D., The Canonical Episcopal Visitation of the Diocese, X-197 pp., 1941.
143. SWOBODA, REV. INNOCENT ROBERT, O.F.M., J.C.D., Ignorance in Relation to the Imputability of Delicts, IX-271 pp., 1941.
144. DUBÉ, REV. ARTHUR JOSEPH, A.B., J.C.D., The General Principles for the Reckoning of Time in Canon Law, VIII-299 pp., 1941.
145. MCBRIDE, REV. JAMES T., A.B., J.C.D., Incardination and Excardination of Seculars, XX-585 pp., 1941.
146. KRÓL, REV. JOHN T., J.C.D., The Defendant in Ecclesiastical Trials, XII-207 pp., 1942.
147. COMYNS, REV. JOSEPH J., C.SS.R., A.B., J.C.D., Papal and Episcopal Administration of Church Property, XIV-155 pp., 1942.
148. BARRY, REV. GARRETT FRANCIS, O.M.I., J.C.D., Violation of the Cloister, XII-260 pp., 1942.
149. BOLDUC, REV. GATIEN, C.S.V., A.B., S.T.L., J.C.D., Les Études dans les Religions Cléricales, VIII-155 pp., 1942.
150. BOYLE, REV. DAVID JOHN, M.A., J.C.D., The Juridic Effects of Moral Certitude on Pre-Nuptial Guarantees, XII-188 pp., 1942.
151. CANAVAN, REV. WALTER JOSEPH, M.A., LITT.D., J.C.D., The Profession of Faith, XII-143 pp., 1942.
152. DESROCHERS, REV. BRUNO, A.B., PH.L., S.T.B., J.C.D., Le Premier Concile Plénier de Québec et le Code de Droit Canonique, XIV-186 pp., 1942.

153. Dillon, Rev. Robert Edward, A.B., J.C.D., Common Law Marriage, X-148 pp., 1942.
154. Dodwell, Rev. Edward John, Ph.D., S.T.B., J.C.D., The Time and Place for the Celebration of Marriage.
155. Donnellan, Rev. Thomas Andrew, A.B., J.C.D., The Obligation of the Missa pro Populo, VII-131 pp., 1942.
156. Eltz, Rev. Louis Anthony, A.B., J.C.L., Cooperation in Crime.
157. Gass, Rev. Sylvester Francis, M.A., J.C.D., Ecclesiastical Pensions, XI-206 pp., 1942.
158. Guiniven, Rev. John Joseph, C.SS.R., J.C.D., The Precept of Hearing Mass, XIV-188 pp., 1942.
159. Gulczynski, Rev. John Theophilus, J.C.D., The Desecration and Violation of Churches.
160. Hammill, Rev. John Leo, M.A., J.C.D., The Obligations of the Traveler According to Canon 14, VIII-204 pp., 1942.
161. Haydt, Rev. John Joseph, A.B., J.C.D., Reserved Benefices, XI-148 pp., 1942.
162. Huser, Rev. Roger John, O.F.M., A.B., J.C.D., The Crime of Abortion in Canon Law.
163. Kearney, Rev. Francis Patrick, A.B., S.T.L., J.C.L., The Principles of Canon 1127.
164. Linahen, Rev. Leo James, S.T.L., J.C.D., De Absolutione Complicis In Peccato Turpi, 114 pp., 1942.
165. McCloskey, Rev. Joseph Aloysius, A.B., J.C.D., The Subject of Ecclesiastical Law According to Canon 12, XVII-246 pp., 1942.
166. O'Neill, Rev. Francis Joseph, C.SS.R., J.C.D., The Dismissal of Religious in Temporary Vows, XIII-220 pp., 1942.
167. Prince, Rev. John Edward, A.B., S.T.B., J.C.D., The Diocesan Chancellor, X-136 pp., 1942.
168. Riesner, Rev. Albert Joseph, C.SS.R., J.C.D., Apostates and Fugitives from Religious Institutes, IX-168 pp., 1942.
169. Stenger, Rev. Joseph Bernard, J.C.D., The Mortgaging of Church Property, 186 pp., 1942.
170. Waldron, Rev. Joseph Francis, A.B., J.C.D., The Minister of Baptism, XII-197 pp., 1942.
171. Willett, Rev. Robert Albert, J.C.D., The Probative Value of Documents in Ecclesiastical Trials, X-124 pp., 1942.
172. Woeber, Rev. Edward Martin, M.A., J.C.D., The Interpellations, XII-161 pp., 1942.
173. Benko, Rev. Matthew Aloysius, O.S.B.. M.A., J.C.L., The Abbot *Nullius*.
174. Christ, Rev. Joseph James, M.A., S.T.L., J.C.L., Dispensation from Vindicative Penalties.
175. Clancy, Rev. Patrick M. J., O.P., A.B., S.T.Lr., J.C.L., The Local Religious Superior.

176. Clarke, Rev. Thomas James, J.C.L., Parish Societies.
177. Connolly, Rev. John Patrick, S.T.L., J.C.L., Synodal Examiners and Parish Priest Consultors.
178. Drumm, Rev. William Martin, A.B., J.C.L., Hospital Chaplains.
179. Flanagan, Rev. Bernard Joseph, A.B., S.T.L., J.C.L., The Canonical Erection of Religious Houses.
180. Kelleher, Rev. Stephen Joseph, A.B., S.T.B., J.C.L., Discussions with Non-Catholics: Canonical Legislation.
181. Lewis, Rev. Gordian, C.P., J.C.L., Chapters in Religious Institutes.
182. Marx, Rev. Adolph, J.C.L., The Declaration of Nullity of Marriages Contracted Outside the Church.
183. Matulenas, Rev. Raymond Anthony, O.S.B., A.B., J.C.L., Communication, a Source of Privileges.
184. O'Leary, Rev. Charles Gerard, C.SS.R., Religious Dismissed After Perpetual Profession.
185. Power, Rev. Cornelius Michael, J.C.L., The Blessing of Cemeteries.
186. Shuhler, Rev. Ralph Vincent, O.S.A., J.C.L., Privileges of Religious to Absolve and Dispense.
187. Ziolkowski, Rev. Thaddeus Stanislaus, A.B., J.C.L., The Consecration and Blessing of Churches.

www.ingramcontent.com/pod-product-compliance
Lightning Source LLC
LaVergne TN
LVHW050246080826
844660LV00012B/601

* 9 7 8 0 8 1 3 2 2 3 6 6 7 *